OLIVER CROMWELL

In this concise and accessible new biography, Martyn Bennett examines the life of Oliver Cromwell – one of the most controversial figures in world history. Elected to parliament in 1640 Cromwell played a major role in challenging the excessive powers of Charles I. As Lieutenant General, his military campaigns were crucial to victory during the Civil War and he was instrumental in the trial and execution of the king. As Lord Protector of the Commonwealth he remains the only non-royal head of state in British history. His rule was characterised by unprecedented religious freedoms and is seen as laying the foundations for the modern British constitution. However, Cromwell's legacy in Ireland and Scotland has greatly troubled his reputation. Furthermore, Cromwell's government is often viewed as an anomaly – a temporary hiatus before the re-establishment of the monarchy.

Martyn Bennett challenges these long-held perceptions of Cromwell and the Commonwealth, arguing that in his role as 'God's Constable', he needs to be placed at the core of early Modern British and Irish history. Charting his early career, the origins of his political and religious thought and the development of his notions of governance that influenced him as Lord Protector, Martyn Bennett contests the post-Restoration vilification of Cromwell to examine how his influence has shaped notions of citizenship, identity and governance and informed the relationship between religion and the state in Britain.

This radical new interpretation will give students a clearer view of the motivations and achievements of a fascinating and pivotal figure in British history.

ROUTLEDGE HISTORICAL BIOGRAPHIES

SERIES EDITOR: ROBERT PEARCE

Routledge Historical Biographies provide engaging, readable and academically credible biographies written from an explicitly historical perspective. These concise and accessible accounts will bring important historical figures to life for students and general readers alike.

In the same series

Bismarck by Edgar Feuchtwanger

Neville Chamberlin by Nick Smart

Churchill by Robert Pearce

Edward IV by Hannes Kleineke

Gladstone by Michael Partridge

Henry VII by Sean Cunningham

Henry VIII by Lucy Wooding

Hitler by Martyn Housden

Jinnah by Sikander Hayat

Lenin by Christopher Read

Louis XIV by Richard Wilkinson

Martin Luther King Jr. by Peter J. Ling

Martin Luther by Michael Mullet

Mary Queen of Scots by Retha M. Warnicke

Mao by Michael Lynch

Mussolini by Peter Neville

Nehru by Ben Zachariah

Emmeline Pankhurst by Paula Bartley

Richard III by Ann Kettle

Franklin D. Roosevelt by Stuart Kidd

Stalin by Geoffrey Roberts

Trotsky by Ian Thatcher

Mary Tudor by Judith Richards

OLIVER CROMWELL

Martyn Bennett

Routledge
Taylor & Francis Group

LONDON AND NEW YORK

First published 2006
by Routledge
2 Park Square, Milton Park, Abingdon, Oxon OX14 4RN

Simultaneously published in the USA and Canada
by Routledge
270 Madison Ave, New York, NY 10016

Routledge is an imprint of the Taylor & Francis Group, an informa business

Typeset in Garamond and Scala Sans by
HWA Text and Data Management, Tunbridge Wells
Printed and bound in Great Britain by
TJ International Ltd, Padstow, Cornwall

British Library Cataloguing in Publication Data
A catalogue record for this book is available from the British Library

Library of Congress Cataloging-in-Publication Data
Bennett, Martyn.
   Oliver Cromwell / Martyn Bennett
      p.   cm. – (Routledge historical biographies)
   Includes bibliographical references and index.
   1. Oliver Cromwell, 1599–1658.   2. Generals – Great Britain
   – Biography.   3. Heads of state – Great Britain – Biography.
   4. Great Britain – History – Puritan Revolution, 1642–1660
   – Biography.   I. Title.   II. Series
DA426.B$^ 2006
941.06´4092–dc22   2005034764

ISBN10: 0–415–31921–8 (hbk)
ISBN10: 0–415–31922–6 (pbk)
ISBN10: 0–203–08845–x (ebk)

ISBN13: 978–0–415–31921–8 (hbk)
ISBN13: 978–0–415–31922–5 (pbk)
ISBN13: 978–0–203–08845–6 (ebk)

FOR DEBORAH

Contents

LIST OF PLATES

ACKNOWLEDGEMENTS

Writing a biography is an experience quite different to experiences of writing that I have previously undertaken and so I would like to thank the readers who commented on my original proposal for the book for their suggestions, comments and guidance. I would like to thank Professor Ronald Hutton in particular for letting me see a pre-publication copy of his chapter on Cromwell from his *Debates on Stuart History*, it was enlightening and instructive. I must thank the staff of all record offices and libraries I have used in collating the material for the book, especially those at the Huntingdonshire Records Office and also the staff of the Cromwell Museum who collaborated in securing access to the records displayed at the museum. I need also to thank my colleagues at Nottingham Trent University for their enthusiasm and willingness to have ideas tested out on them, and for reading parts of the book. My thanks also go to my third-years students over the past three years who have likewise had theories and ideas thought out with them. I must also thank the Graduate School administrators, in particular, Terry McSwiney, for the unfailing support that allowed me the space to devote time to this book. Finally, thank you to Deborah for enduring the presence of the ghost of a man over four hundred years old, stalking our house, sometimes at weird hours of the day.

CHRONOLOGY

	Personal events	National events
1599 25 April	Oliver Cromwell born	
29 April	Oliver Cromwell baptised	
1603		Death of Elizabeth I and succession of King James VI of Scotland to the crowns of England/Wales and Ireland
1616	Cromwell at Cambridge University	
1617	Death of Oliver's father: Oliver left Cambridge	
1620 22 August	Oliver married Elizabeth Bourchier	
1621	Son Robert born	
1623	Son Oliver born	
1624	Daughter Bridget born	
1625		Death of James VI and I: succession of Charles I
1626	Son Richard born	
1628	Cromwell elected to Parliament	
	Son Henry born	
1629	Daughter Elizabeth born	Parliament dissolved
1630	Fishbourne bequest crisis, Cromwell loses position on Huntingdon crisis and leaves the town for St Ives	
1632	Son James born, died same year	
1633–4	Cromwell involved in parish management of St Ives	

	Personal events	National events
1636	On the death of Sir Thomas Steward the Cromwells moved to Ely	
1637	Daughter Mary born	Charles I's attempt to change the liturgy of Scotland provokes revolt
1638	Daughter Frances born	
1639		1st Bishop's War
1640	Cromwell elected to Short and Long Parliaments	Charles I called Short Parliament. Defeat of the king's forces in the 2nd Bishop's War. Charles called Long Parliament.
1641 21 May		Root and Branch Bill introduced to parliament
22 October		Irish Rebellion
27 November		Grand Remonstrance
1642 August	Cromwell raised a troop of Horse	
23 October		Battle of Edgehill
1643 13 May		Battle of Belton
July	Cromwell became governor of Ely	
20 July		Battle of Gainsborough
20 September		1st Battle of Newbury
1644 January	Cromwell appointed Lt General of the Eastern Association Army	Scotland entered the war on the side of parliament
5 February	Signed the Solemn League and Covenant	
7 February	Appointed to the Committee of Both Kingdoms	

	Personal events	National events
2 July		Battle of Marston Moor
27 October		2nd Battle of Newbury
November–December	Conflict over army leadership leading to the Self-Denying Ordinance	
1645 January		Creation of the New Model Army begun
14 June		Battle of Naseby
10 July		Battle of Langport
10 September		Capture of Bristol
13 September		Conclusive defeat of royalist forces in Scotland at the Battle of Philliphaugh
14 October		Storm of Basing House
1646		End of First Civil War in England and Wales
13 January	Marriage of daughter, Elizabeth to John Claypole	
15 June	Daughter Bridget married Henry Ireton	
1647	Cromwell attempted to ameliorate differences between the army and parliament	
4 June	After meeting Cromwell, Cornet Joyce seized the king Heads of the Proposals presented to the king and rejected	
October–November	Cromwell chaired the Putney Debates	
11 November		Charles I escaped from Hampton Court

	Personal events	National events
15 November	Cromwell put down the Corkbush mutiny	
1648		Vote of No Addresses
May – July	Cromwell's campaign in Wales	Fairfax on campaign in south-east England
17 August		Battle of Preston
October	Cromwell in Scotland	
December		Establishment of the process for the king's trial
1649 January	Cromwell one of the king's judges and a signatory of the death warrant	
30 January		Execution of the king
15 August	Cromwell landed in Ireland	
11 September		Storm of Drogheda
11 October		Storm of Wexford
1650 February–May	Cromwell campaigning in south and midland Ireland	
June	Appointed commander in chief	
July	Beginning of campaign in Scotland	
3 September		Battle of Dunbar
1651 3 September		Battle of Worcester
1652		Anglo-Dutch war
1653 20 April	Cromwell expelled parliament	
4 July		Opening of Little Parliament

	Personal events	National events
12 December		Little Parliament dissolved itself
16 December	Cromwell became Lord Protector	
1654 April		End of Dutch War
4 September		Opening of the First Protectorate Parliament
November	Death of Oliver's mother	
1655 22 January		Dissolution of Parliament
March		Penruddock's rising
July	Cromwell aware of the failure of the Western design in May	
9 August		Major Generals inaugurated
1656		
12 September		Second Protectorate Parliament
1657 February	Proposals to make Cromwell a king in the Humble Petition and Advice presented to Cromwell	
8 May	Oliver refused the crown	
26 June	Cromwell reinstalled as Lord Protector under the terms of the Humble Petition	
November	Marriages of Cromwell's daughters Frances and Elizabeth	
1658 4 February		Dissolution of Parliament
6 August	Death of daughter Elizabeth	
3 September	Death of Cromwell	

1

BY BIRTH A GENTLEMAN...
1599–1617

The novelist and biographer John Buchan, Lord Tweedsmuir, felt that Oliver had underplayed his origins. Cromwell once said 'I was by birth a gentleman, living neither in any considerable height nor yet in obscurity'. Buchan suggested that he might 'have put the claim higher', because of his family's prominence in the region. Many biographers and historians across the past three and a half centuries have been mesmerised by Oliver's apparent rise from obscurity to prominence and national leadership. To some nineteenth century commentators, imbued with the virtues of Samuel Smiles's 'self-help' mentality, Cromwell's 'self-made man' image was irresistible. It still lingers in recent works, although over time historians have questioned it. Maurice Ashley stressed that the Cromwell family's status meant that the implication of obscurity is hard to justify. Yet it has almost become a commonplace in many ways to see Cromwell appearing as it were from nowhere. Several factors have been ascribed in this rise, a combination of his natural talents with the cataclysmic movements of class struggle unleashed by the revolutionary times, or to the rise of the puritans, with which Cromwell has been long associated. The notion of obscurity is a complex phenomenon with at least two facets appropriate to Cromwell's life. One facet is the aspect of being hidden or lost: this can be examined with regard to Cromwell's early life and development. A few of the usual records, those confirming birth and baptism exist, but there are few details of Oliver's childhood.

Yet familiar tales of Cromwell's early years abound. Stories of his being abducted by a monkey and carried onto his uncle's roof and of a punch-up with the infant Prince Charles are well-known, as is the story that he was rescued from drowning by a local man who later in life regretted doing so having seen Oliver fighting against his king. There is also a story about him placing a stage-prop crown on his own head during a school play. It has to be said that these stories probably all had their origins much later in Oliver's life or even afterwards. Oliver himself left little record, contemporary or recalled in adulthood, of his intellectual or spiritual development, as indeed few people did or do. For someone who was to achieve such prominence this may seem a regrettable case of negligence, but the absence of such records even in such a family as his branch of the Cromwells is by no means unique.

Obscurity too can refer to the social background of a person and this is also applied to Oliver Cromwell, and depends far more upon perspective. The progression from a gentry background to national leadership was dramatic. Clearly, to many who looked upon Cromwell whilst he was head of state, his rise must have been remarkable in a society in which even usurpers to the throne had at least tenuous claims to royal blood, and there were attempts to link Oliver through his mother's family to the deposed Stuarts. Yet to a far greater number of observers Oliver would not have been an outsider to the world of politics: for perhaps 95 per cent of the people in Oliver's world he would have been quite simply out of their class, gifted as he was by birth with property and social position which would entail political and administrative power and authority at some level. People like Oliver, even at his most lowly, organised and ran other people's lives, employed them, marshalled them in communal responsibilities, propelled them into court if necessary. Oliver, during the 'obscure' parts of his life, played this role to the full: as a councillor at Huntingdon, he served as a borough justice of the peace; he may have been part of the rural administration in St Ives. As MP in the late 1620s he had a role in deciding the fate of taxpayers' income and fiscal duties. It cannot be doubted that the political controversies of the 1630s and the civil wars which followed propelled Cromwell into the public arena. Yet here he was not alone; civil war companies, troops and even regiments of both sides were led by men originally of lesser standing than Oliver Cromwell even at his lowest. Many of these men sought to use the war to rise from obscurity. Colin Davis, in his thoughtful and thought provoking biography of Cromwell, underlined that rising to high political power was not unique, citing the cases of William Laud, the Archbishop of Canterbury who was the son of a draper, and a parliamentarian contemporary of Cromwell's, Major General Phillip Skippon, a working-class lad made good.

Cromwell had two major advantages in his career: membership of the gentry and the revolution. The latter, when coupled with his instrumental involvement with the 'winning side', formed the background to his rise to power. It was this which distinguished him from many other contenders who had been on the starting line of 1640. As with all individuals who rise to prominence, Cromwell both shaped and was shaped by the times in which he lived. If Charles I had not had a contentious relationship with parliaments, there might have been no Personal Rule between 1629 and 1640 and Cromwell's life would have been very different. His career as an MP may have come to an end in 1629 because only shortly after that he lost his place as a burgess in Huntingdon, the town he represented in the Commons. With no Personal Rule, there would have been less need for his more powerful cousins and associates to place him in the Cambridge seat in 1640: he may never have represented Cambridge at all. Yet this counter-factual discussion has little value: the purpose of this chapter is to explore Cromwell's early life and set a context for it.

Oliver Cromwell was born on 25 April 1599 the second, but eldest surviving son of Robert and Elizabeth Cromwell of Huntingdon, the county town of one of England's smallest counties. Unusually, and therefore somewhat suspiciously, his baptismal record in the register of St John the Baptist church, dated 29 April 1599, is in Latin (as is the following entry for Mary Wallis).[1] These are the only two Latin entries, all the other births, deaths and marriages within the parish are recorded in English. One other thing makes Cromwell's entry stand out: it includes the date of birth. All other entries simply record the date of baptism. It would seem clear that Oliver's record has been entered later, perhaps replacing the standard English language version made at the time of his baptism, which may have been pumiced out and written over like a palimpsest. The change may have been made during his lifetime, possibly whilst he was famous, and therefore it takes its place alongside the contemporary myth-making that generated stories of monkeys and fights. This near contemporary alteration was only part of a long-term process for the replacement of the entry was not the only bit of writing on the page. Oliver's record is the first actual entry on the page, but Immediately above his entry, another person wrote 'Englands plague for five years'. Yet another hand crossed that out. The page has been so heavily examined that the vellum is polished; at the centre of the fly, it is almost transparent.

Whatever date Oliver's entry was re-written, back in 1599, he was one of six children baptised in the church. Unfortunately for those born in the same year as Oliver, with the exception of Mary Wallis, this interest in Oliver's birth has almost resulted in their entries being expunged from the record as arms rested on the lower half of the page have faded entries. Sadly this erasure is mirrored in the physical structure of Huntingdon, for St John's church was demolished in the mid-seventeenth century, probably during Cromwell's lifetime. The place of Oliver's birth has likewise gone. The present Cromwell House, a private clinic, is on the site of the family home but incorporates nothing of it. Heavy reconstruction before 1724 had changed the building dramatically, but had left the room where Cromwell had been born in place as a curiosity. By 1810 the last vestiges of the original building had gone. We are left with an intangible early life, which enables the myth of obscurity. Yet there are real structures into which the baby Cromwell fitted, which remove the obscuring veils.

Robert, Oliver's father was not an obscure man, he was the son of Sir Henry Cromwell a star of Queen Elizabeth's court, who in turn was the son of one of her father's King Henry VIII's favourites. Robert had been an MP, a county high sheriff and now he was a county JP, as well as a bailiff in his home town of Huntingdon. Robert's elder brother Oliver, was even more prominent; he would in 1603 inherit the family's principal estates and would in turn become an associate of King James VI and I and the centre of the county's political and cultural milieu as Sir Oliver Cromwell resident in the nearby sumptuous house, Hinchingbrooke.

Although at the time of his early children's baptisms Robert Cromwell was referred to as gentleman, a title applied in the Latin entry for Oliver's birth and baptism, he was, after his father's death in 1603, referred to as esquire at the baptism of Oliver's sister Elizabeth in 1606. Robert's elder brother Oliver on the other hand was referred to as esquire when his daughter Katherine was born in 1594, but he was soon elevated. Queen Elizabeth knighted him in 1598: and at King James's Westminster coronation Oliver was made a Knight of the Bath. Sir Henry's two eldest sons (he had five in total, four of whom survived into adulthood) served as MPs in Elizabethan parliaments, Robert just the once in 1593.

Baby Oliver's mother Elizabeth was a member of the Steward family; a family of successful gentlemen who farmed land belonging to Ely cathedral. Her brother Thomas took over the lands after their father's death. Both the Stewards and the Cromwells had benefited from the sixteenth century's cataclysmic social restructuring attendant upon Henry VIII's break from the Roman Catholic church. The two families were able to take advantage of the break-up of the church's estates, buying into the massive property market and deriving increased wealth and status as a result. Elizabeth had married John Lynne of Bassingbourn in the 1580s, but he and their baby daughter Katherine had died by 1589 and were buried in Ely Cathedral. Into her second marriage Elizabeth took a jointure worth £60 a year and a small brewery. At Oliver Cromwell's birth Robert and Elizabeth lived on the site of the Friary on the High Street, bought by Sir Henry Cromwell in 1568. Four years later it was still referred to as the 'Fryers', even though it was over thirty years since it had been closed down. On one side there was a common drain and on the other Friar Lane. Sir Henry gave the site to Robert who turned it into a building site, which when work was over revealed the family home in which Oliver would be born.[2] Christopher Hill believed that this gave the Cromwells a vested secular interest in the Reformation: the Cromwells' Protestantism was tinged with a realistic materialism. Any restoration of Catholicism would undo their fortunes, even if some of those fortunes were relatively meagre.

Robert Cromwell was not a wealthy man, the estates which he was given brought him an income of about £300 a year. This was not a remarkable amount for members of the gentry; being about the average income for a lesser gentleman, but for an esquire who was expected to be a public role, it was low. It would seem to be the case, that Robert Cromwell was not amongst those gentry who increased their wealth during the pre-civil war period through estate improvement or office holding. In Huntingdonshire the numbers of the gentry seem to have declined during the seventeenth century: certainly Robert's failure to improve his income between the 1590s and his death in 1617, put his nuclear family at risk. They could have become what Hugh Trevor-Roper classified as declining 'mere-gentry'.[3] Nevertheless, £300 a year was an unimaginable sum for the vast majority of Oliver's contemporaries, sixty times what a ploughman could earn by the sweat of his brows in a year, and Robert did not need to sweat a drop through physical exertion to earn it. Other people earned the Cromwells' income.

Oliver was the fifth of the Cromwell children, Joan was the eldest, but died before she was ten, then followed Elizabeth , the only girl baptised at St John's that year on 14 October 1593. Oliver's elder brother Henry died at some time during his childhood, having been baptised on 31 August 1595. Katheren was born in early 1597 and Oliver himself a couple of years later. He was in turn followed by Margaret in 1601, Anna in 1602, Jane in January 1605, Robina some years later and finally by Robert, who was born in January 1609: he was buried on 4 April.[4] Oliver and his young siblings were fortunate children. In 1603 plague struck Huntingdon. Most of the casualties recorded at St John's, opposite the Cromwell's home, were adults. The Cromwell family remained intact. It seems unlikely that Oliver's elder brother died in these years, the plague deaths are well-documented, although we do not know when the boy did die.

In terms of the fortunes of the Cromwell family as a whole Oliver was born just as the upward trajectory slowed. In the sixteenth century the Cromwells had appeared not from obscurity, but from Wales. With a surname of Williams, Cromwell's ancestors had prospered in the reign of Henry VII. Morgan Williams married Katherine Cromwell, sister of Henry VIII's future chief minister Thomas Cromwell. Their son Richard also married well, gaining ownership of property in Cambridgeshire through his marriage to Frances Murfyn daughter of a Lord Mayor of London. Richard worked with his uncle as a regional commissioner in charge of the dissolution of local monasteries, and served as high sheriff of Huntingdonshire and Cambridgeshire. The dissolution was profitable and Richard's reputation survived the disgrace and execution of Uncle Thomas. Former church property was bought in Huntingdonshire, including Hinchingbrooke Nunnery and Ramsey Abbey, as well as the smaller Augustine Friary in Huntingdon and a couple of priories at St Neots and Huntingdon and another abbey at Sawtry. Richard Williams had during his rise (and before his uncle's fall) adopted the surname Cromwell. This became the family name thereafter, but legal documents continued to bear the name Williams as well. Oliver Cromwell himself was styled Cromwell alias Williams as late as 1627.[5] Richard and Frances's first son Henry was born in 1537 and seven years later he inherited the property. Fortunately his experience of wardship was a happy one and his proprietorial guardian Sir Edward North managed the estates well. Henry married Joan Warren, daughter of a Lord Mayor of London, like his mother. Once again marrying into a wealthy business family brought a large financial benefit to the Cromwell family. Hinchingbrooke Nunnery was demolished and an impressive lavish home was constructed and the gateway of Ramsay Abbey dismantled, the stones were shipped to Hinchingbrooke and rebuilt as the grand entrance to the new home. Henry entertained Queen Elizabeth there in 1564, where she knighted him. The family fortune was spent generously on such entertainments, and Sir Henry gained the nickname 'The Golden Knight'. Henry and Joan had a large family: five boys, of whom four survived into adulthood, and five daughters. Two of the daughters' marriages produced men with a role in Oliver's future. Elizabeth married John Hampden and their son John became the future ship money protestor and politician. Frances married Richard Whalley whose son Edward by his first marriage would be one of the major generals in the 1650s. This pattern continued; Sir Henry's granddaughter Elizabeth married Oliver St John, the man who defended John Hampden when he was prosecuted for not paying ship money. Oliver was therefore by birth tied into the leaders of the revolution. Yet we must not read too much into this, for Cromwell was also tied into the families which supported the king's cause too. His extended family included Thomas, Lord Cromwell who would become a royalist administrator during the civil war. A cousin, son of Uncle Sir Oliver, worked for Charles I's sister Elizabeth Queen of Bohemia. A half-cousin from the same branch of the family, James, would fight for Charles I as a colonel. Another, Henry, descended from Uncle Sir Phillip would also become a royalist colonel as would his brother Thomas (although he married in to the Leicestershire Dixie family after the wars; they were parliamentarians). The young Oliver was not a parliamentarian-in-waiting in his childhood, he was a part of a broad network of family and social class which would participate in the wars because of their birth and connections. It must be remembered that the royalist Cromwell would have had the same vested economic interest in the survival of Protestantism as Oliver. If the origins of the family wealth made the Cromwells Protestant, it certainly did not make them parliamentarians. David Smith and Peter Newman have both shown us that royalists were adherents of the established state church and the property redistribution of the sixteenth century which had created it.

Cromwell's cocoon was class based, but not unique to his class. Indeed there is a suggestion that there was already in place horizontal stratification of the 'class' system. The family contacts which would work for Oliver Cromwell throughout his life were within the gentry. Through the gentry he would gain his political office, his administrative and legal appointments and the basis of his family wealth. This is not to say that this was a rigid structure: the entry into the gentry of his maternal relations and the maternal relations of his ancestors proved that the access to the gentry was possible, and Cromwell's own economic decline in the early 1630s, proved that it was possible to fall out of it too. Uncle Oliver's failing fortunes showed that there was room to rise and fall within the gentry cadre too; indeed because his fall was related to his court ambitions, he fits, like his father, into Hugh Trevor-Roper's category of 'falling gentry': those who invested their family wealth into maintaining a social position, which in the end brought no economic or financial return. Such a cocoon was not unique to the gentry: recent work on credit and community structure shows that other 'classes' of early modern men and women had networks of their own which functioned in the same way. Cromwell's family and connections do not therefore make the unique man, but they explain the way his life functioned in those first forty years of his life.

The large family and generous spirit of grandfather Sir Henry was beginning to stretch the family fortune yet his sons and daughters married well, but not as spectacularly as Sir Henry or his father Sir Richard. The apex of the family's success lay in the years before Oliver's birth and in his youth, when his father and uncle Oliver served as MPs in Elizabethan parliaments and upon her death, when James VI and I, Queen Elizabeth's successor, visited Hinchingbrooke just a couple of months after he came to the throne of England. In the short term, this visit, the first of many, paid dividends. Uncle Oliver was knighted. He became a creditor to the crown and as a result received grants of lands. In the long term, entertaining the monarch began to cost more than it returned. Grandfather Henry died shortly after his queen, and the post of royal entertainer passed to Sir Oliver. Lavish entertainment began to sap the family resources, but during Oliver's childhood, there would be no outward sign that the apex of the family had been reached and passed. Unlike the rising upper gentry and aristocracy, which Lawrence Stone[6] identified in the early seventeenth century, the Cromwells were on the way down, largely through an association with the court that entailed a greater outlay than income.

Cromwell's immediate and extended family smoothed his passage through early life, securing him a comfortable childhood, good schooling at the nearby grammar school and a place at Sidney Sussex College, Cambridge University. In later life, the fall of the family would mirror and contribute to Cromwell's own decline in fortunes, but later still it would drag him back from rural obscurity and place him again into parliament. Much of this network of support would be in place before Cromwell was born, the rest was assembled in his youth and early manhood, and he continued the process as he matured and married. At its heart was the Cromwell family, centred at once in the old friary with Oliver's mother and father, but also at Hinchingbrooke the home of Sir Oliver. This part of the network was to fail the young Cromwell, the heart of the family sustained a shock in 1617 when Robert died, but the wider circle went into financial and thereby influential decline by the 1620s. Cromwell's economic and social resurgence was related to another circle, that of his wife. Political resurgence was owed however to the links made by the Cromwells. As yet of course all of this was to play out in Oliver's future but the foundations appeared contemporary with the most obscure years of Cromwell's life. His Aunt Elizabeth had married John Hampden, cousin Elizabeth was married to Oliver St John, sister Margaret married Valentine Walton, a local gentleman and future deputy lieutenant for the county. All would play a part in the young man's future.

There would of course be a range of other influences within the British Isles and Europe which would impinge upon Cromwell's life. The religious and political world was shifting throughout his early years, England for example was at the centre of changing relationships within the British Isles. As the Williams-Cromwell family continued to rise in the world during the Reformation England and Wales, their home country, were unified. By the time Oliver was born the union was in its seventh decade and well-established. On the other hand, England's imperial ambitions in Ireland were not quite as successful. The monarch's authority had increased from the Pale – the Leinster based English administration and other pockets of English control around major market towns and ports since the 1530s – but major rebellions in the 1580s and 1590s demonstrated serious weakness in England's power.

In 1599 the O'Neill, Hugh O'Neill, Earl of Tyrone and his principal ally Hugh O'Donnell, Earl of Tyrconnell dominated the north of Ireland and defied Queen Elizabeth's Dublin-based administration. Within a few years of Cromwell's birth the situation changed dramatically. The succession to the thrones of England/Wales and Ireland of the Scots king James VI brought a new impetus to the imperial processes at work. In the last years of her reign Elizabeth's forces had defeated O'Neill at Battle of Kinsale and driven him into hiding. Peace was achieved as James came to the throne, and by 1607, with the flight of the two earls from Ireland, complete control of Ireland was effectively achieved. But James had brought with him a design to fully unify England/Wales and Scotland, and he had himself proclaimed king of Great Britain. This part of the plan proved easier than creating a political union between the two nations. The English/Welsh parliament proved unwilling to enact an equal union with a nation which it long perceived as inferior and in Scotland there was a fear that England, with its superior economic power, would dominate any union. For most of Oliver's life, the union remained partial, with both nations maintaining independent governments and parliaments, united in the figure of the king, first James VI and I and then Charles I. It was Charles's attempts to alter the relationship between the churches of the two nations which precipitated the crisis which threw Cromwell onto the national stage. During Cromwell's later life the relationships between the three kingdoms became central to his life.

Cromwell's environment was the bustling town of Huntingdon. This is still a small town, marred by a horrible set of modern roads, which coupled with the rail line, severs the direct route to Hinchingbrooke in a savage way. Huntingdon is pretty, despite some ugly modern building lurking behind the genteel eighteenth century frontages. Although no towns are left behind by the centuries through which they pass, some might mistake Huntingdon for a laggard. This would seriously underplay its role in the world. In the seventeenth century it was a prosperous town surrounded by a prosperous champaign. Moreover, it was on the main road leading to and from London, the route between the capitals of King James's two main kingdoms. It was also close to one of the two universities in England. The Huntingdon of Cromwell's childhood is perhaps deceptively familiar. The road layout of the part of the town which embraced Cromwell's world is almost the same as it was at the beginning of the seventeenth century. The boundaries of the shops detectable in the town survey of 1572 and on Speed's 1610 map seem to have been preserved by the later buildings constructed on their plots. It was a modernising town, as commercial, educational and private concerns replaced the religious houses and their properties. Oliver's Huntingdon was concentrated at the north-west end of the town. The family house stood on High Street, next to a drain. Across the road was St John the Baptist church. Further south down the High Street was the school. Had Oliver taken a right-turn just before reaching his school along the side of All Hallowes or All Saints church along what has been George Street since the eighteenth century, but was known as St Georges then, he could have walked a mile or so to Uncle (Sir) Oliver's home.

As a young lad Oliver went to school, just a hundred yards or so from his house, underlining the close world in which he lived and grew up. The school, like Robert and Elizabeth's house, owed its existence to the Reformation, being established in the buildings once occupied by the Hospital of St John the Baptist, and remained closely linked to the church where Oliver was baptised, for the head teacher, Thomas Beard was also the minister of the church. The role of Beard in Oliver's education has been the subject of much speculation. Much of this speculation has centred upon Beard's religious perspective. As with much of Cromwell's history, a good deal about Beard was read backwards. Starting from the assumption that Cromwell must have imbibed his later puritanism somewhere, Beard became a distinct possibility. He taught Cromwell at school on weekdays and from 1610 preached at him on a Sunday. The connection seems clear; but it depends much upon Beard being identified as a 'puritan' himself. As John Morrill has convincingly shown, this identification is now in doubt.

Seven years before he took up his place as minister and teacher at Huntingdon, Dr Thomas Beard had published a book, *The Theatre of God's Judgement*, in which he demonstrated himself to be a providentialist, amongst other things. There is certainly something in this which would appear to link the text with Oliver for Cromwell would later show himself to be a providentialist, believing that God's plan for humanity could be discerned by observing closely the course of worldly events. Yet in attempts to encapsulate Cromwell's religious outlook, historians from a wide spectrum of thought, including Christopher Hill and Maurice Ashley and even John Buchan, have conjoined Beard's providentialism with a dislike of the structured religion of a state church. If this were the case, it would tie in with what Colin Davis has called Cromwell's 'antiformalist providentialism', combining distrust of a single 'formalised' national church with the belief that god was instrumental in everyday life. The question of Beard's influence on Cromwell turns upon a question – could Beard be described as one of the Godly, potentially a separatist? The answer given by recent examinations appears to be no. Beard was able to work easily within the regime as it existed in James VI and I's reign, and more importantly within the changing religious regime of Charles I. Beard did believe the pope was the antichrist, something which Charles's Archbishop of Canterbury, William Laud and his ilk, did not, preferring to see the head of the Roman Catholic faith as an erring brother; but even this would not automatically make Beard a puritan or separatist. John Morrill has presented him as a 'greedy pluralist' who lived in great comfort with income derived from a number of posts. In Huntingdon alone he held the living of All Hallowes (All Saints), and then St John's. He also held the mastership of both the school and the hospital. Until he took up the post at St John's he also was the absentee incumbent of Kimbolton. In 1612 he gained a prebend's chair at Lincoln Cathedral, increasing his income yet again. Beard was distinctly un-puritan in another way too: he played a full, and later acrimonious, role in the civil government of the town. Beard was not the source of Cromwell's puritanism.

It is far safer to assume that Beard was influential only in a general sense: Cromwell's religious awakening was probably located later in life, and it may have been more closely associated with his social and temporary mental problems in his late twenties, than with his school life. Within the Huntingdon Free Grammar School, which unusually for buildings associated with the young Oliver, still exists in part (it is the Cromwell Museum), Master Cromwell studied the liberal arts programme of early Stuart England, largely unchanged from that imbibed by his father. This would be the old trivium, consisting of Latin, grammar and rhetoric, subjects based in the classics which served as a preparation for the quadrivium, that would be studied at university. If he was lucky there would have been a chance to study other things, Greek, Hebrew, French, Italian and perhaps even music. Later commentators suggested that he had a fairly lax attitude to schooling. Cromwell is said to have been something of a naughty boy, stealing apples, playing the rough games of boyhood. It was claimed that he read little, but again this may be the product of later imaginations, as we know he enjoyed Sir Walter Raleigh's *History of the World*, published in 1614 whilst Oliver was still at school. Cromwell's Latin, a mainstay of a gentleman's education, was sometimes referred to as weak, but on the other hand he seemed adept at using it as a means of communication with foreign diplomats later in life. In short though, we do not know what Cromwell did at school. The tick-box mentality of examination-dominated twenty-first century education has no seventeenth century parallel from which we could derive a statistical impression of the boy's attainments, nor do end of term reports exist to provide us with Beard's impression of his pupil. We are left with the impressions of people who were not present or who were not contemporaries of Oliver. Having had our collective fingers burned over Beard's 'puritan' influence, it is best to stay clear of unfounded speculation. That Cromwell went on to university offers little guide either. It was a social, political and economic decision, rather than an educational one. Cromwell followed his uncle and father to Cambridge, but not to their college, Queens, instead he went to Sidney Sussex College on 23 April 1616: it was the day William Shakespeare died.[7] Two days later Oliver Cromwell was seventeen years old. Cromwell's status was that of one of the dozen gentlemen commoners. He would pay fees and eat in the common hall. He was not a scholarship boy and he would not be in the ignominious position of having to double as a college servant. This would have eaten into the family's income considerably; it has been estimated that it cost between £30 and £50 a year to be a student.

Oliver Cromwell was enrolled under a tutor, Richard Howlet. Sidney Sussex had a growing reputation for puritan scholarship. The college had been founded by the Montagu family, which was closely associated with the Cromwells as it was also located in Huntingdonshire and moved in the same circles of power and influence. The master of the college was Dr Samuel Ward who was a determined Calvinist, convinced of the essential truth of predestination. To Ward there was no salvation to be expected other than that predicated by God at the world's creation. No good works, no amount of prayer and certainly no intercession by saints could impinge upon one's election or damnation. This was certainly a more promising environment in which the young Cromwell could imbibe a puritan outlook. The purpose of university education is the subject of much discussion. It has been claimed that they performed the function of a 'finishing school' and the formal education played a less-important role than the socialising between the young gentleman and the extra-curricular activities, such as music and dancing, fencing and hunting. On the other hand, as Felicity Heal and Clive Holmes have reminded us, we must not overstate this centrality of the socialisation process at the expense of education: members of the gentry themselves viewed the courses followed as important to establish themselves as cultured and intellectual men.[8] Of course there was time for more raucous activities, often centred around alcoholic drinks. Some things do not change. Yet, because Cromwell left no comprehensive account of his education, we are only able to speculate about his education. His later love of music and dance may have been cultivated at university as it was for many of us. In any case Oliver's time at the university was destined to be short.

2

A CHIEF OF SINNERS
1617–1637

Cromwell's higher education came to an abrupt end in June 1617, because of the death of Robert Cromwell. Earlier that same month the Cromwells' personal network expanded as Oliver's sister Margaret Cromwell married Valentine Walton at St John's church across the road from the family home. Robert's death cast a massive pall over the family. Aside from the trauma of a father's death, which in itself is a life-changing event, the death of the *pater familias* had enormous legal and financial consequences. Even counting Margaret's marriage there were still five girls at home, the estate income had not been improved and the male heir was not old enough to inherit control of the estate.

With the death of Robert Cromwell, Oliver became the only male member of his nuclear family. Because of Oliver's age there was the possibility that the estate would fall under wardship. Part of the estate was held from the crown by what was still referred to as knight's service (or *per capite*), even though the mediaeval military dues were no longer exacted. Such tenure would have entailed Oliver being made a ward of the court, especially as Elizabeth had inherited the *per capite* for life. Cromwell would have to sue for his inheritance, and this would have been awkward and costly for the small estate. Fortunately the Court of Wards decided that the liberty of the estate had been sued by Robert, in other words confirmed, during the life of his father, and Oliver did not have to.[1] Nevertheless, with four more daughters to be provided with dowries the estate would be severely tasked. What was a young man of 18, separated by two generations from a knighthood, and thus by one from being truly regarded as an esquire going to do? Earning a living would have to have been a serious consideration, and the law was a possibility by which a gentleman could work for a living without imperilling his social status. It was the means by which an estate could be enhanced. There has been a great deal of speculation about Cromwell and the pursuit of a career in law. Early biographers, including S. Carrington[2] and James Heath,[3] suggested that Robert and Elizabeth had intended that Oliver study civil law, and went on to say that the lad attended Lincoln's Inn. Lincoln's was the Inn where Sir Henry, Sir Oliver and Robert had been students themselves.

Maurice Ashley once suggested that Cromwell 'appears' to have attended one of the 'law schools' the Inns of Court. However, there is no hard evidence, and historians have been reduced to searching for circumstantial proof. For instance, the best case that can be made for Cromwell having attended Gray's Inn is that some of his cousins were there and the Inn's records are incomplete. Gray's Inn did draw students from East Anglia, according to Wilfred Prest's work, which identified regional links with the four Inns. Historians speculate that Cromwell did attend one of the Inns between 1617 and 1620, and he certainly spent some of his time in London. Attending the Inns was a similar experience for young gentlemen as attending university. Many young men who had attended university, whether taking a degree or not, progressed to the Inns to gain a training in law which would be useful in later life when dealing with real estate law as landowners. For Cromwell and his contemporaries, training in law would be useful when they became justices of the peace in counties or towns. For the Cromwell estate attendance at an Inn would have been expensive: there were no fee concessions or scholarships as there were at university. If Cromwell attended an Inn then he would have had to pay from the small income of the estate. Life at the Inns of Court had certain similarities with life at Cambridge. There was a wealth of extra-curricular activity to indulge in, and of course, the spectacle of the court. Again, however, we know little of the life of the teenage Cromwell, except that he fell in love.

Cromwell's possible presence in London begs a question about the management of the estate. Another assumption about this period of his life is the possibility that he spent some time in London and some in

Huntingdon helping his mother manage the estate. This would probably be unnecessary. Recent work, such as that by Amy Louise Eriksson,[4] on early modern women, has clearly shown that women managed estates alone in a number of circumstances; widowhood being a major cause of female management. One clue to Elizabeth Cromwell's ability is the fact that Robert had named her sole executrix of the estate.[5] Men who understood and appreciated their wives' managerial capacities would in the right circumstances appoint them to execute the will. Sometimes this would be in conjunction with another relative, if there was some perceived limitation to a wife's capacities, including age or ill-health. With a wide network of family near at hand Robert would have had no shortage of suitable co-executors or even alternative administrators. Instead, he nominated Elizabeth alone, and this must be a clue to her capacities. Far from guiding his mother, perhaps young Oliver would be learning estate management from her. It would certainly leave it possible for the young heir to spend a considerable part of the period 1617–1620 away from the family home, pursuing a legal career or simply gaining the gentleman's quotient of legal training.

One thing we do know for certain about Cromwell's time in London is that he met and married Elizabeth Bourchier. She was the daughter of a London fur-dealer, Sir James Bourchier. The Bourchiers were friends of the Barringtons. Joan Barrington, wife of Sir Francis Barrington, was Oliver's Auntie Joan, his father's sister. John Morrill suggests that Oliver lived at Auntie Joan's London home, but there is speculation that the young couple meeting at Joan's country home where she was a neighbour of Sir James at Little Stambridge in Essex. Of course this speculation removed the need for a London connection at all, until the marriage at St Giles Cripplegate on 22 August 1620. The marriage entailed more of a drain on the meagre gentry estate, for the marriage settlement alienated £40 a year from the general family income as Oliver, having come of age at his twenty-first birthday the previous April, was able to settle the parsonage of Hartford on his wife.[6] On the other hand this Barrington-Bourchier circle brought Oliver into contact with another political circle, that of the Rich family, and its head the Earl of Warwick, a personal link re-cemented near the end of Oliver's life. A series of circles, Cromwells, the extended circle of cousins and the political elites' circles were revolving around the young Cromwell in ways which were both visible, such as the ever-developing family relationships of marriage and birth, and invisible, revolving around politics and religion. Within these circles there would be people to whom the young Cromwell would, if he were able to prove himself within his own at present limited spheres, become useful.

The newly married Cromwell returned to Huntingdon and established the family home as their home. Within a few months of his marriage, Oliver came of age and became the legal as well as titular head of the family. In common with many families of all classes the Cromwells consisted of two and then three generations in close proximity. There was one member of the oldest generation, mother Elizabeth, then there was Oliver and wife Elizabeth, and those of Oliver's sisters who had not yet married. Soon a third generation, the children of Oliver and Elizabeth, would be added: Robert in 1621, Oliver in 1623, Bridget in 1624, Richard in 1626, Henry in 1628, Elizabeth in 1629, James in 1631 and later, Mary in 1637 and Frances in 1638. The birth of Richard in 1626 occasioned the earliest known letter from Oliver Cromwell, dated 14 October 1626. He wrote to his old college friend Henry Downhall, who unlike Cromwell had completed his degree and was now a Fellow at St John's College and asked him to be godfather to Richard.[7]

Within his own 'limited spheres' Oliver Cromwell began to make his mark: he was not the country squire that his father still had claims to be, he was very much the urban gentleman. Whilst many members of the 'urban gentry' had tenuous claims to gentility, at least before the Restoration (or before they bought rural estates), Cromwell had full credentials for being addressed as Mister, even if he lacked his father's qualification as an esquire. Cromwell's status came far more from his own demonstrable assets than did his father, making him at once less high in status but more certain of a place in the urban sphere. In the town's tax roles Cromwell paid tax on moveable goods (in the category of men who paid *in bonis*), indicating that he was not amongst the town's wealthiest men, who paid tax on income from property (the category known as *in terris*). He paid £4 suggesting an income of £100 a year. In 1627 Cromwell sold a piece of property in Huntingdon known as barnes close to a draper, Arthur Ashton, for £104. The land consisted of two closes (enclosed fields) with the eponymous barn and a cottage occupied by the blacksmith Owen Mayfield. The property had been given to Elizabeth Cromwell by Sir Henry, perhaps as part of her marriage settlement although in theory this could have remained in mother Elizabeth's possession.[8]

Oliver began, at some time in the 1620s, to take up the responsibilities attendant or expected of an urban gentleman taxpayer or subsidyman. At sometime during the decade Oliver Cromwell became a member of Huntingdon council like his father. We do not know when, because the records of the borough are fragmentary. He would have been one of those men who annually elected the twenty-four burgesses comprising the Common Council and before January 1621 he was elected himself to be one of them. On 9 January 1621 Cromwell signed the borough's return of MPs Sir Miles Sandys and Henry St John to parliament.[9] Huntingdon was governed by two bailiffs and a common council which was responsible for all financial and civil affairs. It was not a refined borough structure: although it had a recorder by the sixteenth century, it is clear that this was not a full blown legal official as in more sophisticated urban governments, but strictly an official who stored the towns records. From 1295 the town was given the right to elect two MPs. The MPs were to be selected from the town's burgesses, but by the seventeenth century as in many boroughs, the MP were outsiders to the town, intruded into it by powerful magnates on the eve of the polls. The candidates would pay the required dues and complete required formalities to become burgesses of the borough and thus eligible for election but probably thereafter play little part in its affairs.

We can surmise that Cromwell was doing well in his small pond. In 1628 the fruits of this appeared. Oliver Cromwell was selected as one of the town's two members of parliament. This is generally seen to be the last gasp of the Cromwell network in the immediate area. The family was on the decline. Sir Oliver's mounting debts entailed the sale of the mansion at Hinchingbrooke to the Montagu family who also supplied the other MP. For much of Cromwell's life hitherto national politics had had minimal impact. There have been suggestions that Cromwell gained some military experience fighting on the continent in the early stages of what would become the Thirty Years' War, in which case international politics would have impacted upon him, but this is in doubt. The subtle religious changes imposed by James VI and I as he sought to impose some sort of conformity or comparability of worship across England and Wales probably had little impact. Had Dr Beard been the puritan of supposition, this would have been different for James's denial of puritan ambitions for further reform within the church, would have angered Cromwell's teacher. However, as we have seen Beard seemed happily encompassed within James's church. In 1625 King James died and was succeeded by his son Charles. Charles did not have his father's subtlety with regard to either religion or politics. In both he would appear to be abrasive. Despite a warm welcome from his first parliament, some members of which had high hopes for a good working relationship with the new king, things changed quickly. There were concerns that the king would spend money on unwise military interventions in the continental wars by his favourite, the Duke of Buckingham. On a wider scale there were general concerns about taxation and efforts were made to retain fiscal control in parliament's hand, by voting the new king the income from customs duties, known as Tunnage and Poundage after liquid measures and dry weights, for one year only; normally these rights had been granted for life by the accession parliament. After a year the aggrieved king would continue to collect the tax illegally. Furthermore only two subsidies – the normal taxation levies – were approved. Inflation had destroyed the value of the subsidies and they were now completely inadequate for present needs, especially given the king and the Duke's military ambitions. There were also concerns about Charles's religious policy. There was a group of churchman who wished to reduce the Calvinist tone of the Church of England and supplant it with a variation of the forms suggested by the Dutch theologian Arminius. Arminianism rejected the harsh notion of predestination, which allowed the individual no role in his or her salvation, and introduced the notion of salvation through active participation in the sacraments of the church and through 'good works'. To critics this seemed very close to Roman Catholic belief, and they coupled this concern, wrongly, with Charles's marriage to a French Roman Catholic, Henrietta Maria, into an apparent conspiracy. Nevertheless, the King and Buckingham were both enamoured with a leading figure in this reform movement, William Laud, Bishop of Bath and Wells, and this further worried a significant section of the parliament. Any hope that the king and this parliament would work well together, was soon dashed by this mutual suspicion and antagonism. The parliament was dissolved without any long term solution to the financial problems. The parliament of the following year was no more successful, and Buckingham's disastrous attack on Cadiz seemed to confirm the worries many MPs had had about his suitability as a leader. The king still required money, loans secured on the crown jewels had funded the war, but nothing costs more than a defeat. Charles had tried to lessen the opposition by appointing some troublesome MPs to the post of county high sheriffs thus preventing them from standing in the elections. By such an appointment, these men become the supervisor of elections in their county and ineligible to seek election themselves. However, even without these activists, the new parliament focussed its attention on Buckingham as much for his increasingly apparent Arminianism as for his disastrous campaign. At the same time as discussing proposals for four subsidies, parliament planned to impeach Buckingham, prompting Charles to dissolve it, in order to protect his favourite.

Without parliamentary finance, the king and privy council sought to finance the continuing war without access to the normal means of supply. Two methods were tried, firstly a Benevolence or 'free gift' by which taxpayers were asked to voluntarily loan money to the king. This met with a poor and sometimes derisory response. The second method was a Forced Loan, by which the taxpayer was 'obliged' to lend money to the crown. Although this was financially successful to some extent, the levy was unpopular and provoked a high profile law suit against prominent 'refusers' known as the Five Knights' Case, which as Richard Cust[10] has shown, instigated a habit of resistance to the king's fiscal policy that refused to go away. Buckingham continued to spend money on disasters: his attempt to provide military support to the trapped French protestants at La Rochelle and the Isle de Rhe failed. The 1628 parliament met in the subsequent contentious atmosphere. Cromwell was one of its members.

We are not certain of the process by which Cromwell was chosen as member for Huntingdon alongside James Montagu.[11] Montagu gained the highest number of votes, reflecting his family's pre-eminence in the area. A year earlier Sir Oliver had had to sell Hinchingbrooke to Sir Sidney Montagu for £3,000; after which he retired to his other home Ramsey. It is perhaps possible that Oliver was still helped into the selection by family influence, but friendship and economic ties with the Montagus might have also been an influential factor. Huntingdon's members of parliament were chosen by the burgesses of the town, theoretically from amongst their number but they were often outsiders chosen by powerful landed magnates from the area, such as the Montagus and the Cromwells and 'imposed' on the town. To qualify for election outsider nominees would be made burgess before the election. In Cromwell's case this would not have been necessary as by 1628 he would be cementing his claim to be one of Huntingdon's urban gentry elite. The 1628 parliament was an exciting one which set down principles which were adhered during the English revolution. Cromwell played a low key role as befitted a new member, but even so he was involved in a religious debate, which was integral to the declining relationship between parliament and the king. Yet Charles had opened the session with conciliation in mind and encouraged the commons to discuss a range of grievances centring on the recent Forced Loan and the billeting of soldiers along the south coast. In response to the king's apparent acknowledgement of previous wrongs, parliament responded with an offer of five subsidies. Nevertheless, parliament continued to discuss grievances and drafted the Petition of Right, which asserted its authority over the collection of taxation and the preservation of subjects' rights against the imposition of martial law. This angered Charles as he had presumed that he deserved the trust of parliament, especially after he had honestly acknowledged his mistakes, put down he argued to youthful enthusiasm in the dire circumstances of war. He prevaricated in signing the petition and in the end, did so confident that as it was a petition, he could not be held to its terms later. When the commons then passed a remonstrance (or complaint) about the Duke of Buckingham, Charles prorogued the session. Before it met again, Buckingham was murdered by John Felton who claimed to be inspired by God and by the recent remonstrance; a claim which did nothing to enamour the king to his parliament.

Whilst at Westminster, Cromwell became ill, with what we might call depression, and what Cromwell's contemporaries termed melancholy. He consulted the well-known physician Sir Theodore Mayerne. Mayerne, a French immigrant, had conducted the postmortem on the king's elder brother Prince Henry, and had a formidable list of clients by 1628: he was perhaps the most famous physician in the country. Mayerne was probably recommended to Cromwell by one of his extended family or their associates; the Whartons and the Russells were represented in the doctor's case notebook.[12] Cromwell consulted Dr Mayerne on 19 September 1628. His symptoms were physical, bad stomach aches after meals, excessive phlegm and a cough. Yet he was labelled *Valde Melancholicus*: truly melancholic.[13] There has been much discussion of this part of Cromwell's character. It has been noted that he was a man of extremes: he could be plunged into the deepest despair, yet reach the heights of elation. It is always problematic making diagnoses for long dead 'patients', but there has been a long tradition of looking at Cromwell's health. A Huntingdon based Doctor Simcott implied that Cromwell was a hypochondriac who during the mid-1630s would have him dragged out of bed at all hours on the premise that he was dying. In 1628 on the other hand Mayerne seemed to take the symptoms seriously and prescribed a series of remedies. Cromwell's mood swings bear some resemblance to bi-polar disorder. This would account for the extremes of mood, the inability to sleep during the 1630s and the bizarre thoughts that allegedly ran through his head during the 1630s health crisis: at one time apparently he thought that he would be come the greatest man in the kingdom – although this is from the less than reliable evidence of Dr Simcott. Yet this diagnosis is purely speculative. There are other traits that apparently do not fit with bi-polar disorder, Cromwell's fierce demonisation of enemies, his inability to distance the person from an argument with which he disagreed, may also be the result of a mental problem.

Cromwell's illness in 1628 has often been linked to his religious outlook. Coming out of deep depression into exultation may have been related to Cromwell's religious experience or his being 'born again' into a firmer faith. It might explain how he came to identify himself with the Godly, as it does not seem that there was any discernible external experience, now that Beard, Howlet and Ward's collective influence have been ruled out completely or seen as minimal. We are left with a ten-year period during which at some point Cromwell underwent this 'conversion' experience, but we have no firm date. We do know that it was intensely personal and perhaps born of the effects of melancholia upon his psyche.

Parliament was not recalled until the beginning of the following year, and it was clear that the king did not wish it to sit much longer and he had done his best to limit the impact of the Petition of Right by printing along with it a long exculpation. The issue of Tunnage and Poundage reappeared and Charles urged parliament to discuss a formal grant, but the house debated the actions of the king's customs collectors and summoned them to the bar of the house to explain their actions. It was also preoccupied with religious issues, and Cromwell was involved in the work. Indeed the only record of his activities in the House of Commons comes from the committee debates in February 1629 in the last weeks of the parliament. The committee was investigating the spread of Arminianism in the church, in particular Bishop Richard Neile's actions in securing pardons. Two Arminians, John Cosin and Sidney Montagu, had been pardoned and two others, Roger Mainwaring and Robert Sibthorpe who had declared that obedience to the Forced Loan was the only justified response had also been released, having been imprisoned on the orders of parliament during the first session. Cromwell presented evidence about Neile's previous activities, involving Dr Beard.[14] It was an old story, over a decade old by the time Cromwell raised it. It centred upon an alleged papist sermon preached at St Paul's Cross in the open air sermons behind St Paul's cathedral by Dr William Alabaster. Alabaster had converted to Rome in the 1590s and returned to the Church of England flock around 1610, but his sermon was apparently dubious and Beard was asked to refute it. However Neile, as Bishop of Lincoln, tried to stop Beard so doing. In the end Beard did give a response, on the Bishop of Ely's orders. Neile had summoned Beard and angrily berated him for disobedience. As an old story with little corroboration, Cromwell's contribution would hardly enliven the debate, but it would add to the general background of distrust centring on Arminians' supposed engagement with popery.

Such discussions ran contrary to the king's religious ambitions and Charles suspended the session for five days. During the recess, members of the commons drafted a declaration on religion calling for adherence to the tenets of the church in opposition to Jesuits and Arminians. On 2 March 1629 parliament reassembled, but it was quickly clear that Charles wished to suspend the session again, preparatory to dissolution. As the Speaker got up to end the session, MPs Denzil Holles and Benjamin Valentine pushed him back into his chair. The king's ministers leapt to aid the speaker and a scuffle broke out around the chair, but the king's opponents managed to restrain Sir John Finch until declarations against innovations in religion and collecting, or voluntarily paying tunnage and poundage, were read by Sir John Eliot and others, and passed by acclamation before Finch was allowed to stand. It was high drama set against the hammering of Black Rod's staff upon the doors of St Stephen's chapel. It was the last session of parliament until April 1640. Cromwell returned home.

At home Cromwell resumed his role as a burgess governing Huntingdon, expecting, no doubt, that should a new parliament be summoned, he would stand a good chance of representing the town again. Meanwhile, there was a decision to be made about a donation made to the town council. The property or cash stock of a town could often be enhanced through legacies made by prominent townspeople in their wills. Often these could be given for the town's use with few conditions attached. On other occasions there could be strict terms to be applied, so that the money should be invested to provide an income for the poor and so on. During the 1620s mercer Richard Fishbourne died. Although he lived in London, Fishbourne had been born in Huntingdon and when he died he left £2,000 to the town. The terms of the bequest were vague enough to allow the town to make decisions upon its use. There were two main options after investing the money in property to produce an annual rental income: one option was to use the income to provide work for the unemployed. Another was to use at least part of the money to pay a lecturer to deliver godly lectures-cum-sermons in the town. Both of the ideas had merit, but some councillors pointed out that Dr Beard already gave lectures on Wednesdays and Sundays and so another lecturer would be superfluous.

The process of deciding upon the Fishbourne bequest was a long one, beginning before Cromwell left for parliament. It took three years to buy the property from which the annual income would be derived. Then the arguments began. One of the wealthier members of the council, Thomas Edwards, went to the Court of the Mercers' Company which was administering Fishbourne's bequest and put the argument against the lectureship in January 1630. He was followed by the big guns of the council, the recorder – the man who kept the council's papers – Robert Barker and Thomas Beard himself to the court to argue that of the annual income, £40 be spent on the lectureship and the remaining £60 be devoted to creating an employment scheme. It was Edward's case which impressed the Mercers, as they could see that the majority of the council were trying to simply offset council expenditure – it paid Beard's lectureship fees – against the new money. Instead the Mercers' Court suggested setting up a completely new lecture given by a new man, but then the king took a hand and ordered the appointment of Dr Beard. This did not end the argument and eventually the king was persuaded to allow a new post to be advertised and Beard was considered as one of the applicants, although the job was offered to Richard Proctor. The council, still aiming to offset Beard's wages, prevaricated over paying Proctor's salary. It was not until the middle of 1631 that the first Fishbourne lecture was given.

By the time Proctor entered the pulpit of St Mary's the arguments in council had moved on. In order to clear the air after the years of argument, it was suggested that the town government be reorganised. A new charter was issued, reshaping the town government: henceforth the council would consist of a mayor and twelve aldermen, rather than of 24 burgesses. Thirteen of the 'better' burgesses would be selected and the remaining eleven would become the lower house or council, who would 'attend and advise' when called upon. Thomas Beard, Oliver Cromwell and Robert Bernard would be JPs; but Cromwell was not made an alderman. Thomas Edwards the man who had opposed the lecture scheme was not among the new aldermen either, despite his clear suitability as a 'better' burgess and neither was William Kilbourne.[15] These three men were not happy at the decision and Cromwell and Kilbourne began to argue with the newly appointed aldermen, and Cromwell did not take up his appointment as JP. The argument quickly got out of hand and Cromwell and Kilbourne were sent for by the Privy Council after the aldermen complained about their attacks on the mayor.[16] On 26 December 1630 the two men arrived at the council and were remanded in custody. On 1 December the case was handed to the Earl of Manchester, new owner of Hinchingbrooke in his position as Lord Privy Seal. Cromwell's objections were to the councillors not the new structure of the council. He and Kilbourne, according to a sworn statement by Beard, 'with free assent and consent did agree to the renewing of our late charter and that it should be altered from bailiff to mayor and that did hope it would be for the future good and quiet of our town'. When the new charter was presented to them all the burgesses, Cromwell and Kilbourne included, 'did like it very well'. Thomas Beard's evidence did not harm Cromwell, it made clear the distinction between his belief that the new charter, issued by the king, was a good thing, and his dislike of the personnel appointed.[17] It is clear that this evidence was influential with Manchester as his judgement reflected this perception exactly: Cromwell thought that the newly created aldermen would alter fundamental precepts of the government in order to 'line their pockets', by selling off town property amongst other innovations. The earl, whilst he may not have agreed with Cromwell, did oblige the aldermen to formally agree to not sell town stock and had the charter altered to ensure that this was the case. Within the judgement Manchester acknowledged Cromwell's regret at his language. Nevertheless, clearly

Cromwell's attacks on the new Huntingdon elite had been so voluble and personal that it could not be ignored. The result was none-the-less climatic for Oliver: he was forced to make a very public apology, as part of the process of reconciliation.[18] A public apology of this kind, enforced by the Privy Council, was a personal and political humiliation. Oliver was in disgrace in his own town.

Such disgrace would make it difficult for Cromwell in his own town. He could not and did not take up the post of JP, which in any case was not one which would have carried much prestige: John Morrill compared its authority to that of a village constable, but this may be understating the case. There would have been mundane ward-based duties, but an urban JP did have magisterial power too and would with his colleagues hold the borough courts, the urban equivalent of the county quarter sessions. Nevertheless Cromwell could not really take a position on the bench sitting next to men whose honour he had impugned. Honour was crucial to the gentry, the integrity of a gentleman was central to the way he would be perceived by his peers and those whom he would govern. Manchester's judgement reflected the way Cromwell had called into question the aldermen's honour, and the punishment meted out impinged upon his.

The Cromwell family responded by leaving Huntingdon. They sold the vast majority of their Huntingdon estate for £1,800 and moved to St Ives, a small farming community, five miles away. John Morrill has speculated on the reasons why St Ives was chosen and concludes that it was a combination of things, proximity to his former home, where his mother remained, a vacant tenancy and the incumbency of a university friend, Henry Downhall. The Cromwells probably moved to a house leased to them by a distant relative and future president of the Protectorate Council of State, Henry Lawrence. It was behind Slepe Hall, where Henry Lawrence lived as lord of this adjacent manor. Cromwell was distinctly moving down the social ladder at this point, but the process would not have been straightforward. As the last stages of his humiliation at Huntingdon were being played out, Cromwell was charged with paying distraint of knighthood. Distraint of knighthood was a money-making scheme adopted by the king in the wake of his dissolving parliament and thereby depriving himself of regular taxation. Essentially it was a 'trick-shot'. Centuries earlier a suitable income rate for a man bearing a knighthood had been decided upon: it was an income of £40 *per annum*. It was incumbent upon such men to attend the coronation of a new monarch and be knighted. Failure to attend entailed payment of a fine. The income rate, after years of inflation, meant very little now, but Charles's financial advisors found the practice and employed it and thus in 1631 everyone with that rate of income was charged the 'non-attendance' fine. For some years, it was thought that Cromwell had made a political stand on the question of paying this levy, based on a list of names of men who had paid the composition or fine to the commissioners charged with collecting it. What made this paper seem important was the clear indication that Cromwell's name had been added after the list was originally compiled. Over a century of speculation followed this discovery in 1860; and commentators decided that Cromwell had paid late, and this tardiness was due to his antipathy to the government. It was suggested that Uncle Sir Oliver had paid the fine on Cromwell's behalf. Again a soufflé had been made from poor ingredients. Brian Quintrell showed how the reality was far less exciting. Cromwell probably had not demurred at all and his late payment was due to a combination of circumstances, sometimes out of his control. Again the early roots of Cromwell's opposition to the king's government are rendered less visible. Cromwell was not the only future parliamentarian who paid without qualms: his cousin, John Hampden, who would soon make a very public stand against the king's extra-parliamentary taxation policy, paid his £30 fine even more quickly than Cromwell. Cromwell had only been expected to pay £10: his tenuous claim to gentility, never mind the squirearchy, was underlined.

In St Ives Cromwell lived a life nearer to that of a yeoman, the amorphous group of wealthy farmers from amongst whom new gentry arose, and into which falling gentry sank. Yeomen could be richer than gentlemen but they lacked the essential armigerous qualifications: coat of arms, livery, shield, etc. of a gentleman. Cromwell retained these badges of rank, but had one of the periodic visitations of the genealogists of the Court of Heralds been made to Huntingdonshire between 1631 and 1636, he may well have lost them. He was now in the pasture farming business, managing a dairy herd. One of the few pieces of evidence of his life in St Ives confirms that Cromwell was now a pasture farmer.[19] One other mooted reason for Cromwell's move to St Ives is that he had a friend there from his student days. Henry Downhall, godfather to Richard Cromwell, was now vicar of St Ives. Downhall is another person often associated with Cromwell's religious outlook, and he was appointed to his parish by Bishop of Lincoln, John Williams and the Earl of Holland, men of very different outlook to the king and Archbishop Laud. However, Downhall was not one of the godly, as John Morrill has pointed out he had wanted Buckingham to be Chancellor of Cambridge and he would later be a royalist, as indeed would Williams during the first civil war and Holland in the second. So their friendship, trust and family link were not related to Cromwell's profound religious experience or politics. This brings us back to accepting that Cromwell found his own path to being one of the Godly, perhaps through the health crises of 1628 and the mid-1630s. Depression would be the depth of his sinful life and the exultation of release from its cloying grip, the light of his assuredness of election: at least until the next bout of melancholia.

We can obscure Cromwell's real status by concentrating upon his entitlement to be called Mister as he undoubtedly would have been called in St Ives to his face, if not behind his back and closed doors. Cromwell has assumed the gentlemanly duties of administration in Huntingdon. He seems to have played such a role in St Ives, but the evidence is small, partly because Cromwell lived there for so short a time. There is an intriguing excision in the signature in the town's vestry book, for 22 April 1633, when Mr Thomas Filby, John Ibbit and Thomas Larkin were nominated as officials for Slepe, Cromwell is supposedly one of the signatories to the appointment, but where his name was is now a hole in the page: a later churchwarden John Bentley cut out the name in 1732.[20] We are on firmer ground a year later.[21] On 7 April 1634 the 'vestry' a semi-formal gathering of the town's wealthiest men appointed the new officials for the forthcoming year. Small towns and villages which were not incorporated were managed by a series of officers who were appointed annually. St Ives had an administration complicated by its history as a wealthy market dominated by the nearby religious houses. Administration was divided in two: the vestry, a committee named after the room in the church in which they met appointed some officials, whilst the manor court appointed the constables and market officials. There is no doubt that the vestry appointed the most prestigious officials, the churchwardens. It also appointed the surveyors of the highways. Churchwardens in St Ives had the usual range of duties associated with church management, maintenance of order in church, upkeep of the fabric and tithe collection, but they also fulfilled duties done in other communities by constables.

Until 1668 they also fulfilled the duties of Overseers of the Poor. The churchwardens were appointed from amongst the men defined as the inhabitants of St Ives. Cromwell immediately seems to have qualified for this group of men. The surveyors of the highways were not from the same social circle. Instead they were appointed from amongst the 'parishioners' the rest of the male community of St Ives. It would seem that 'promotion' was possible and that successful 'parishioners' could rent better properties and thus become 'inhabitants'. Those 'inhabitants' who were not in office audited the accounts of those who were. On that April day in 1634 the four overseers of the highways were appointed: John Johnson, William Chadbourne for the street and Thomas Fielde and Daniell Golde for the other division of the town. The rest of the 'vestry' signed the note of appointment, at the head of the list is Oliver Cromwell. If this is a genuine signature, it has been questioned several times, then it suggests that Cromwell was by 1634 recognised as part of the town's administrative circle. This would imply that Cromwell would have at some time held one of the offices himself. It is interesting that Cromwell does not sign the list again and does not hold office between 1631 and his move from the town three years later. It may be possible that assertion of Edmund Pettis, St Ives's eighteenth century historian, about Cromwell's decline in status whilst in St Ives has some possibility of truth. Pettis suggested that the Cromwells could not afford the rent of the large farmhouse and had to sublet parts of the building. If true this would explain Cromwell's absence from later vestry minutes. On the other hand had he simply been absent for the appointment meetings, he would not have been unusual, sometimes Henry Downhall (who had a say in the nomination to the churchwardenship) or his curate Edward Bell did not sign the minutes either.

One other potential way by which we underestimate Cromwell's status in these years is by ignoring the fact that he and everyone else around him knew that Cromwell's position as tenant at St Ives was temporary. His mother's brother Sir Thomas Steward had no offspring and nephew Oliver was named as his heir. This inheritance would elevate Cromwell from his pasture farmer status and move him to a larger town. Sir Thomas was farmer of the tithes of Ely cathedral and he had a fine house within sight of the cathedral. The income he would pass on to his heir would be in the region of £500 a year, far more like the income of the esquire Cromwell purported to be. In 1637 Sir

Thomas died and the Cromwell family moved to Ely before the middle of the year.

Cromwell was by this time thoroughly in line with opposition politics even if not yet involved with them and part of the group of people who opposed the direction of Charles I's religious policy. His conversion, whenever it had occurred, marked him as one of the godly. That he had undergone a profound religious experience is not in doubt. In January 1636 Cromwell wrote to Mr Storie in London, thanking him for sending a lecturer, Dr Welles to St Ives. In it he makes it clear that in common with those who would describe themselves as 'Godly', he privileged the word of god over other physical manifestations of 'godliness' such as hospitals and temples.[22] Whilst he does not go as far as to reject the value of temples in 1636, he is clearly on a journey from conformity to a more radical stance. Cromwell's letter of 13 October 1638 to cousin Elizabeth, daughter of Uncle Henry, now the second wife of Oliver St John, makes this clear. Oliver described his old self as 'a chief, the chief of sinners'. But then the lord

> ... accept[ed] me in His Son, and give me to walk in his light – and give us to walk in the light, as He is the light! He it is that enlighteneth our blackness, our darkness. I dare not say, He hideth his face from me. He giveth me to see light to see in His light. One beam in a dark place hath exceeding much refreshment in it: – blessed be His Name for shining upon so dark a heart as mine!

Oliver likened his conversion to a well in a barren area, and God had blessed him, but it carried responsibilities too. Conversion required action, as Cromwell wrote: 'Truly no poor creature hath cause to put himself forth in the cause of god than I'. In practical terms this implied connections with the king's opponents. 'Salute all my friends in the Family whereof you are yet a member. I am much bound to them for their love.'[23] There are both immediate and long terms inferences here. Cromwell had asked Oliver St John for a favour, as yet unfulfilled and thanked them for a kindness regarding one of his sons; John Morrill suspects that this entailed getting him into Felsted School which was associated with the Earl of Warwick's circle, into which the Barringtons and Bourchiers were entwined. St John had other things on his mind, just under a year earlier he had begun his involvement in the court case which sprang from another of Oliver's cousins, John Hampden's refusal to pay Ship Money. The longer term implications of Oliver's remembrance to Elizabeth's 'Family' bound him into this political network, for it was through this network that Cromwell could 'put himself forth'. And the time was at hand.

3

... A GENTLEMAN ... VERY ORDINARILY APPARELLED
1638–1641

Oliver Cromwell had little time to make himself at home in Ely, before he was to become embroiled in national politics, nevertheless just as in St Ives he was quickly involved in urban affairs. With the post of collector of the tithes, it would be expected that Cromwell would play a role in Ely society, and there is some evidence to suggest that he did. He was involved in the administration of Parson's Charity. He was involved in the purchase of medicine for one of the charity's beneficiaries and was embroiled in the leasing of property by the charity.[1] However, the affairs of the fens seem to have dominated this period of his life. This is an area of Cromwell's life which is embroiled in myth, exaggerated when during the civil wars royalists dubbed Cromwell 'lord of the fens'. In many areas of England there were extensive drainage schemes in waterlogged areas, promoted by groups of powerful landowners or the king himself. The aim was to improve farming conditions (and profits) by making the ground more suitable for modern farming methods and the work was undertaken by experienced drainage engineers from the United Provinces. Such a scheme was undertaken in the Ely area by a group of aristocrats and gentry, including relatives of the Cromwell family. Oliver Cromwell himself was not opposed to the principle of drainage, and years later he argued that it was a good idea. If he played any substantial role in the drainage dispute at the end of the 1630s it was because he was concerned at the practice not the policy. John Morrill sees that the core of the issue for Cromwell was the allocations of rights and drained lands to the community's poor, the group which lost most in the drive to drain lands. It was alleged that Cromwell was funded by such a group to maintain a lawsuit against the drainers in 1638. The extent of Cromwell's involvement may have been over-exaggerated but it is clear that as he later said he had an interest in the equity of the division of the spoils of improvement. However it would be wrong to use this possible involvement with the cause of the poor fen farmer, or his ill-thought out campaign against possible corruption in Huntingdon council to suggest that Cromwell was a politically active, let alone a radical activist. It might be overstating the case to suggest as J.S.A. Adamson does that Cromwell was a nonentity until he entered the Long Parliament, but Cromwell was hardly at the centre of national events during the 1630s. However, some of his relatives were and they would soon have an impact upon Cromwell's future.

Cromwell's return to higher gentry status coincided with the beginning of what Professor Conrad Russell has rightly called the fall of the British monarchies. As Cromwell moved from St Ives to Ely, and cousin Oliver prepared cousin John's Ship Money case, the king's government in three nations began to unravel. In England there was little trouble in the 1630s. Charles's dismissal of parliament in 1629 was unpopular at the time, but except for the political elite of the country, the anger faded and seems to have been at best low key for some years. Long gaps between parliaments were not uncommon in this period, James VI and I had called only one brief and unproductive parliament between 1610 and 1621, and so for the first years of the 'thirties, it could be argued that nothing out of the ordinary was experienced. However, the absence of parliament had cut the king off from regular financial supply and the 1628 Petition of Right had underlined the illegality of his continuing collection of Tunnage and Poundage. Nevertheless money was required and Charles and his advisors had begun to develop alternative strategies. A series of measures, including Distraint of Knighthood were adopted. The levy which was perceived as most pernicious by contemporaries was Ship Money. Normally Ship Money was a coastal county levy to cover sea-borne defence, it had originally been a mediaeval levy charged on the Cinque Ports on the south-east coast. Charles extended it to all counties, so inland shires like Rutland found themselves technically responsible for building ships and transporting them to London. Another innovation with the tax was the regularity of collection. Ship Money was an extraordinary tax collected in times of emergency; Charles issued warrants year after year. He could justify the collection: there were threats to the coastal communities and the fleet was in need of rebuilding and refurbishing as the disastrous campaigns of the Duke of Buckingham had shown during the 1620s. Dutch fishing craft regularly encroached on British waters and 'Barbary pirates' were landing on the Cornish coasts and kidnapping men and women and carrying them into slavery. Yet the continued collection of the levy was unpopular, partly at least, because it reached into pockets not normally touched by subsidy collection. Historians have long debated the effects of this levy upon the nation's politics. Recently, revisionist historians have suggested that Ship Money was not problematic. Charles needed and got a new navy and thereby prestige and security increased, disputes over collection were in the main over local issues such as allocations and fairness, not political issues. In some cases this is true, but it must not be over stated, some of the disputants did call for a parliament and there is evidence to suggest that opposition increased and filled the country's court rooms with defaulters. It is, perhaps, a pattern of tax refusal that began with the opposition to Charles's collection of the Forced Loan in the late 1620s.

The most public opposition to Ship Money involved Cromwell's cousins by marriage, John Hampden and Oliver St John. In 1637 Hampden refused to pay his Ship Money levy of just 20 shillings on his Buckinghamshire estate. The case was pursued through the courts and ended in being a test case before the twelve judges of the central courts. Oliver St John acted as Hampden's lawyer and argued that the king had every right to declare an emergency and collect extraordinary taxation when parliament was not sitting. Nevertheless, by 1637–1638 three years had passed since the levy had been first collected and there had been plenty of time to call a parliament and raise ordinary levies. St John and Hampden had opened a very contentious case and one of the judges arguing the king's case, Sir Robert Berkeley, argued that the king's word was law, and thus there were no grounds for questioning the king's right to raise such levies. In one sense the argument was over whether or not a king in England and Wales could rule without a parliament. The judgement in the end favoured the king, but only by seven to five and many opponents of Ship Money claimed something of a victory, other observers were worried by Berkeley's argument about royal powers. Events outside England quickly swept away the advantage the king had gained.

As several historians have pointed out, Charles I's religious policy in England and Wales had provoked few martyrs and little noise. In summer 1637 three religious radicals, William Prynne, John Bastwicke and Henry Burton, suffered the disgusting punishments of being pilloried, branded and having their ears cropped (Prynne for the second time), for publishing and broadcasting their religious beliefs. In Llanfaches, Wales an 'alternative' religious community had taken shape and there were pale imitations of such a thing in other parts of the country and in England. Some people simply 'sermon-hopped', illegally going from church to church in order to find a minister of their liking. Generally speaking this was a low-key opposition to the king's policies, and what some historians of past generations have seen as a radical re-structuring of the church by Archbishop Laud and the king has been seen more recently as a kind of liturgical tidying-up, bring a semblance of unity to a fairly lax church. Even if this revisionist perspective is somewhat overstated, because it underplays the commitment of anti-Laudians like Cromwell and others, England and Wales remained quiet relatively compared to Scotland. North of the border, there is no way of referring to the king's religious policy as 'liturgical tidying-up'. The king aimed to subvert the Presbyterian church by strengthening the Episcopal strand injected into it by his father James VI and I. This would undermine the very structure of the Kirk and bring its government under the control of the king completely instead of being a representative organisation grounded in parishes and regionalised synods. As for the liturgy, this was to be re-drafted based on the Church of England Book of Common Prayer. In the same summer that crowds stood and verbally sympathised for the bleeding Prynne, Bastwicke and Burton in London, crowds across Scotland rejected the new liturgy with violence. Riots at St Giles Cathedral in Edinburgh greeted the official reading of the new prayer book and in the days and weeks following the same pattern emerged across the country.

Charles proved incapable of compromise with his Scottish people and failed to understand that opposition to the prayer book united class and gender as well as the geographical entity of his northern kingdom. In October 1637 the leading opponents issued a Supplication urging the king to take action against those who had drafted the prayer book and placing the blame on the bishops. The king responded by assuring the supplicants that the prayer book was his own responsibility, effectively trying to force his opponents to back down believing that they would not attack him personally. Instead he only hardened and broadened opposition, for the response was the drafting of a National Covenant, incorporating his father's so-called 'negative oath' of 1581 which abjured the pope and the Roman Catholic church, alongside a declaration that the reforms of the church made by James VI and I and Charles I were illegal and a band enjoining all Scots to defend the Kirk against its enemies: ostensibly the king. Once drafted, the covenant was signed in St Giles by leading politicians and ministers on 28 February 1638, the next day city officials signed it and then in Greyfriar's kirkyard the citizens of Edinburgh subscribed and then the text was sent out into the nation to be signed in the parishes. When Charles responded with force, he effectively engaged the whole of the Scottish nation. A century and a half before the French Revolution's *levée en masse*, Scotland was mobilised: an army was formed supported by the money and industry of the Scottish people as a whole. The christening spoons could be removed from the bairn's mouths; such was the intrusiveness and effectiveness of the county-focussed taxation. The practical necessity of defying a king who was determined to destroy the Kirk, with force if necessary, entailed governmental restructuring which comprised a political revolution effectively removing the monarch from the political equation.

In 1639 King Charles I mobilised England, Wales and Ireland against Scotland, but his ambitious plans stalled and the main effort amounted to an English and Welsh army encamped on Scotland's southeast border with a similarly scaled down amphibious force off Scotland's east coast. A royalist rising in the Aberdeen region was the only armed manifestation inside the country of support for the king. A small scale reconnaissance force was sent into Scotland in early June and after an embarrassing encounter with a section of the Scottish Covenanter Army retreated back to England. The Aberdeen royalists were defeated on 18 June by which time negotiations had opened between the king and the Scottish government. Although negotiations continued through the summer, it was not long before both sides were preparing for new war. However, whilst the Scots perfected their nascent taxation system, the king was bankrupt. Charles's plans for financial recovery would entail Cromwell, as he had once written to Elizabeth St John, in 'putting himself forth for the lord'.

A plan was put forward by Sir Thomas Wentworth the Lord Deputy of Ireland, who suggested that the only recourse was to parliaments from which the king could ask for money. Wentworth would call a parliament in Ireland, which he believed he could influence sufficiently to succeed in getting taxation approved. This would meet in spring 1640 and close on the eve of the opening of an English/Welsh parliament and act as an influence upon it, inspiring a patriotic fervour which would be converted into money for the king's war chest. The first part of the plan appeared to go well; four subsidies were approved in Dublin and collection begun. The Westminster parliament was not similarly inclined. The tumultuous closing of the 1629 parliament and the imprisonment of some MPs still rankled. Moreover, opponents of the king had been highly organised during the elections, seeking to secure the selection of trusted men to parliamentary seats. Cromwell was one such man. We are not fully aware of the mechanics of Cromwell's selection for a Cambridge seat. Despite his renewed social status, Cromwell was not associated with the town, until with apparent suddenness on 7 January 1640 he was presented to the corporation by the mayor, paid the customary penny to the poor and sworn in as a freeman of the borough, thus becoming eligible for election to parliament for the town.[2] Shortly afterwards, he was elected as an MP for the parliament by Cambridge burgesses who gathered in the Guildhall on 25 March to vote. Following the election he joined the MPs who assembled in Westminster on 13 April 1640. It would seem that the section of Cromwell's kin network that was associated with the Earls of Holland and Warwick had sought his election. As John Morrill suggests, it was probably through the Warwick links with the Barringtons and Bourchiers that Cromwell was absorbed into the circle of opposition MPs. There are other possibilities: Cromwell's sons were at Felsted School, the master of which had links to another opponent of the king Lord Saye and Sele. Cromwell can also be associated with Saye and Sele through the St Johns. There is another possibility: the corporation of Cambridge saw in Cromwell a man who could develop links between it and the leaders of a powerful political faction which included (in Warwick) the elder brother of the university chancellor, the Earl of Holland with whom the town was in dispute and therefore Cromwell was approached by the councillors just as the election got going. For whichever reason, Cromwell, alongside Sir Thomas Meautys a court candidate sponsored by Lord Keeper John Finch, was elected MP for Cambridge and attended Westminster on 13 April.

This was to be a brief parliament and Cromwell was not able to make any kind of mark on its proceedings. As soon as parliament opened, the king asked for twelve subsidies and offered proof of the treacherous behaviour of the Scots, who he claimed had been in contact with a foreign power. For its part the House of Commons sought redress for grievances dating back to Cromwell's last appearance in Westminster. These included the breach of parliamentary privilege, committed when Charles arrested the MPs responsible for holding Speaker Finch in his chair, but also to national issues like perceived illegal taxation and religious changes. John Pym the leader of the Earl of Bedford's group in the Commons summed these three causes up on 17 April 1640:

> I shall ranke these grievances under these 3 Generall heads;
> Greivances:
> 1 Ag[ains]t Liberties of Parliament
> 2 In matters of Religion
> 3 In Affaires of State or matters of propertye
> In all these I shall take care to maintaine that the great prerogative of the King that hee can doe no wrong[3]

In effect Pym set out a political programme for the king's opponents which would transcend the current parliament. It was an agenda that Cromwell would be closely associated with executing over the next year: but not in this parliament. The king's agenda was very different. He needed money and pressed for a quick vote for supply, whereas the Commons insisted that their grievances be dealt with first. It was an impasse. The king attempted to break deadlock in several ways, firstly by intervening in the House of Lords and asking them to press the financial issue. The Commons resented this as interference in their business, seeing in it another breach of privilege. The king then tried offering to discuss grievances if they voted four subsidies immediately; in return he would stop collection of Ship Money but some MPs pointed out that Ship Money as it was being collected was probably illegal and therefore this was in effect no deal at all. On 5 May the king dissolved parliament, it had sat for just three weeks. Cromwell and his fellow MPs went home. Some MPs were despondent, Sir Edward Hyde recorded both the country's and his misery: 'there could not a greater damp have seized upon the spirits of the whole nation ...'. On the other hand, members of Cromwell's circle were far happier: Hyde met Oliver St John 'who had naturally a great cloud in his face and very seldom known to smile, but then had a most cheerful aspect'. St John and others believed that the Short Parliament had not been sufficiently determined to tackle the king. Moreover, St John believed that the king would have to call another parliament, because his determination to go to war would require money in quantities which only Parliament could provide. That parliament would be far more capable of 'what was necessary to be done'.[4] We are left to assume that Cromwell shared St John's perspective.

Within weeks Charles had prepared for war and the English and Welsh part-time militia, the Trained Bands, assembled and marched northwards. This time there was a great deal of disorder as soldiers rioted and attacked churches and in some cases murdered their officers. The Scots, in the meantime, had undertaken what amounted to a political revolution which had reduced the role of the monarch in government. Of more immediate importance was the thorough organisation of a county-based military organisation, which provided the resources for a politically and religiously committed Army of the Covenant. On 20 August 1640 this army crossed the border and eight days later defeated the English and Welsh forces at the Battle of Newburn. Following this victory the Scots pushed the king's forces before them and occupied the North East of England. They were to remain there for the next year. On the same day as the battle, a group of peers forwarded a petition to the king calling for a parliament. The peers were the public face of a larger group of men centred upon the Earl of Warwick and Lord Saye and Sele. It has been suggested that Oliver Cromwell was involved in the drafting process, Oliver St John in his old age was supposed to have recalled taking Oliver along to the meetings. However the evidence for this is quite limited, and Cromwell himself never referred to it.

The pressure for calling a parliament in England and Wales was mounting and was within a British Isles context. In Ireland the second session of the once compliant parliament had been a very different affair. With the Earl of Strafford absent in England the Dublin House of Commons retracted its early enthusiastic support and revised the value of the subsidies, reducing their value from £45,000 to under £10,000 each. In Scotland, the estates had been responsible for the war and had set the conditions of the ensuing peace to include the calling of a parliament south of the border to ratify any treaty. Charles tried to head off a parliament by calling a Council of Peers to York instead; however, once assembled the nobles demanded a parliament. In the face of this Charles issued the warrants for a new Parliament to assemble at the beginning of November 1640. Cromwell stood again at Cambridge, and this time he was elected alongside Cambridge councillor and chandler John Lowry on 27 October.[5] Finch's candidate Meautys, Cromwell's former fellow MP was beaten soundly at the polls.

Parliament assembled on 3 November and Cromwell swiftly became involved in important matters. In previous parliaments Cromwell had been generally low-key, but in this new parliament, which became known as the Long Parliament, he was soon visible. Within the first week he presented the petition of John Lilburne, imprisoned for publishing and distributing the works of William Prynne, and John Bastwicke, the 'martyrs' of William Laud's attack on puritans. At this point he was noticed by Sir Phillip Warwick who later recalled:

> The first time I ever took notice of Mr Cromwell was in the beginning of the Parliament held in November 1640 ... I came into the House ... and perceived a gentleman speaking, (whom I knew not), – very ordinarily apparrelled; for it was a plain clothe-sute, which seemed to have bin made by an ill country taylor; his linen was plain, and not very clean; and I remember a speck or two of blood upon his little band which was not much larger than his collar; his hatt was without a hatband. His stature was of a good size; his sword stuck close to his side: his countenance swoln and reddich, his voice sharp and untunable, and his eloquence full of fervor; for the subject matter could not near much of reason; it being in behalfe of a servant of Mr. Prynn's who had dispenst libels against the Queen ... I sincerely professe, it lessened much my reverence unto that great council; for this gentleman was much harkened unto.[6]

Cromwell was also quickly appointed to a series of parliamentary committees; he sat alongside relatives, Hampden and St John and opposition leaders John Pym and Denzil Holles in a committee examining the case of another 'martyr', this time of the Star Chamber, Alexander Leighton. In the first year of the Parliament Cromwell sat on eighteen committees. Historians have debated the meaning of this sudden appearance in at least the fringes of the limelight. Cromwell was not wealthy, nor prominent on the eve of 1640. He had rebuilt his social status with the benefit of a timely family death, but although he was firmly in the gentry cadre again, he was not a leading light in any sphere. John Morrill sees Cromwell as a collaborator, working with family members in the circle of the opponents of Charles I. J.S.A. Adamson, on the contrary, sees instead Cromwell as a loner and loose cannon. It would be possible for Cromwell to operate alone in the Commons, and Adamson points out that even in the high profile cases, like Lilburne's, Cromwell was not backed up by many people and so his efforts were slow to bear fruit: Lilburne's case, Adamson shows, was not concluded until after the first civil war, and Leighton's took even longer. Yet this is not conclusive, Lilburne was released from prison after Cromwell's intervention and Leighton's case was in the hands of a committee, which included very powerful figures. Cromwell was probably working on the fringes of the organised opposition. It was this circle of men who put him into Cambridge at the beginning of 1640 to counterbalance the government's nominee Meautys and again in October 1640 to destroy the town's royal party's political representation.

The first sitting of parliament, lasting into the summer of 1641 dealt with the major issues which had arisen during the Personal Rule of Charles I, beginning with the three issues raised by Pym in the Short Parliament and highlighted in a number of petitions sent in from around the country and awaiting MPs when they arrived at Westminster, but extending into other areas too, including the causes of the two wars against Scotland, foreign policy and the education of the king's children who were felt to be vulnerable to the Roman Catholicism of their mother. The attack on the personnel of the king's executive government began very quickly. The targets were some of the most important men in government: Thomas Wentworth, Earl of Strafford was held to be responsible for trying to establish absolutist government in Ireland and of fomenting war against Scotland and perhaps even against the

Westminster Parliament itself; William Laud, Archbishop of Canterbury was accused of preparing the ground for the reintroduction of Roman Catholicism, both were imprisoned in the Tower of London. Secretary of State Francis Windebank and former Cambridge MP Meautys's sponsor Attorney General John Finch were also targeted, but they did not hang around to be arrested. There were attacks on the institutions identified as pillars of tyrannical government: the Star Chamber, the Court of High Commission and the Court of Wards. Also in line for action were the financial expedients Charles had used during the 1630s, especially Ship Money. Cromwell was involved in some of this. The things with which he was most directly involved were amongst the least successful items of parliamentary business.

Naturally, the king also had an agenda, changed in detail, rather than in general thrust, from his plan for the Short Parliament. In November Charles wanted parliament to finance a military effort to dislodge the Scots from the north-eastern English counties: he still hoped to persuade parliament that the Scots were rebellious subjects and believed that their demands for £800 a day would cause anger and resentment in parliament. In return Charles offered to discuss grievances once the Scots had been dealt with. However, parliament quickly accepted responsibility for paying the maintenance the Scottish army required and indicated that it believed that the Scots had been justified in going to war against the king. Following this initiative, the business of dismantling the king's government began. Wentworth and Laud were imprisoned during November and parliamentary committees were established and began to gather information about Ship Money, the Court of Wards and other hated features of the 1630s. Oliver St John led the Ship Money committee and his report followed the arguments presented in his case in the Hampden trial. It was this report which sealed the fate of John Finch, because of his role in the judgement against Hampden.

Religious reform was prompted by a petition from London with 15,000 signatures demanding comprehensive restructuring of the Church of England. Petitioners wanted the existing structure of the church, from bishops downwards, to be dismantled and replaced. The comprehensiveness of the petition's demands for the dismantling of the episcopacy led to it being referred to as the Root and Branch petition. Parliament established a committee to discuss the petition and prepare legislation, and Cromwell was included on it. By May a draft was ready and submitted to the House of Commons. It was a long process, based on the Root and Branch petition sent to parliament in late 1640, but based on discussions and research during winter and spring 1641. Cromwell himself wanted to work out the Scots' intentions with regards to England and Wales's religious affairs. The Scottish army remained in the north-east of England over the winter and their motives were suspected. Some were wondering if the Scots sought to ensure the imposition of a Presbyterian system in England. In February 1641 Cromwell sought clarification of their intentions from a friend. Within article eight of their peace proposals was the suggestion that there should be uniformity of religion within the two kingdoms. As he prepared the bill Cromwell wrote to a friend, George Willingham, a London merchant with Scottish trading connections, to ask 'the reasons for the Scots to enforce their desire of Uniformity in Religion ... I would peruse it against we fall upon that debate, which we will speedily'.[7] Cromwell's timing was optimistic for several other matters, including the trial of Thomas Wentworth, Earl of Strafford intervened before the debate began, for in the meantime parliament had been dismantling the king's government. Wentworth was brought to trial in spring 1641 on a general charge of treason consisting of 28 accusations drawn up across the British Isles. However, the charges were in some cases supported by weak evidence, and the case seemed in danger of collapse. Instead a bill of attainder was passed against the earl: it was a mediaeval instrument which had the effect of finding someone guilty because they were suspected of treason. On 12 May Wentworth was executed.

By that time a whole range of reforms were in place, confirmed by the powerless king's assent. Oliver Cromwell and William Strode, one of the men imprisoned in 1629 after the dissolution of parliament, worked on a bill which would entail the calling of parliaments annually. This bill was eventually transformed into a version of the Scottish Triennial Act which had provided for the calling of the Estates every three years; it became law on 15 February 1641. Three months later another act had made sure that the present parliament could only be dissolved if it consented to it. In February Oliver St John was appointed Solicitor General. A complex plan to embrace some others of the leaders of the opposition, including the Earl of Bedford and Pym, had also made some progress until in mid-May Bedford died. This was concurrent with the revelation that the king was at the very least tangentially involved with the Army Plot, a plan by junior officers from the king's army, based in Yorkshire, to attempt an armed rescue of Wentworth as the opening stage of a *coup* in support of the king, which would see the seizure of strong-points around the country. The plot was exposed in early May and the leaders imprisoned.

At around the same time Cromwell and Sir Robert Harley completed the draft of the Root and Branch Bill and presented it to Sir Edward Dering to introduce into the House of Commons. Even then the fruit of Harley and Cromwell's labours floundered in the Commons and it went no further. The bill, for 'utter abolishing and taking away all Archbishops, Bishops their Chancellors and Commissaries, Deans, Deans and Chapters ...' was introduced into the House of Commons by Sir Edward Dering and the House of Lords by Bishop of Lincoln John Williams on 21 May 1641. However, debate was minimal and it did not progress to a vote. When a re-drafted bill on religious reform was presented to the Lords, it owed something to the original petition's and the first bill's general premise, but now it was a proposal for 'better regulating of Archbishops, bishops, deans ...'; it was a considerably muted document. The main thrust of the proposed act was to limit the powers of the church leadership, firstly by dividing the powers of state and church; forbidding ecclesiastical leaders from holding secular legal or political office and secondly by inhibiting their freedom of action within their diocese by making them part of a team, something similar to the regional synods in Scotland, except that the twelve assistants to the bishops would be chosen by the monarch, the lords and the commons, retaining thereby the distinctive nature of the English church and its relationship with parliament and the king. There was no mention of the exclusion of bishops from the House of Lords, something which Cromwell earnestly wanted, and to which he would return throughout the year.[8] There was a significant number of people who did not want such wide scale reform. The removal of Laud had effectively removed the leadership of the Arminians and for some reformers, possibly including the Earl of Bedford himself, that was enough. There was insufficient support for reform at that level, and failure to take the bill any further also began to distance the Scots from their southern brethren, from then on there was doubt that the English and Welsh were as strong in their religious convictions as the Scots.

During that May parliament issued the Oath of Association. This was almost in emulation of the Scottish National Covenant and bound those who swore it to the defence of Protestantism and parliament. Cromwell and John Lowry did their constituency duty and sent the oath to Cambridge council on 8 May 1641, a few days before the Earl of Strafford's execution. The oath was 'accepted with alacrity and willingness' by parliament and, as Cromwell wrote to the councillors, 'dreadful to our adversaries' for it reinforced the people's loyalty to God, the king and the country.[9] The councillors would be responsible for ensuring that the oath would be administered in the town.

Cromwell was still concerned with the fenland drainage schemes that had involved him in the 1630s. On 22 May 1641, the day after the Root and Branch Bill was presented to the commons, Cromwell became involved in a dispute involving Viscount Mandeville, son of the Earl of Manchester, who claimed that their enclosures at Somersham had been destroyed whilst they were being discussed in parliament, because of a petition submitted by the commoners. Cromwell took the side of the commoners, arguing that Mandeville had persuaded the House of Lords to order the Huntingdonshire High Sheriff to use the Trained Bands to deal with the commoners. In June the issue was referred to a committee chaired by Sir Edward Hyde.

Cromwell sat on a series of other committees during the early summer. On 3 July he sat on a committee for the Better Enabling Members of Parliament to discharge their Consciences in the Process of Parliament. At the end of the month Oliver became a member of a committee to consider an act for raising money more speedily and a few weeks later he took part in another, to consider the deforestation of Sir James Thynne's property; an issue that related to a case in the Court of Wards that Cromwell had referred to in the Commons back in early June. Cromwell was showing himself to be consistent in the matters he took up. He presented a petition on behalf of prisoners in the Fleet prison and the King's Bench prison who wanted bail to go away from the prison during an outbreak of 'pestilence' in the city. However it was the religious issue that really enjoyed Cromwell's commitment. Even though the Root and Branch bill and the much watered down July bill had failed to progress through parliament, Oliver continued to press for the disestablishment of the church: he wanted the bishops removed from the House of Lords and argued for this in the Commons on 8 August. He was again to press for this in October 1641. This time he was nearer to success than at any other time, although the victory would not be his or parliament's but that of the people of London.

As the summer approached Cromwell perceived another threat to the victories secured by the king's opponents. Negotiations with the Scots had been concluded and there was pressure on the king to travel to Edinburgh to officially sign it and approve of the stream of legislation enacted by the Estates. In many ways this would be a humiliating experience for the king as it would entail him approving of legislation that diminished his monarchical power. Of course it would also register the finality of his defeat in the second Bishop's war the previous year. On the other hand, the king was optimistic that he could win over a faction within the covenanting movement and turn the tables on his opponents. He had begun to work on this plan before the summer, by conceding to Scots demands in order to get their army out of northern England and thus minimise its impact in English and Welsh affairs. Even at the point of Scotland's greatest victory in the previous year several covenanters had signed the Cumbernauld Bond, in effect creating an opposition to the Earl of Argyll's leadership of the movement. Principal amongst the signatories was James Graham, Earl of Montrose hero of the first Bishop's War, but an opponent of renewed fighting in 1640: by May 1641 his behaviour and correspondence with the king caused the government to arrest him and commit him to prison. Nevertheless, the king believed that he could forge either a 'royalist' party within the Scottish government or influence the Scots into opposing Westminster. This did not go unsuspected. Charles had signed a great deal of legislation in England before preparing to journey north, but he did not react kindly to Ten Propositions for further changes in government submitted to him in June. Cromwell and others opposed the king's going to Scotland, warning that there would be 'danger in this kingdom if he go ...'.[10]

Cromwell was right to be concerned, but in the end there was real danger in Charles's other two kingdoms, rather than in England and Wales. In Scotland the king failed to engineer a political *coup* which left him no choice but to reluctantly accede to the legislative changes. This did not prevent further intrigues, but a violent attempt to take over the government in October was betrayed, leaving the king isolated and making his return to England ignominious. In his wake, the government began to investigate the plot, known as 'the Incident', but they and their Westminster counterparts soon had a greater problem to deal with.

Over the summer John Pym had attempted to maintain the reform momentum, but with little success. Trying to provoke an air of emergency by issuing dire warnings about rebellion in Ireland, or a plot on behalf of the queen to seize control of the royal children, failed to generate a sense of urgency. Nevertheless, the pace of reform continued, even if slowed. After a brief recess parliament reassembled on 20 October, Cromwell returned to the religious debate. He argued that the investiture of five new bishops be postponed whilst the greater issue of bishops in the House of Lords was discussed: he was nominated to a committee to deal with it.

The king's return from Edinburgh coincided with momentous news. On 22 October rebellion broke out in Ulster and Leinster and spread rapidly across Ireland. Such an emergency buried even 'the Incident' as attention turned to raising an army to send to Ireland. On 11 November the Westminster parliament voted to create an army of 10,000 and discussions began about raising a sum of money, eventually estimated to be £400,000, to fund the reconquest of Ireland. It was the outbreak of war in Ireland that would accelerate progress toward civil war in England and Wales. It enhanced mistrust between the king and parliament and led the king to overestimate the amount of support he had in the country at large and in London. These factors would lead to a breakdown in government over the next few months and thrust Oliver Cromwell into a new and unforeseen career.

4

MY ESTATE IS LITTLE ...
1641–1643

The Irish rebellion transformed politics. Cromwell and his colleagues were now faced with a more aggressive king and responded in kind. Against the background of war in Ireland, England and Wales were swept into civil war and Cromwell, for the first time in his life, embarked on a military career. Cromwell had been in the Long Parliament serving on many committees for a year and it could be expected that he had become something of an experienced parliamentarian. There were two clear strands to his political interests by the beginning of the second sitting of parliament in November 1641. Cromwell had demonstrated commitment to religious reform even if the dramatic one-stroke changes proposed in the Root and Branch Bill had been quietly dropped. In October he proposed delaying the appointment of five new bishops and was appointed to a committee to consider the idea. Clearly Oliver Cromwell was now an anti-formalist seeking the end of a single state church such as the Church of England. This concern would resurface within weeks of parliament's sitting. Oliver was also becoming interested in military affairs. Having originally opposed the king's trip to Scotland on grounds of national security, he had subsequently supported the Earl of Essex's appointment as commander of all forces south of the River Trent in the king's absence. In November he proposed that the earl be continued in that office even after the king had returned from Scotland.

By mid-November parliament was busy dealing with the Irish Rebellion and the king was apparently cooperating in a British response to the insurgents. Even so John Pym and his allies had found the impetus they needed for further reform. During the summer there had been a distinct lack of fervour for more reform and even Pym's attempts to sound the alarm over popish plots at home and in Ireland failed to stir up support. The Irish Rebellion of 22 October 1641 seemed to confirm Pym's alarms but in reality it was unexpected: Pym's allies suspected that the Irish Army created by Strafford would be the source of the rebellion, not the seemingly quiescent Gaelic Irish gentry. Nevertheless Pym now had the emergency he needed to provoke concern over the king's intentions: this was enhanced when the leader of the rebellion, Sir Phelim O'Neill claimed to have the king's commission to lead a 'loyal' rebellion and so many refugees were telling government officials in Dublin and in Britain that rebels had told them that they held commissions from the king or queen. Whilst the king had not authorised the rebellion, many could not trust a man who had been implicated in attempted coups in both England and Scotland during 1641 and now appeared to be involved in this new rebellion. Moreover, the king was soon going to seek advantage from the rebellion.

The main thrust of further reform was contained in the Grand Remonstrance presented to the House of Commons in late November 1641. The document had three main elements: a catalogue of the problems caused by the king's Personal Rule; the solutions put in place by the first sitting of the Long Parliament; and most controversially a series of proposals which would put the education and marriage plans of the royal children in parliament's hands, allow parliament to select ministers and to have a crucial role in foreign policy. This was in effect the logical way forward for the political revolution being put in place in England, following many of the precedents established in Scotland's political revolution during the past three years. Cromwell thought it would be an uncontroversial set of proposals and that it would pass the house with little debate; he told Lord Falkland that any debate would be 'A very sorry one' when Falkland suggested that a long debate would ensue. He was miles from the truth. Debate began on 22 November 1641 at 9am and every clause was debated: 'candles being called for when it grew dark' and only at 2am the next day was the division bell rung. The majority for the Remonstrance was only eleven, but immediately John

Hampden proposed printing it in its entirety and making it available for purchase. There was uproar in the house as it was felt that such a move broke all traditions and procedures. A vote was put off for twelve hours, although Hampden's motion was eventually approved. Cromwell admitted to Falkland that he had been mistaken and would listen to his experience in future. According to Edward Hyde MP Cromwell also told Falkland that had the Remonstrance been rejected he would have left the country and emigrated to New England, although there is no other source for this private aside.[1] This was a formative moment for many MPs, some of the king's more moderate opponents felt there was little if any need for further encroachments on royal power and the Grand Remonstrance and its publication drove them into support for the king: this included Falkland and Edward Hyde who had been one of the most vociferous opponents of the Remonstrance.

The king almost threw this new-found support away in January 1642, but by that time events had moved more rapidly than Cromwell or his associates could have expected. The religious issues had remained one of Cromwell's main concerns; he was sitting on the committee investigating the appointment of new bishops when the people of London took the religious cause into their new hands. The appointment of these new men would bolster the votes of the developing royal party in the Lords as well as strengthen the church's input into political affairs in the absence of the imprisoned Archbishop of Canterbury. John Pym had introduced a bill into the Commons proposing the abolition of the bishops' rights to vote in the Lords. Into this heady mix of debate the king threw a direct challenge by replacing the Palace of Westminster guards with his own men. Hitherto, guard duty had been undertaken by the London Trained Bands under the command of the Earl of Essex, now the king gave the job to the Earl of Dorset and a company of the Westminster Trained Bands. There was fighting on the streets around Westminster between apprentices and soldiers at the end of November during which the apprentices shouted 'No bishops!'. The king had played a shrewd game, for amongst his new Episcopal appointments was John Williams, Bishop of Lincoln, who was translated to the Archbishopric of York. Williams was an enemy of William Laud and had been imprisoned in the Tower of London in recent years, he was also related to Cromwell's cousin John Hampden and had appointed Oliver's friend Downhall to the parish of St Ives.

Alongside him was Joseph Hall Bishop of Exeter, known for protecting puritans, who was scheduled for translation to Norwich.

It might have been expected that this would have been accepted as a desire for moderation, but by late 1641 the temperament of parliament and the London streets was such that even these men were criticised for their support of the king's reforms. Williams had written on the placing of altars at the east end of churches and Hall had defended episcopacy in print: these men were tainted. Ominous crowds began to gather around parliament: apprentices, fishwives, oyster women, dockers, hawkers, merchants and traders were about to change parliament themselves. They prepared a massive petition calling for the expulsion of bishops and Roman Catholic peers from the House of Lords. On December 7, to head off the potential for the king to strike at his opponents with force, Cromwell's call for parliament to take command of the armed forces was redoubled by Sir Arthur Hesilrige. At this point too the Grand Remonstrance appeared in print. The king had tried to ignore the remonstrance and had hoped that his public pressure to deal with the Irish situation would win support in London and the provinces. To some extent it did, but it made little impression on the streets of the city where the crisis appeared that much more immediate, especially after the king seized control of the Tower of London. As parliament went into recess for Christmas the apprentices mobbed the Palace of Westminster. Fighting broke out across Westminster over Christmastide and by the end of it bishops were driven out of the Lords, the people of the city achieved that which Pym and his agents, including Cromwell, had been unable to do.

The king's reaction was swift, on 3 January Charles had treason charges drafted against five MPs: John Pym, the leader of the king's opponents in the Commons; William Strode and Denzil Holles, opponents from 1629 who had held Speaker Finch in his chair whilst Charles's policies were condemned; Sir Arthur Hesilrige, a hard-line opponent who had just successfully moved the Commons towards taking control of the armed forces; and Cromwell's cousin, Ship Money opponent John Hampden. A sixth set of charges was drafted against the newly emergent leading opponent in the Lords, Lord Mandeville son of the Earl of Manchester. Accusations against the six were made in the Lords, but the plan to imprison the men immediately failed to materialise. On 4 January the king and an armed guard entered the House of Commons and demanded the arrest of the accused. The intended victims had waited until just before the king arrived at the door and only then fled to the safety of the city of London. The king was humiliated and worse: he was exposed as a man prepared to circumvent political process with force, and he had failed to seize his enemies. Charles's position in the capital became untenable and he was, within days, forced to abandon his palaces. Both sides began to make plans for war. The king sent Queen Henrietta Maria abroad with a portion of the royal jewels to pawn for weapons, after which the king himself headed northwards, reaching York in March. Parliament reopened the debate over militia control, establishing a committee to discuss the issue in mid-January, which by 10 March 1642 had prepared the ground for taking control of the country's Trained Bands. Moreover, parliament established the means by which it would govern during the king's estrangement, because it put the legislation into immediate effect by declaring it to be an ordinance. Just as Cromwell had wanted the previous year, overall command would be vested in the Earl of Essex.

War broke out untidily: it is difficult to precisely date its outbreak, for confrontations and small-scale fighting between rival factions broke out around the country throughout late spring and summer, although the momentum quickened once the king and parliament had assembled significant numbers of troops under their direct command and moved into the Midlands. It was clear that the normal processes of government had become fragmented. The king refused to compromise further on what he saw as his prerogative rights, including control of the armed forces, but extending to his control of government appointments and foreign policy. Parliament for its part could no longer trust the king and was sure of its need to take control of executive power to protect its political gains against Charles's proven aggression. By August Cromwell's commitment moved beyond offering money towards the fund for fighting the war in Ireland to taking up arms himself. The planned use of the trained bands had by now been exposed as a failure. Only in the North West and in London were the Trained Bands used by either side in their entirety. The process of taking over the county forces was slowed in the first instance because of genuine and deliberately provoked confusion as the lord lieutenants appointed in the Militia Ordinance took up the reins of management across the country. By the end of May the king was sufficiently concerned to try and prevent wide scale compliance with the Militia Ordinance and then re-established obsolete commissions of array to try and wrest control of the militia from the new lord lieutenants. This created more confusion in the shires which as June and July progressed, eventually ensured that neither side was able to control the militia in most parts of the country. Both sides then set about asset stripping the traditional defence forces; disarming the soldiers and trying to gain control of the county magazines, particularly in the Midland counties that lay between the king's forces assembling in the north and parliament's forces gathering first in London and then in the southeast Midlands. Private money was being used to provide other weapons. In some cases private enterprise was a temporary expedient: in mid-July Cromwell was refunded £100 he had spent on helping to arm two volunteer companies of foot raised in Cambridge.

Negotiations between the king based at York and parliament continued throughout the summer. On the need to defeat the rebellion in Ireland there was more accord than on other issues, although the means of doing so were controversial once the king suggested placing himself at the head of the army raised for the purpose. Few people felt able to trust a king who had been involved in three attempted coups in the past year, and the need to ensure that he had no military power had driven on the solution to the militia issue. Nevertheless, king and parliament agreed on the need to raise £400,000 to fund Scottish and English/Welsh forces being sent into Ireland. Wales was also of concern to Cromwell. In late March he and Sir Arthur Hesilrige along with John Pym received a petition from a Mr Symonds about gatherings of papists in Monmouthshire. Cromwell was concerned that there was a potential 'Ireland there' and concurred with Symonds that the county magazine should be moved from Monmouth to Newport. Although Pym disagreed, the magazine was eventually moved.[2]

In June parliament set out its political demands framed into Nineteen Propositions which included demands to confirm control of the militia, sought the expulsion of Roman Catholic politicians, the power to oversee the education and betrothal of the royal children and the seizure of initiative in foreign affairs. Knowing that the king would reject the propositions parliament sought to strengthen its own hand by declaring the king incompetent to govern and appointing the Earl of Essex lord high constable of the kingdom.

Money was a major requirement for both sides and the king quickly circumvented the collection process established for the raising of £400,000 to fund the war in Ireland. Little of the money from northwest England and Wales reached Westminster. The king also called upon the resources of individuals and institutions. In August he asked the universities of Oxford and Cambridge to send him their silver and gold plate. Cromwell set out to Cambridge to stop the plate being sent. He and fellow local MPs raced to the university: suspecting that he would need to oppose the royalists by force he raised troops on the way. He took over the castle and posted some of the volunteers on the roads out of the town. The university failed to get more than a small portion of the plate to the king. Of equal importance was securing the county magazine in the castle. At this time the contest for county magazines was reaching a climax: in late July the king had tried to seize the magazines in Lincoln, Leicester and Nottingham, but had been thwarted in each town.

In August Charles organised a rendezvous in Nottinghamshire and set out from the north, heading for Warwickshire, where the skirmishing between parliament's Lord Brooke and the royalist Earl of Warwick was becoming open warfare. The king arrived outside Coventry, where the county magazine was stored and demanded access. Cromwell in Cambridge was in a position to ensure that the king could not enter East Anglia in search of ammunition. During Cromwell's stay in the area he travelled to Huntingdon on a recruitment drive. It was clear that Cromwell intended at this point to command a mounted unit, he clearly had the resources to assist in mounting his soldiers: his financial circumstances had so clearly changed since his days in St Ives: he had already committed £300 to the war in Ireland and now his expenditure on the troop of horse would have bankrupted the younger Cromwell. By 7 September the troop had a near full complement of 60. Within a week it was listed in the Earl of Essex's army as troop number 67 under Captain Oliver Cromwell: he had been commissioned an officer, troop commander with no experience of warfare at all.

The war, given some official status since the king had raised the royal standard at Nottingham on 22 August 1642, was a family affair. The Cromwells' eldest surviving son Oliver, now 19 years old was a cornet in Lord St John's troop.[3] In these early days there is little sense of what Oliver's troop would look like. We know what it should look like: there should have been sixty men and three commissioned officers, a captain, a lieutenant and a cornet carrying the troop colour, there would be a quartermaster too, responsible for the logistical needs of the men and horses. The troop officially consisted of harquebusiers, an outdated term taken from the name of the long-barrelled firearm carried. Although some form of carbine, a smoothbore with a wheel or flintlock, would be carried, horse troops depended more on their heavy sword than on firepower. The troopers would have two pistols in saddle-mounted holsters, and they would wear a buff-coat of tough leather, topped, if they were lucky, with a back and breast plate, thigh-length boots and a hard hat with facial protection in the form of a single or triple barred guard. This at least would be what Cromwell aimed for; also he would be attempting to ensure that they wore the same colour coat, the sleeves of which would be seen under the buff coat, to establish some uniformity and recognisability. The colour should have derived from Cromwell's own coat of arms. His recruitment programme was successful: on 17 December 1642 Cromwell was paid £204 13s for half a months pay for 80 harquebusiers.[4]

In September, Cromwell and his troop were summoned to join the field army. Parliament had appointed Essex Captain General and he began to assemble its forces on Hounslow Heath in early August. On the 8 August Essex led this army northwards, although heading for Warwickshire it encamped in Northamptonshire where newly raised units like Cromwell's joined it when judged ready: parliament's newly formed executive wing, the Committee of Safety, ordered Cromwell to prepare to go to Northamptonshire in mid-September. The king had failed to create an army strong enough to challenge Essex by the end of August and so had returned north to Nottingham where he had raised the standard at the castle, before moving through Derbyshire and Staffordshire to Shropshire and the Welsh borders. There he received regiments and troops from the north-west and Wales that gave him the army he needed to face Essex. Cromwell's troop had Gilbert Baildon as the lieutenant and John Waterhouse as cornet with John Desborough as the Quartermaster.[5] By October the king was moving through the Midlands with the aim of manoeuvring Essex out of the way and advance on London. Morale in the royalist forces had been boosted by a small scale but symbolic victory at Powick Bridge, south of Worcester on 23 September when Prince Rupert, the king's nephew had defeated a small detachment of Essex's army. Essex marched on Worcester and occupied the city in case the king advanced through the west Midlands, but the king instead moved south east from Shrewsbury towards London on 12 October, trying to get between Essex and parliamentarian garrisons of Coventry and Warwick, prompting Essex to also move eastwards to try and intercept him. A mark of the inexperience in the armies was the way in which the rival forces bumped into each other at Kineton in south Warwickshire on the night of 22 October as quartermasters of the rival armies sought out lodgings for their soldiers. On the day following the two armies ranged opposite each other on the field between Edgehill and Kineton. The Battle of Edgehill was a further example of inexperience as neither side proved able to develop initial successes. Initially the battle seemed to go the king's way when both his flanking brigades of horse crushed the opposition ranged against them. Fighting in the centre denied the king the opportunity of a quick victory and then parliament's reserve forces began to put serious pressure on the royalist left flank which had been left unprotected following the royalist horse's pursuit of fleeing parliamentarians. The fighting ground to a standstill and the autumn evening fell.

Cromwell's role that day is not easy to pin down. His troop of horse was grouped with six others under the command of the Earl of Essex for the battle, but he seems to have arrived at the field late in the day, participating, if he did so at all in the fighting, only in the latter stages as darkness fell. It is usually argued that Cromwell learned a great deal about how to fight from what he saw at Edgehill that day. It was his first experience of fighting, although of course he had been leading men under arms for slightly over two months.

It is of major importance that Cromwell, aged 43 had no military experience, for it was in the military that he finally found his metier. This is extraordinary and is difficult to explain. He does not appear to have served in the trained bands in any capacity, but he could have called on the experience of his brother-in-law Valentine Walton, who was a captain of foot in the Toseland and Hunstanton Hundred contribution to the Huntingdonshire trained bands. This contribution also included a detachment of 28 light horse and so cousin Walton may have been able to learn something of cavalry management before raising his own troop in 1642.[6] Of course by having his own troop Walton would have had his troopers to look after and train too. Like many men of little or no military experience Cromwell would have ensured that he associated with, and or employed veterans. We are not certain who Cromwell employed as non-commissioned officers in the troop, but it is probable that some would be professional soldiers with continental experience who could drill Cromwell's troopers in their basic skills. Gentry officers when creating their regiments, troops and companies would also call upon relatives. In 1636 sister Jane Cromwell had married an attorney and farmer, John Desborough. Cromwell gave him the important non-commissioned post of quartermaster during the Edgehill campaign: it would be he who sought out food and accommodation for the troopers and their horses as they moved across country: he would later be a troop captain and then major as Cromwell developed a regiment from his original troop. Cousin Edward Whalley was probably in the troop too.

There were outsiders to this family group, united to Cromwell's religious perspectives and politics, such as William Ayres, later to become a political radical and James Packer later known as an Anabaptist. Another was a man later to take over the running of the original troop by becoming Cromwell's captain-lieutenant, the officer commanding the troop of the colonel (or other field officer), James Berry. It is also possible that the original troop had three other future troop captains in its ranks, a Captain Lawrence, John Browne, and William Evanson.

Within months of the Battle of Edgehill, Cromwell received permission to raise more troops and become colonel of a regiment of horse. His brother-in-law Valentine Walton was an experienced Trained Band officer and he had also raised a troop of horse (no. 73 in Essex's army), but his son, also called Valentine who served in the Edgehill campaign as his father's cornet, soon served under Cromwell as a troop captain. Young Oliver Cromwell would also move into his father's regiment as it grew in size.

This has of course bearing on Cromwell's famous declaration about who he would prefer to lead parliament's regiments, and it adds some perspective, perhaps an air of realism to the statement, to this and other references to the composition of his troops. In his letter to Sir William Springe and Maurice Barrowe, on 29 August 1643 a year after he had first begun assembling his regiment, he made several statements about his requirements for soldiers:

> I beseech you be careful what captains of horse you choose, what men be mounted, a few honest men are better than numbers. Some time they must have for exercise [training]. If you choose godly honest men

to be captains of horse, honest men will follow them, and they will be careful to mount such.

After referring to the troops at the regions disposal as a 'handful' Cromwell went on to underline his thoughts:

> I would rather have a plain russet-coated captain that knows what he fights for, and loves what he knows, than that which you call a gentleman and is nothing else. I honour a gentleman that is so indeed.
>
> I understand that Mr Margery hath honest will follow him; if so, be pleased to make use of him. It much concerns your good to have conscientious men.[7]

It would be easier to prefer a russet-coated officer, if you knew him as a member of family or church, because the character of a person could have been assessed over time, so Cromwell was in the position to have selected men on this basis. Much is made of Cromwell's seeming social radicalism. He appears to reject social standing as a prerequisite for the job, but he does not: he adds that he would respect a gentleman who is a convinced supporter of the cause. That would be the best of both worlds. At the outset of the war both sides appointed men, including Cromwell, for their social status: they had the money required for the expenses of recruiting as well as social standing in the areas from which they would recruit their men. Such men would recruit experienced soldiers to help them through the training process. Cromwell is really arguing for an army led by supporters of the cause, in effect the same sort of men both sides wanted. However, in one particular there is a marked difference, and here Cromwell marks out his belief in spiritual equality as well as his developing understanding that the war was God's cause: he wanted Godly men. In other words it does seem to be an accurate description of the very men that we know he had gathered into his growing troop. It worked for him; perhaps, he suggests, it could be a principle more widely adopted. Cromwell was beginning to believe that God favoured his pre-war cause – the disestablishment of the Church of England.

Cromwell was still a troop captain on 31 January 1643, but by 1 March he was referred to as a colonel in the issue of the newspaper *Perfect Diurnal* published on 6 March.[8] During that period he was working to strengthen defences in the Cambridge area and rarely ventured out of the immediate region: he was involved in skirmishes and watched the bombardment of King's Lynn. His letters show him cajoling local committees, impressing the need to find funding for fortifications at Cambridge and elsewhere. One major concern is evident and it contributed to his success. Cromwell was consistently urging the committees to find money for soldiers' wages. He was, he argued prepared to work for God: 'I count myself worthy to be employed by God' in other words he could live off the income from his estate, but his men were not in such a fortunate position: 'for my poor men, help them what you can for they are faithful' he wrote to the deputy lieutenants of Essex.[9] This is telling, Cromwell might be able to support himself at war, but he could not pay for his soldiers: his estate was simply not sufficient to bear the charge. Cromwell clearly respected his men, by now consisting of thirteen troops. In September 1643 he wrote to Oliver St John:

> I have a lovely company; you would respect them, did you know them. They are no Anabaptists, they are honest, sober Christians: they expect to be used as men.[10]

Clearly, Cromwell was sensitive to suggestions that parliament was employing religious radicals at this point, but as he was writing to one of parliament's leading figures, he emphasised his point about fair dues. 'They expect to be used as men' would refer to the soldiers deserving to be paid for their labours and not to be treated as beasts of burden or slaves.

Cromwell's regiment would no doubt have been trained or 'exercised' during these months of skirmishes and patrols and their preparedness for a larger fight was tested for the first time in May. Much of Cromwell's work was related to the western fringes of East Anglia where it bordered the Midlands. The Midlands region had been placed under the command of a young man, Thomas Lord Grey of Groby the twenty-year old son of the Earl of Stamford. Grey worked hard to control his region, but he was inexperienced and faced by a determined royalist opponent, the second son of his father's rival the Earl of Huntingdon. Henry Hastings proved himself not only able to dominate large parts of the east Midlands, but also influential enough to call upon help from prominent royalists, including Prince Rupert. The Midlands/East Anglian region was a crucial communications route. The king had by spring 1643 established his headquarters at Oxford and his supporters had proved most successful in the northeast and the southwest. Henry Hastings held the middle ground with a series of major garrisons holding open the route north. On the eastern side lay the great north road, which passed through the Midlands/East Anglian region.

Parliament's forces were able to dominate the southern end of the road, but from Newark upwards the royalists held sway. Newark was therefore an important staging post for the Midland royalists. In the spring of 1643 parliamentarians directed their attention to the town. Major General Thomas Ballard attacked the town at the end of February, but failed to make any impression, beyond encouraging the re-development of the town's defences. Around the same time the situation in the north of England further enhanced the importance of Newark. On 23 February 1643 Queen Henrietta Maria returned to England with arms and ammunition purchased abroad. She persuaded Sir Hugh Cholmeley to change sides and take the port of Scarborough into the royalist camp and then set about raising a small army of her own to guard the convoy or weapons that she intended to take southwards to her husband. The route she would take would be down the Great North Road to Newark and then southwestwards though Hastings's territory to Oxford.

In the meantime, Cromwell had to deal with a royalist rising at Crowland on the southern border of Lincolnshire. On 25 March the royalist vicar had galvanised his parishioners into declaring loyalty to the king and had raided Spalding. This contributed to royalist control of western Lincolnshire, for they now held a string of garrisons, Gainsborough, Grantham and Stamford, and had also taken over Peterborough in north Cambridgeshire. Pressure was being put on the Lincoln garrison, and communications with northern parliamentarians was being threatened. Cromwell was given a detachment of the Eastern Association army and advanced upon the garrison at Crowland having first taken over Peterborough. Along with forces from Norfolk under Sir Miles Hobart, Cromwell surrounded Crowland. The small garrison there was largely isolated, forces from Newark and the Midlands had aided the town, but this had been patchy support. The townspeople had beaten off an attack in the middle of the month, but Cromwell's force was dishearteningly large. On 29 April Crowland was surrendered.

Cromwell was able to secure the major crossing points on the River Nene thus putting a substantial natural barrier between East Anglian resources and the royalists, retaking Peterborough had enabled the front line to be advanced from the Great Ouse and its crossings at Ely, Huntingdon and St Ives. The aim would be now to move across Lincolnshire to the next great natural line the River Trent.

In response to the queen's proposed convoy of munitions from the north, the East Midlands and East Anglian parliamentarian officers set about planning the capture of Newark upon Trent. Oliver Cromwell, following his success at Crowland, joined a team which included Lord Grey and John Hutchinson, governor of Nottingham Castle. Cromwell was involved in the plan and marched to join Lord Grey at Stamford, but Grey failed to make the rendezvous. Cromwell wrote and complained to the Lincolnshire committee of Grey's behaviour. Grey had sent Sir Edward Hartopp to Cromwell with the excuse that he could not leave Leicester exposed to attack by Henry Hastings and the royalists from Ashby de la Zouch. 'I perceive Ashby de la Zouch sticks much with him', Oliver explained.[11] Cromwell still hoped that a large rendezvous would take place. He expected Hutchinson and himself to be joined by forces from Hull under Captain John Hotham, Derbyshire forces under Sir John Gell as well as those from Leicester. There were also foot troops heading from Norfolk, but there would not be as many as he wanted or were expected. Cromwell suggested another rendezvous at Stamford on 4 May, but it seems that this did not come about either and Cromwell and Captain John Hotham were left to patrol the area with a force too small to seriously impinge upon the garrison at Newark.

On the night of 13 May Cromwell, along with Hotham, returned to his base at Grantham, probably frustrated at the failure to assemble a larger force to attack Newark. However, a party of royalist horse had followed him from Newark and attacked the outposts around the town. Under attack, Cromwell abandoned Grantham and marched north up the Lincoln road about two miles, as far as Belton, where he turned on his attackers and drove them off. Belton was one of Cromwell's earliest tests as a commander of independent forces. Cromwell's report on the fight was also his first communiqué to go into print. Cromwell sent the letter to Miles Hobart, who was leading the Norfolk detachment; from him it was passed to the editor of *Perfect Passages* and published in the 22–29 May edition. In common with many of his later reports,

Cromwell overestimated the size of the enemy facing him, suggesting that the royalists had 21 troops of horse and three or four of dragoons. This would have totalled about 1,200 horse and 180–240 dragoons, probably more than were based at Newark at the time. Of course it is possible that there were that number of cornets carried into the field, but that each did not represent the full complement of soldiers in a troop. Even so the effect of Cromwell's opening paragraph would be to create a sense of contrast between his embattled 'handful' of 'poor and broken' troops and overwhelming odds – he declared having 12 troops himself.[12] The parliamentarian victory was the result of one charge against the royalist horse which seems to have chosen to stand still and receive the assault. This was a flawed tactic which could alone account for Cromwell's victory. Casualties on neither side seem to have been high, Cromwell thought some of his men had killed only two or three royalists apiece, although he was not sure, but he had captured 45 royalist soldiers and five colours. Despite being a minor victory it would have strengthened the morale of Cromwell's regiment. It was essentially a tactical success, for there had been no overall victory in the field: Hotham's troops had not met with success and the parliamentarians continued their withdrawal to Lincoln. Nevertheless the fight at Belton was Cromwell's first major fight whilst in command of a detachment, even if the numbers were small.

The campaign had however failed, Newark remained secure in royalist hands and late in May the first shipment of royalist ammunition passed through the town under a guard led by Sir Charles Cavendish. Henry Hastings also sent reinforcements to ensure the continued safe passage. At the beginning of the following month the queen and her small army also marched through Newark, and the assembled parliamentarian commanders, now including Hobart and the Norfolk detachment, wrote to Lord Fairfax, parliament's commander in the north, to explain their failure.[13] As further humiliation, Stamford, Cromwell's proposed rendezvous site, fell into royalist hands.

Part of the reason for the parliamentarians' failure lay in the treasonable activities of Sir John Hotham and his son Captain John. They had been negotiating the surrender of Hull with the Earl of Newcastle and their commitment to the seizure of Newark was compromised by their negotiations and need to demonstrate to the earl their bona fides. The Hothams were eventually arrested and shipped to London to await trial. Cromwell had however made an important friendship during the campaign, with 32-year-old Henry Ireton of Attenborough in Nottinghamshire. Ireton was a major in Hutchinson's Nottingham garrison, where he had played an important part in the development of the stronghold, but he took the opportunity to leave his post there and joined Cromwell. He was appointed deputy governor of Ely, probably on the strength of his work at Nottingham, and became quickly indispensable to Cromwell. Ireton was embarking on what would be for him a lifelong association with Cromwell that would extend into his political and personal life, and both men rose together in importance to parliament.

In July, however, with the Hothams out of the way, the East Anglian parliamentarians began to increase their hold on the area again, in contrast with their colleagues further north who lost control of large parts of Yorkshire in the wake of the Battle of Adwalton Moor on 30 June. The commander of parliament's forces in Lincolnshire, Lord Willoughby of Parham attacked the royalist garrison at Gainsborough and captured the town, and a few days later Cromwell recaptured Stamford. However, Gainsborough was an important town and by nightfall on 16 July it was besieged by royalists and for ten days remained surrounded by forces led by Sir Charles Cavendish. Willoughby's capture of Gainsborough and Cromwell's reoccupation of Stamford had been part of a strategy aimed at blocking the East Midland royalists from eastward expansion; and in particular the Newark garrison's ability to control and impose taxation on Lincolnshire. There was a larger context too: these occupations effectively created a line of garrisons, running from Gainsborough in the north, through Lincoln and Grantham to Stamford in the south, linking up with the parliamentarian controlled counties of Northampton and Bedfordshire. This would also open up control of an alternative route to the Great North Road, which the royalists controlled from Newark northwards. Parliamentarians could use the main road up as far as Stamford and then could go northwards via Lincoln and Gainsborough. At the end of one northward route from Gainsborough was Barton on Humber, a ferry-crossing point by which the parliamentarian garrison at Kingston upon Hull, and the Fairfaxes who had taken refuge there after Adwalton Moor, could be reached. If the north was ever going to be reconquered by parliament, then a secured route northwards was needed. Royalist counter-strategy was clearly aimed at rolling up this line, starting at Gainsborough. In any case, the capture of any one of these outposts would inhibit movement north to south. It was therefore important to the region's parliamentarians to hold on to this northern outpost.

Within days Cromwell strengthened his hold on Stamford by capturing Burleigh House outside the town as well. From there he marched to join the Nottinghamshire horse under Sir John Meldrum at Grantham. With Meldrum in command, the parliamentarians marched to North Scarle, ten miles south of Gainsborough, where they joined forces from Lincoln. Early on the morning of 28 July the assembled parliamentarians marched towards Gainsborough, via Marton and Torksey parallel with the River Trent to their left hand. This brought them onto the southern approaches to the town, and they were clearly expected. A royalist vanguard had set off southwards from the leaguer to meet them. It was clear that their plans were well known and the attack was no surprise. The first skirmish of the battle took place between Gainsborough and Lea as parliamentarian dragoons attacked the royalists and at first gained an upper hand before being forced to withdraw rapidly as greater numbers bore down upon them.

The royalist horse, under Sir Charles Cavendish, stood upon a rising plateau known as Foxby Hill. Cromwell advanced upon Cavendish, up hill and across broken ground. It was a move full of risks and Cavendish knew it, waiting until the parliamentarians began to move up the hill before attacking them. The fighting was ferocious, Cromwell 'recovered the top of the hill', whereupon Cavendish attacked and the fighting was again hard, once more the royalists were defeated and the front line troops began to retreat. However, Cavendish had retained a full regiment in reserve and as some parliamentarians pursued the retreating royalists, two groups of parliamentarians faced Cavendish. A section of the Lincolnshire horse had become separated from Cromwell and his cousin Major Edward Whalley who were ranged on the top of Foxby Hill. Cavendish could not divide his regiment, but knew he had to recover the hill if he was to protect the royalist foot comprising the leaguer around Gainsborough. He gambled on attacking the Lincolnshire horse, presumably hoping to defeat them and turn his troopers around, before Cromwell could reach him. He almost managed it, the Lincolnshire horse were quickly defeated, but before he could turn about Cromwell attacked the royalists in the rear and drove them down the hill. It was close hand-to-hand fighting and Cromwell's troop fought Cavendish's troop as the clash moved downhill. At the foot of the hill Cavendish was caught in a bog and killed by Cromwell's captain-lieutenant James Berry. The royalist horse was routed, and the foot moved away from Gainsborough, allowing Meldrum to put supplies and reinforcements into the town. Cromwell and some of the garrison decided to push the remains of the leaguer further from the town and marched after them, northwards of the town towards Morton.

It was then that the day turned from an apparent victory into a complete disaster. Cromwell described the unfolding catastrophe, from the point at which he believed he was driving the besiegers away from the town.

> When we recovered the hill, we saw in the bottom, about quarter of a mile from us, a regiment of foot; after that another; after that the Lord Newcastle's own regiment; consisting in all of about 50 foot colours, and a great body of horse; which was indeed Newcastle's Army ... our foot retreated in disorder and with some loss got into the town; where now they are. Our horse also came off with some trouble ...[14]

Willoughby was abandoned in Gainsborough and left to face the might of the Northern Army. Two days later he surrendered. Willoughby was allowed to retreat to Lincoln, but within days this city too fell to Newcastle. The route to the north opened painstakingly during July was closed, and Newcastle, having bought time and security to the south of his command, turned on Hull. The attack on Gainsborough had been a disappointing and potentially frightening one for Meldrum and Cromwell, but up until the arrival of Newcastle's army it had been a successful one. Cromwell had proved his ability to handle cavalry in the field. He exhibited one of the traits for which he would later be known, the initial withholding of and then successful deployment of a reserve force. In must be remarked that Cavendish had also done this, and the only marked difference was that either his luck and or his timing was out, whereas Cromwell's timing and luck most definitely were spot on. Possessing both factors makes a good leader, and Cromwell clearly had both.

Despite this setback attempts to control Lincolnshire and the East Anglian borders continued, and the defeat at Gainsborough forced a re-think of organisation. As with other areas under parliament's control,

East Anglian counties had been associated with each other to maximise the use of resources. The armed forces of the region had been brought together, under the command of Major General Lord Grey of Warke. This command had provided the troops that Cromwell had drawn upon during his forays into Lincolnshire. One result of the Battle of Gainsborough was the possibility that the Earl of Newcastle could advance southwards into East Anglia and perhaps even onto London. Although Newcastle did nothing of the sort, seemingly mesmerised by the Fairfaxes' garrison at Hull to the extent that he concentrated upon capturing the port, parliament felt that a stronger bastion was needed. The Eastern Association forces were turned into an army, with the creation of new regiments authorised and a new commander put in charge: Cromwell's relative Edward Montagu, Earl of Manchester was appointed to the post. The earl was asked initially to raise an army of 20,000 men, but impressments proved unreliable: on the other hand Montagu's reputation as a principal figure in parliamentarian religion and politics attracted radical officers from the main field army, like John Lilburne and thus the new army developed a leadership committed to parliament's victory even if from differing religious perspectives.

Manchester knew that Lincolnshire was important, both as a communications route and as barrier to any royalist southward march. Newcastle's obsession with Hull gave Manchester the time he needed to act on this knowledge and he firstly moved on King's Lynn. The royalists in the northwest Norfolk port were, like the Crowlanders before them, quite isolated from the royalists in Lincolnshire and Nottinghamshire. With a growing army settling around the town the royalists' isolation was enhanced and on 13 September the Eastern Association Army met with its first success when the port was surrendered. Cromwell had advanced into Lincolnshire; using the small garrison at Boston as a pivot provided a screen of cavalry across southeast Lincolnshire. He was not impressed with the new units under his command. He wrote a letter to his cousin Oliver St John from Boston, in which he extolled his own men's worth. On the other hand the troops coming from Manchester were 'very bad and mutinous, not to be confided in'. One thing however bound all the troops together; a lack of pay, Manchester's men had only a week's pay, and Cromwell had not got any money to support the new regiments. He had been allocated sequestration money from Huntingdonshire, Norfolk and Hertfordshire, but he had seen little of it come his way.

Cromwell may have been in a position to support himself, but he was now strapped for cash:

> I have little money of my own to help my Soldiers. My estate is little. I tell you the Business of Ireland and England hath had of me, in money, between Eleven and Twelve Hundred pound: – therefore my Private can do little to help the Public. You have had my money.[15]

Despite the lack of pay, Cromwell imposed sufficient discipline into the Eastern Association horse and in mid September led them into north Lincolnshire to support the evacuation of the Yorkshire horse from Kingston upon Hull. Horse is of limited tactical value to a besieged garrison and moreover it is expensive. Newcastle's siege of Hull was close enough to prevent the Fairfaxes from using the horse and as such it became and expensive commodity. Taking it across the river Humber would remove the expense and provide Manchester with extra resources against the Lincolnshire royalists. Cromwell's screen worked effectively, preventing the Newark and Lincolnshire troops from interfering. Sir Thomas Fairfax was able to evacuate 22 troops. These were marched to Boston which became the base for them and the Eastern Association horse and where they were soon joined by Manchester and the foot, fresh from King's Lynn.

Manchester went onto the offensive in early October, besieging the small royalist garrison in Bolingbroke Castle. The point was to draw royalists from the west of the county into an open fight and it worked. The governor of Newark assembled a force of east Midlanders and Lincolnshire troops and attacked the parliamentarian cavalry screen near Horncastle north of Bolingbroke on 10 October. It was a brief running battle and the parliamentarian horse fell back towards the siege. On the following day Manchester moved towards the royalists who had remained near Winceby. The royalists had assembled 74 troops of horse and 21 companies of dragoons. These were drawn from the garrison at Newark, the Lincolnshire garrisons and some were from Henry Hastings's North Midland army, the commander was Thomas, Lord Widdrington, the commander of Lincolnshire appointed by Newcastle during his July foray into the county. Had these been full troops then there would have been about 5,700 men; yet royalist troops were notoriously under-strength. Cromwell and Fairfax mustered about half the number of troops, but his troops were more likely to be full strength and numbers thus were likely to be even at something under 3,000 a side.

Cromwell and Fairfax led the horse ahead of the main army and encountered the royalists at Winceby. The parliamentarians were in three bodies as they advanced up the Bolingbrooke to Winceby road; Cromwell was at the fore, with Fairfax following and Manchester with the foot in the rear. Dragoons from both sides engaged in the vicinity of the town and then the parliamentarians attacked the royalists around noon on 11 October, with Quartermaster General Vermuyden's regiment of five troops leading as a forlorn hope, Cromwell with his regiment and some of the earl's troops were in the second line and Fairfax third. Vermuyden's charge defeated Widdrington's front line, which then became entangled on broken ground north of the town. Cromwell's second attack followed on taking advantage of the royalists' problems. The royalist dragoons were quick of the mark, getting two volleys off before Cromwell got near them: it was a difficult moment for Cromwell's own horse was shot dead under him during by royalist carbine and he was quickly attacked by Sir Ingram Hopton who tried to ride him down as the royalists counter-charged. Nevertheless, the royalist response appears to have been scrappy and Cromwell was able to get up a second time and find another horse. He remounted to continue the charge and the royalist counter attack was defeated. As the first line was driven back onto the second retreat developed into a rout and the parliamentarians caught the royalists in an area now known as Slash Hollow and Slash Lane and royalist casualties mounted, Cromwell's attacker being one of the casualties. The battle, a fast moving fight of about half an hour, was largely over before Manchester and the foot arrived on the field.

Winceby may have been a brief battle but the consequences were great. Lincoln was surrendered to Manchester just over a week later. Cromwell took the horse into western Lincolnshire, the riding of Kesteven, which bordered the royalist north Midland counties. As winter approached Cromwell skirmished with the Newark garrison's forces whilst trying to prevent regular royalist taxation collection in Lincolnshire. The county was steadily occupied by the eastern Association forces, as the coastal garrisons were taken over and on 20 December 1643 Sir John Meldrum avenged his defeat in the summer by retaking Gainsborough. This time when the now marquis of Newcastle moved his army south from Hull, having finally acknowledged his inability to take the town he stayed away from Lincolnshire and kept to Derbyshire and Nottinghamshire, where he bolstered Henry Hastings, now Lord Loughborough's control of the central north Midlands. Colonel Oliver Cromwell's role in the reconquest of Lincolnshire had been crucial in this reshaping of territorial alignment in the region.

In the new year the Eastern Association was again reorganised and Cromwell's role enhanced. At the beginning of the war the Earl of Essex had been appointed captain general or commander in chief of all parliament's forces. Since that time, every military appointment was in effect made by him, and all the nation's forces, whether brought into existence by the Fairfaxes, the earls of Manchester or Denbigh or by Oliver Cromwell were effectively under Essex's command. By mid-1643 Essex's reputation was beginning to tarnish, and his clear desire for a negotiated settlement was apparently affecting his judgement. His standing had been restored somewhat by his relief of Gloucester and his subsequent victory at the battle of Newbury during September 1643. However regional commanders resented Essex's imperious summonses and, like Cromwell who ignored a demand to join Essex's march to Gloucester in August 1643, tended to find reasons to circumvent the commander's orders. Naturally Manchester resented Essex's position and the Eastern Association's friends in parliament joined others in pressing for a change in the command structure. In January 1644 the Eastern Association was granted new powers freeing it from the Earl of Essex. The association was given a central committee comprising representatives from all of its individual county committees, which was to meet at Cambridge with new taxation powers. The central committee was granted revenue 50 per cent higher than previously: Cromwell's complaints about under-funding had finally hit the mark. The army's size was to be more realistically set at 14,000 men, recognising the impossibility of Manchester's earlier target: it was later reduced to 7,500 foot and 3,000 horse. Oliver Cromwell's hard work the previous year was appreciated and recognised and he was promoted to lieutenant general. Cromwell was now the second in command of an army, with particular command of the horse. Cromwell was also appointed, along with his commander to the newly formed executive committee in London. He was now in a position to try and influence the course of the war.

Whilst Cromwell and Manchester had been absorbed in the reconquest of Lincolnshire the war had changed. John Pym, whose faction Cromwell had been a part of for three years had died in December 1643, and the structure of the group had altered even before that for Cromwell's cousin John Hampden had died during the summer of wounds received at the small battle on Chalgrove Field. These deaths left another of Cromwell's cousins, Oliver St John as the most prominent figure in the faction known by historians as the Middle Group. Pym had made one last major contribution to the war before his death; he had arranged a treaty with Scotland. The king had rejected Scotland's offer of mediation and instead pursued a peace effort in Ireland which would firstly free the English and Welsh forces sent into the country in the wake of the rebellion to return home and be enlisted in the king's army and secondly would potentially enable the king to seek military aid from the Irish government, the Confederation of Kilkenny. Both these factors made Scotland receptive to Pym's overtures and in the wake of a cessation of hostilities in Ireland Scotland allied itself with the English/Welsh parliament. Parliament agreed to impose the treaty's religious terms, involving the signing of the Scottish National Covenant in conjunction with terms of the alliance itself – the Solemn League upon officials and soldiers and eventually a wider net of the English and Welsh people. In return for the acceptance of the Solemn League and Covenant, Scotland would raise an army in the name of the treaty, whilst parliament would raise the funding for it. The Army of the Solemn League and Covenant marched into northeastern England in mid-January 1644.

The two nations acknowledged themselves bound in a union and so appointed a joint committee to execute the course of the war against the king: this was the Committee of Both Kingdoms to which Oliver Cromwell and the Earl of Manchester were appointed. This committee contained elements of the three developing factions from within parliament; the War Party, the Peace Party and the Middle Group. It was the latter group that held the balance of power on the committee and thus largely speaking controlled it. This group comprised Lord Saye and Sele and Oliver St John amongst its numbers: in other words this was the very group to which Cromwell had belonged since parliament opened back in November 1640. Once again, political allies embracing members of his extended family had ensured the rise of Oliver Cromwell, general and politician. Whilst his political expertise was probably still of questionable worth his developing military prowess was not. Cromwell was still some way from being an acknowledged skilled commander in the field, but he had received positive press attention. In the space of two years the war had thrust Cromwell into the limelight.

5

THE GREAT AGENT IN THIS VICTORY

1644–1645

The war as much as the political scene changed complexion whilst Cromwell was in the process of being promoted. Against the background of fear engendered by the possibility of a treaty in Ireland, which would free large numbers of soldiers for the king's forces, John Pym had negotiated a treaty with Scotland over the summer of 1643. For the Scots, a treaty in Ireland posed the threat of Irish forces landing on the southwest coast. Their attempts to mediate between the king and parliament had also been rebuffed in Oxford. In September 1643 the fears of parliament and the Scottish government came to fruition; the king's representative in Ireland, James Butler, Marquis of Ormond concluded a cessation with the Catholic Confederation of Kilkenny. Although this was a prelude to negotiations rather than a full-scale treaty, it did allow the return to England and Wales of a large number of soldiers sent to Ireland in 1642. The king was able to monopolise this army and despite personal political loyalties the returnees were 'dragooned' into the royalist cause.

The impetus on the negotiations between parliament and the estates was great and a treaty between the two parliaments was concluded less than a fortnight after the cessation. The implications of this treaty were immense for it entailed English and Welsh officials, MPs army officers and ministers and later, an increasingly broad spectrum of people, signing the Solemn League and Covenant. The Solemn League bound signatories' loyalty to the treaty; the Covenant section committed those who signed it to defending the Scottish National Covenant. This latter part would later in 1644 centre in the dangerous controversy over Cromwell's own religiosity, but for the time being it was the military consequences of the treaty which impinged upon Oliver Cromwell and the Eastern Association.

Over the winter of 1643–1644 the Marquis of Newcastle and the king's Northern Army had been based in the North Midlands, chiefly in north Nottinghamshire and Derbyshire. This had bolstered the royalist hold on the region but seemed a tacit acknowledgement of Cromwell's victory in Lincolnshire. Regiments raised in the region which had subsequently served elsewhere were recalled to their home territory: Lord Loughborough was given the rank of lieutenant general. The boldness of the Newark forces was reinvigorated and in January they had attempted to capture Nottingham. The menace they posed to parliament's recently established control over Lincolnshire increased too. However, this all changed rapidly once the Scots honoured their military commitment to the treaty. The Marquis of Newcastle left the Midlands, leaving behind Sir Charles Lucas to create a reserve force from recruits from within Lord Loughborough's command weakening his recently bolstered hold on the region and exposing it to attack.

Cromwell spent early January embroiled in the duties of governor of Ely. This involved strengthening the defences and ensuring the 'godly' nature of the services at the cathedral. This was a time of change, for the Solemn League and Covenant did not establish a Presbyterian church system in England and Wales, although there was a clear expectation on behalf of the Scots and of their English and Welsh counterparts that this would come about eventually: an Assembly of Divines from a diverse spectrum of standpoints was appointed to debate and decide the future of the church in England. In the meantime the Church of England liturgy and its accompanying ceremonies had been abolished. In their place was a vague system defined more by what was not desirable than by what was. In some places the prayer book was used undisturbed, and in Ely just a hundred yards or so from the governor's own house a full choir-service was in place under the charge of Reverend Hitch. Cromwell ordered him to stop 'Lest the soldiers should in any tumultuary or disorderly way attempt the reformation of the Cathedral Church.'[1] Cromwell was clear on what he wanted to replace the choir service in the short term: catechism and exposition of the scripture, but he did not know what would come next. At this point in time he trusted to parliament and more specifically to the Assembly of Divines at Westminster to 'direct ... further'. Hitch ignored the warning and Cromwell with his soldiers, as he had predicted, effected the necessary reformation within days.

Shortly after 'cleansing the church' Cromwell made his way to Westminster complaining about the lack of strong leadership in Lincolnshire, blaming Lord Willoughby for the failures of the previous summer. Cromwell also suggested that the county be added to the Earl of Manchester's responsibilities and included in the Eastern Association. It was whilst he was in London that Oliver was promoted to the rank of lieutenant general and given command of the Eastern Association horse. On 5 February Cromwell signed the Solemn League and Covenant. Much has been made of the fact that this was the very last day upon which parliament's officials and officers had to sign before becoming ruled ineligible for office, and Cromwell's signing so late has been linked with his recent promotion. There have been accusations of reluctance. However, Cromwell was exceedingly busy in the months before, serving in the field in East Anglia, out of parliament. His return was brief and equally busy, and shortly after signing the covenant he was in the field again, this time in the south Midlands near to Newport Pagnell, where his eldest son Oliver was stationed, ensuring the safe dispatch of a munitions convoy heading via Warwick towards Gloucester. On 4 March he captured a small garrison, Hillesdon House, Buckinghamshire. Cromwell's apparent tardiness was really the result of his being intensely occupied during the signing period: he was second in command of the Eastern Association, overseeing the restructuring of the Eastern Association's logistics, and he was also involved in executive government joining Manchester on the newly formed Committee of Both Kingdoms. Cromwell had acknowledged parliament's right to establish the nature of religious worship in England and Wales having been a leading figure in parliament's attempts to restructure the church before the war, but, on the other hand political alliances were changing with the proposed settlements, and Oliver may have been becoming aware of the intolerance of Presbyterians.

In the early weeks of the year young Oliver Cromwell died at Newport Pagnell, the garrison commanded by Sir Samuel Luke, parliament's Scoutmaster General. Cromwell had probably left the area by the time his son died of small pox, a garrison-town disease. He was later to say that it cut him to the heart, although there are no contemporary letters dealing with the death of Oliver directly, but in the wake of the Battle of Marston Moor, Cromwell did refer to his loss when commiserating with Valentine Walton.

In March Cromwell became involved in a religious controversy, which would continue to echo through the next few years and in particular provide material for the argument between Cromwell and Manchester late in 1644. On his return to Cambridge on 10 March Cromwell arrived to find Lieutenant Packer under arrest on the orders of his own colonel, the Eastern Association's third in command, Major General Edward Crawford. Crawford was a Presbyterian Scot: Packer was accused of being an Anabaptist. Anabaptists were associated with radical politics as well as for their rejection of infant baptism. They argued that entry into the fellowship of the church should only be undertaken voluntarily, by someone capable of understanding such a commitment. The collapse of the Church of England in 1641 had consequences, perhaps unseen at the time: it had allowed the fragmentation of worship in England and Wales and moreover, with the church's role as censor in abeyance, religious sects which had been underground were enabled to publish tracts outlining and explaining their beliefs. Anabaptists were amongst these burgeoning groups, although there had been Anabaptists in the country since 1570. Packer, being commissioned officer, was holding his position in contravention of the orders of parliament relating to the Solemn League and Covenant which should have obliged Packer to sign. Crawford reported him to Manchester, who, being a Presbyterian could have been expected to sympathise with Crawford's position. However Manchester was in Cambridge to reform the university in accordance with parliament's instructions, and he left the matter to Cromwell.

Cromwell contacted Lawrence and asked him to reconsider. Despite having signed the covenant himself, and having seemingly repudiated Anabaptists in the letter to Oliver St John in September 1643, Cromwell did not condemn Packer. Instead he questioned the wisdom of removing him from his command. After opening the letter by explaining Manchester's failure to respond, Cromwell affirmed Packer's commitment to his regiment and his desire to join it as it went into the field again. His main point was to effectively discount Packer's religiosity:

> Ay but the man 'is an Anabaptist' Are you sure of that? Admit he be, shall that render him incapable to serve the Public? "He is indiscreet" It may be so, in some things, we all have human infirmities.

It seems possible that Packer may not have been, at that point, an Anabaptist, and that Crawford may have used a convenient detrimental label, for Anabaptists were associated with anarchy and social disorder. Cromwell certainly seemed to question Crawford's assertion, although he may not have enquired too deeply into Packer's conscience himself. The core of the problem seems to have been Packer's opposition to the Solemn League and Covenant. This is probably the source of the accusation that he was 'indiscreet': Packer must have made his opposition known to others, and it was this that may have forced Crawford's hand. Cromwell did not care much about the indiscretion (he could of course be indiscreet himself as at Huntingdon fourteen years previously). Packer's own commitment to the parliamentarian cause was all that really concerned Cromwell at this point and he had no doubts about Packer's commitment.[2] His argument seems to have won Crawford over at this point and the opening of the campaigning season meant that a committed experienced lieutenant was needed in the field, especially after the Newark campaign.

Crawford, whilst apparently accepting Packer's return, forwarded Cromwell's letter to Manchester. This would go on to form a part of a wider net of accusations being recalled and gathered about Cromwell's seeming latitude toward individual religiosity. Cromwell had attracted adverse attention already, and his letter to Oliver St John which included the abrupt 'They are no Anabaptists' could have been a response to adverse criticism. Someone already believed that Cromwell was selecting officers on grounds of their religion: one critic was collecting information that would be used later in 1644 against Cromwell when his argument with Manchester became public.[3] Some of the accusations related to the early months of the war and some focussed directly on Cromwell's attitude to religiosity in the army:

> Not such as were soldiers or men of estate but such as were common men pore or of meane parentage only he would give them title of godly pretious men yet his common practise was to cashiere honest Gentlemen & soldiers yt were stout in the cause ... look upon his owne regiment of horse see what a swarme ther is of them that call themselves the godly.

The regiments were captained by men 'such as have filled dung carts both before they were captains and since'. The writer accused several Eastern Association officers of being Independents: Colonels Charles Fleetwood, Thomas Rainsborough, Francis Russell, John Pickering, and eighteen year-old Edward Montagu. The range of accusations relating to Cromwell himself stretched to his winter activity as Governor of Ely. Acknowledging his desire to make the isle a fortress, the author suggested that Cromwell was doing so to make a haven for 'the godly': 'to put in godly and pretious people' and make it 'a place for good to dwell'. The effect was to make Ely 'a meare Amsterdam' where soldiers preached in churches and ministers dare not leave their seats. Whole families of independents had moved into the town from London the writer alleged. For good measure this was all tied to alleged financial peculation: claims were made that Cromwell was over-taxing the local communities personally and through his deputy Henry Ireton. Money it was said was being paid from public funds to Elizabeth Cromwell: 'I am sure' wrote the author, 'that there is noe ordinance of Parliament for that'. There was no ordinance but the money only came from wages already due to Cromwell. The writer of the catalogue of Cromwell's activities continued assembling information throughout the remainder of 1644 and it was to be put forward to the enquiry into the military crisis at the end of the year.

In the meantime the military situation began to impinge upon the Eastern Association. With royalist troops being withdrawn from the midlands for the campaign against the Scots Lord Loughborough's command and adjacent areas became vulnerable. In late February troops from the east Midlands and Lincolnshire under the command of Sir John Meldrum surrounded Newark. Attempts to relieve the royalist garrison were set in train by Lord Loughborough, but he now lacked the manpower to do anything but circle the besiegers with patrols to prevent them exploiting the region's resources effectively. Loughborough solicited the help of Prince Rupert who was currently reorganising the royalist administration in the west Midlands. By 17 March a joint operation was in progress and on 21 March, Rupert and Loughborough attacked Meldrum at Newark and by the early hours of the morning had captured his entire army and its weapons. The effect of this success was electric: even though Prince Rupert and his small 'flying army' returned quickly to the west Midlands, the tables were turned in the east Midlands: Lincoln was abandoned by its parliamentarian garrison two days later.

The military situation in the north and the Midlands soon involved the Earl of Manchester and the Eastern Association. The earl quickly began to assemble troops in south Lincolnshire to restore control of the county, but this was soon to become part of a much more ambitious project. In the north of England, the Marquis of Newcastle had failed to draw the Scots into an open battle, but had held them to a slow progress and had effectively stopped them in County Durham. However, in Newcastle's rear his commander in Yorkshire was failing to hold back the resurgent Fairfaxes and their parliamentarian incursions into south and west Yorkshire: Loughborough's involvement in the Newark prevented him diverting troops to Yorkshire until early April. On 11 April at the Battle of Selby the Yorkshire royalist army was defeated and destroyed. Newcastle was forced to retreat from Durham to York and abandoned the north of England to the Scots. The Fairfaxes advanced on the city from the south and appeals were sent to the Earl of Manchester asking him to join in an attack on the rapidly isolated royalist Northern Army: the siege of York got under way on 22 April 1644. Manchester and the army remained in the Stamford area during April, which had the effect of preventing Lord Loughborough from responding to calls from York for help in preventing the Northern Army's isolation by joining forces with Lord Goring and the Northern Horse, which Newcastle had sent south to avoid being trapped. On 6 May Manchester's forces recaptured Lincoln and Loughborough's Midland counties were hemmed in, with the Eastern Association army on the eastern flank and Lord Denbigh attacking the western flank. However, Manchester responded to calls from the north and Cromwell was sent northwards with 3,000 horse to help confine the Northern Amy foot in York. The earl himself followed on behind in the last week of May.

The Eastern Association army arrived outside York on 3 June with around 4,000 horse and the same number of foot. The army was inserted into the leaguer in the northwestern side of the city between the east bank of the River Ouse as it flowed into the northwest of the city and the west bank of the River Foss as it flowed into the east of the city, with its headquarters at Clifton Without. The Eastern Association Army's arrival made possible the sort of close siege that had hitherto been impossible even with the combined Scots army and the Fairfaxes numbering around 20,000 in total. With a completed circle around the town the royalist sallies could be kept under control and work to advance the circumvallation of the city could begin, Manchester's forces quickly built a bridge of boats across the River Ouse near Clifton at Poppleton to make communication with the Scots easier. Mining operations began and in Lord Fairfax's sector a mine was begun under Walmgate Bar, but it was discovered and counter-mined, whilst the mine begun in the Eastern Association sector was followed through.

Opposite Manchester's section of the leaguer was a weak spot in the city's defensive line. In the thirteenth century the Abbey of St Mary's outside the city's northwest wall had constructed a boundary wall around itself which effectively added a compound to the city walls. In the early fourteenth century this boundary wall had been crenellated and converted to a defensive structure. By the seventeenth century this section of the city was less well maintained than the main walls and was in any case of lower defensive capability. The Eastern Association began a mine under the northwest corner's Marygate Tower. This mine was not detected and it was exploded on 16 June. Major General Crawford led the attack which followed and the Eastern Association Foot fought their way across the bowling greens inside towards the King's Manor complex of buildings – the seat of the Council of the North. However, once inside the abbey precinct the attackers were cut off, effectively trapped inside these quasi-separate defences; forty were killed and 216 captured when the breach was sealed. Cromwell and the horse played a fairly small role in the siege of York, most of the work was done by foot soldiers, but patrols to provide early warning of approaching relief forces and escorting supplies to the besieging forces was necessary if not exciting work, and he hardly merited attention in the reports of the action. In fact this underlines the importance of this campaign to Cromwell. The newsbooks covering the campaign in the north such as *Newes from the Siege Before York,* published on 14 June 1644 did not mention him at all, whereas after the Battle of Marston Moor Cromwell would make the papers.[4]

York was an important city, it was still reckoned to be the country's second city, and its centrality to the royalist war effort in the north was undoubted: because of this the king ordered a large scale relief effort; the men and resources of the west and east midlands were to be combined with the Northern Horse under the command of Prince Rupert in an attack on the leaguer at York. There was also a positive strategic aim as well. Since the early months of the war Lancashire had been largely controlled by parliamentarians: Rupert on his way north would relieve the long-beleaguered garrison at Lathom House and seize the county from parliamentarian forces. This part of the mission was successful and on 25–26 June Rupert crossed the Pennines and advanced towards York. He crossed to the east bank of the Ouse. The commanders of the allied armies outside York assumed that Rupert would advance down the west bank of the Ouse to drive a wedge between the Scots and the Eastern Association forces. To prevent this Manchester moved his army over his bridge of boats to join the Scots on the west bank ready to meet the prince's advance. Lord Fairfax marched round from the northeast of the city to join them, and together the three commanders pulled away from the city to protect themselves from being attacked in the rear by the Earl of Newcastle. But Rupert had outwitted them. The road to York along the east bank of the river was open and he marched to the city unopposed through what had been the Eastern Association's sector. He entered the city in triumph on 1 July. Manchester, Leven and Fairfax pulled their forces back to Tadcaster. Oliver Cromwell's first experience of a major siege had been that of a failure.

Rupert was not minded to allow the allied forces to withdraw, he determined to pursue them and force a battle by making it too dangerous for them to divide their forces. Accordingly during the night of 1–2 July Rupert's army left York and advanced towards the parliamentarian forces, using Manchester's bridge of boats at Poppleton: Newcastle followed him at dawn on 2 July, but his army did not. On that morning Lord Leven ordered a retreat to Tadcaster. As the vanguard approached within a mile of the town, the rearguard, comprising the Eastern Association forces, was leaving the vicinity of the village of Long Marston and its neighbouring moor, when Prince Rupert and his vanguard appeared. The three allied commanders received news of the prince's approach and began to turn their armies around, by doing so they committed their forces to fighting the Battle of Marston Moor. The three second in commands, Oliver Cromwell, Sir Thomas Fairfax and David Leslie, organised the immediate response to Rupert's advance and began to challenge the prince's horse as it moved from Marston Moor towards the small rise in the ground known as Bilton Bream. Artillery fire directed at the prince's horse enabled the parliamentarians and Scots to successfully keep the royalists on the moor, denying them the ridge of cultivated land to the south that overlooked it.

The two armies assembled on the field in a process that took most of a day marked by light drizzle. Rupert and Newcastle marshalled their forces on the moor, whilst the allied forces drew up firstly on the ridge and then in the hollow beneath it, between it and the moor. The allied forces completed their positioning first. The royalists were hampered by the delay to getting the Northern Army foot out of the city. For a variety of reasons Lord Eythin only got the army onto the field at around 4pm, a manoeuvre which resulted in reshuffling the royalist line lasting into the early evening. Cromwell, having just participated in his first major siege, was about to take part in his first major battle: it was to be the biggest pitched battle of the war, the allies totalled about 28,000, the royalists about 18,000.

Cromwell, because the largest body of horse in the combined allied army was his Eastern Association horse, was given command of the allied left wing. He had eight regiments of horse and two regiments of dragoons under him. His own regiment was in the front line with the Earl of Manchester's with one other regiment of horse and Colonel Hugh Fraser's regiment of dragoons. The second line had two regiments from the Eastern Association, led by Commissary General Vermuyden. The third line had three Scottish regiments from the Army of the Solemn League and Covenant under Major General David Leslie. In Cromwell's command was a total of 4,000 horse, 500 dragoons and about 600 musketeers interspersed amongst the horse to fire upon attacking forces. This was Cromwell's largest command in the field to date. He had already demonstrated tactical skill in the use of artillery to clear the royalist horse from Bilton Bream, and he was to use the field to his advantage once the attack began. The brief preliminary engagement had ensured, according to Peter Newman, a battle would take place. If the royalists could have taken the rising ground at the Bream then the entire ridge upon which the allied forces were drawing up would have been vulnerable to being flanked from the west. Cromwell had followed his artillery barrage with an attack on the royalists with horse dragoons and artillery and drove the royalists back onto the cultivated land and moorland north of the Tockwith–Long Marston road.

As the allied forces moved into position, to Cromwell's right was assembled the 11,000 or so foot soldiers from the regiments of the three armies, Eastern Association forces were adjacent to Cromwell, Scottish regiments were to their right and at the extreme right was Sir Thomas Fairfax and the rest of the horse, comprised, as was Cromwell's command, of three lines. The Fairfaxes's army provided the first two lines of these regiments, and again, three regiments of Scots formed the third line. Facing Cromwell across the cultivated land and moor was John, Lord Byron with around 2,400 horse in two lines. Rupert had placed Byron behind broken ground, comprising a rabbit warren and a slough. The idea was that Byron should wait until the enemy attacked him across this rough ground and then counter attack whilst they navigated the difficult terrain. This plan was not followed.

The battle began late in the day about 7pm. Peter Newman has argued convincingly that Lord Leven ordered the attack when he observed continuing disorder in the royalist centre. When Rupert had arrived on the field he had sent horse regiments to the west, Tockwith village side of the moor, lodged another body of horse at the Long Marston end and placed his foot regiments between them, the intention was to bolster the thinly scattered foot regiments with the Northern Army regiments from York. These regiments arrived late and when they arrived, fitting them into the battle line caused disorder. Leven attacked to try and take advantage of this disorder. The wings began to move and the foot in the centre began moving off the ridge, building up momentum as they went downhill. On the royalist right, opposite Cromwell, Lord Byron's wing literally bridled under the pressure. They had been fired on by artillery during the day and the day-long drizzle had sapped their patience. In the late 1970s Peter Newman argued that lord Byron precipitated catastrophe by forgetting orders to stand until Cromwell crossed the broken ground, instead the royalists moved forward and were caught in the trap Rupert had intended for their opponents. As the royalist front line lost cohesion crossing the ditch in front of them, Cromwell led his men forward and caught Byron's men on the rough ground with a momentum gained from crossing relatively clear ground. This momentum allowed Cromwell to push the royalist front wing back and to break its cohesion and eventually its morale. However in his last book, written with Peter Roberts, Newman revised his view. In the revised interpretation, Byron led his men forward to try and prevent the right wing from the disastrous effect of being attacked whilst totally unprepared. The foot regiments placed ahead of Byron's men to try and break up parliament's expected advance on that wing had been stood down and were incapable of meeting the attack. Byron was trying to offset this situation when Cromwell's forces hit his. This revised view sets out to underline just how unprepared the royalist army was when the allied forces attacked.

As neither the foot regiments, nor Byron was able to react quickly enough, Cromwell's men caught the royalists at a disadvantage and defeated them, with little difficulty: he wrote 'God made them as stubble to our swords' of this part of the fighting.[5] Even so Cromwell's own regiment had not had it all its own way, some royalist artillery had been able to fire into it as it charged. Troop Captain Valentine Walton was hit in the knee by a cannon shot and his leg irreparably damaged. He was carried from the scene of the fighting, but although his leg was amputated the wound was so serious that it seems that the bleeding could not be staunched and he died. According to Cromwell the cannonball killed Walton's horse and three others behind it. The cannon fire did not slow Cromwell significantly and his forces broke the royalist first line which disintegrated and fled, crashing into the second line before moving, south of Wilstrop Wood, back towards York. The second line tried to stem Cromwell's advance and were bolstered by Prince Rupert and a few reserves. This was a harder fight and Cromwell had already been wounded and was temporarily absent. It was argued by Denzil Holles that fellow Presbyterian Major General Lawrence Crawford took over and led the second charge but it is more likely that whilst Cromwell's wound was dressed it was David Leslie who took charge and it was certainly he who led the third line, consisting of the two Scottish regiments into the flank of the royalists and finally breaking their spirit: they too fled towards York. It is important to recall the important part played by Leslie and the Scots, and also to recall that Cromwell referred to them only as 'few Scots in our rear' when he wrote of the battle. The parliamentarian horse then began to attack the scattered royalist foot regiments which had been attempting to join the battle lines.

On the other flank there was almost a mirror image: Sir Thomas Fairfax had himself been defeated by Lord Goring's horse and his wing disintegrated and began to flee the field. Goring occupied the ground originally occupied by the parliamentarian right wing and attempted to roll up the flank of the Scots foot regiments, without success. The fight in the centre had been more evenly balanced, and Peter Newman asserts that the royalists were unable to coordinate their foot regiments because they had not been able to draw up into proper battle-lines. Nevertheless, in many places, the veteran royalist foot more than held their own and some parliamentarian regiments were forced to retreat too. The three commanding generals, Leven, Manchester and Lord Fairfax at one point fled the field believing the fight lost. Cromwell was about to change this apparently disastrous course of events.

As at the battle of Gainsborough, Cromwell, on the left wing at Marston Moor, had ensured two things: that there was a reserve force, this was Leslie's line of Scots on their small horses, and that sufficient numbers of the first and second lines had disengaged from the enemy once they had been induced to flee. This meant that there remained sufficient numbers under arms to continue fighting. News arrived of the catastrophe on the parliamentarian right. Various parliamentarian officers and a few scattered troops of horse left adrift by the Goring's attack on them found themselves on the site of the royalist left flank. Sir Thomas Fairfax was amongst these men and he and they now made their way towards Cromwell and Leslie round the rear of the royalist foot in the centre of the battle. Cromwell then attacked the remaining royalist units on the east of the battlefield. Goring counter attacked, but found himself caught up in the network of small lanes and enclosures that had earlier hampered Sir Thomas Fairfax's attack on him. Cromwell defeated him, whilst Crawford turned on the whitecoated regiments of the Northern Army. With Goring driven from the field, Cromwell could turn upon the whitecoats too and ensured that this rearguard action was also defeated. He was ecstatic when he wrote of the battle:

> Truly the Church of God hath had a great favour from the Lord, in this great Victory given us, such as the like never was since this War began. It had all the evidences of an absolute Victory obtained by the Lord's blessing upon the Godly Party principally. We never charged but we routed the enemy.

This letter,[6] one of Cromwell's most famous, is actually a letter to Oliver's brother-in-law Valentine Walton, to tell him of his son Valentine's death in the attack.

Cromwell had achieved a notable success in the action, in which about 4,000 royalists and 1,500 parliamentarians died, his control of the horse under his command and his obvious successful liaison with Leslie and Crawford during the fighting had contributed to the victory enormously. Moreover he received national coverage in the newsbooks. Lionel Walton wrote of him as 'the great agent in this victory'.[7] The author of *A relation of the good success of the Parliaments forces under the command of General Lesley, the Earl of Manchester and the Lord Fairfax*, accorded the defeat of the royalists to

> Collonel Crumwell then leading up our Brigade of horse, gave then so brave an onset, that God seconding it with his blessing, in lesse than an houre we had totally routed their foot on the right wing ...[8]

A Scottish newssheet linked Cromwell and Leslie and described them as 'under God a maine occasion of our victorie'.[9]

Clearly Marston Moor made an impression on Cromwell and on the country as a whole and Cromwell's name would be linked with the battle. It is interesting to note Cromwell's attitude towards the victory in his letter to Valentine Walton. He attributed the victory to God, but it was a blessing upon the 'Godly Party'. The question here is what did he mean by Godly Party? The term is often interpreted as being exclusive, a name by which 'puritans' referred to themselves. If Cromwell was using the term in this way, he would mean that within the allied forces were a few men to whom God had awarded the victory, but he would not include the 'few Scots in our rear', probably not the Scots foot which had held the line against the royalist attacks on the right of the field, nor the majority of the Fairfaxes' army, nor even many of the soldiers in Manchester's army. God, to award victory to the few would have to have given it to the many – the majority of the largest army to take the field during the civil war period. By the time Cromwell wrote the letter he had had three days to think over the battle. Even if fully cognisant of his own role in the victory, he would have had time to understand the course of the whole battle and the roles played in it by a range of Protestants: Scots Presbyterians like Leslie, English Presbyterians like Fairfax, Independents like John Lilburne.

The alternative proposition is that Cromwell saw all the parliamentarians as comprising the godly faction: the officers had one thing in common: they had all sworn to defend the protestant faith and they were signatories to the Solemn League and Covenant, fighting for a parliament currently undertaking one of the greatest discussions of the future of the church in England since the Synod of Whitby. If Cromwell believed this to be the case, he would not be alone. The multifarious nature of the allied forces was noted by many commentators: Captain W.F., the author of *A relation...* made a good deal of the composite nature of the army. Thomas Stockdale, whose letter to John Rushworth[10] was read in parliament, ensured that he showed how the three armies co-ordinated their dispositions according to the 'General Lesleyes direction whose great experience did worthily challenge the prime power in ordering of them'. The author of *The Glorious and Miraculaous Battell at York*, likewise ensured that he referred to all the forces involved in the victory it 'hath pleased God to bestow on us far above our deserts'. To these authors, God was rewarding a multifarious army. To argue differently, Cromwell would have had to have possessed an extremely distinctive self-perception as early as mid-1644. Given the patchy progress of his career to date, it is difficult to see what would have given him such a view, which would involve rejecting many people, including Sir Thomas Fairfax with whom he had worked closely, and those who he had defended against attacks, like Lieutenant Packer.

After the battle the allied army began a second siege of York and by 17 July had forced the royalist garrison to surrender. The Fairfaxes and the Scots remained in the area to complete the destruction of the royalist war-effort in the region. Manchester marched southwards into the north Midlands and began to destroy the royalist hold there. The presence of the Eastern Association army enabled local parliamentarians to capture a string of garrisons in north Nottinghamshire and Derbyshire. Despite local and national expectations that Manchester and Cromwell would go on to attack Newark or Ashby de la Zouch, the region's two principal royalist strongholds, the Eastern Association Army swung eastwards and entered Lincolnshire.

Marston Moor was a major victory for parliament, but within months the national picture was far less positive. A concerted attack on Oxford by the Earl of Essex's and Sir William Waller's armies had failed to achieve any material results. On 6 June the two generals, bridling in each other's company, separated their forces and Essex moved towards the southwest, leaving Waller in the Midlands. On 29 June King Charles's forces had defeated Sir William Waller's army at the Battle of Cropredy Bridge and had then set off to follow Essex's forces. By 3 September the king had caught and defeated Essex's army at the Battle of Lostwithiel in Cornwall. Essex's cavalry had escaped the catastrophe, and his foot, although disarmed were released to return to London. By late September Essex had begun to reassemble his army in the south joined again by Waller and his new forces the following month. The Earl of Manchester somewhat reluctantly joined Essex and Waller on 18 October.

In the weeks since Marston Moor, the Eastern Association Army had nursed its wounds. Manchester reckoned that he had lost about 25 per cent of his strength since recapturing Lincoln: his army was in arrears to the sum of £3,000. Parliament had no army in the centre of England at this point, with Essex in the southwest and Waller forced to recruit a new army altogether. The response was to order Manchester to march south. The earl would not do so until the arrears had been paid and his army recruited to strength. Cromwell was of a different mind. He wrote to Valentine Walton in the wake of Lostwithiel:

> We do with grief of heart resent the sad condition of our Army in the West, and of our affairs there. That business has our hearts with it; and truly had we wings, we would fly thither! So soon as my Lord and the Foot set me loose, there shall be in me no want to hasten what I can do in that service.[11]

Eventually Manchester got his way, 1,800 recruits were raised and money urgently dispatched, but the earl did not bring the army southwards until the end of September, reaching Reading on 29 September.

Other problems beset the Eastern Association Army, Cromwell and Crawford were involved in an increasingly bitter dispute. Stories were beginning to circulate of a very different Cromwell at Marston Moor than that which appeared in the papers and some letters. This was Cromwell the coward, who left the battlefield because of a very slight wound, of a man paralysed into inaction during the fighting and needing the goading of Major General Crawford to compel him to action. These were rumours which surrounded the kernel of the argument between the two men, that centred upon religious differences and Cromwell's heightened profile after the battle. Manchester, at one point, asked parliament to intervene in the argument. Cromwell alluded to this in his letter to Walton. In the first paragraph he implied that Manchester and the foot held him back from setting off to the west: he may have meant Crawford when he said foot as Crawford, as major general, commanded the foot. His second and third paragraphs referred directly to the argument:

> ... indeed all other considerations are to be laid aside, and to give place to it [the current military emergency], as being of far more importance. I hope the kingdom shall see that, in the midst of our necessities, we shall serve them without disputes ...
>
> We have some amongst us slow in action; – if we could attend to our own ends less, and our ease too, our business in this Army would go on wheels for expedition ... But because some of us are enemies to rapine, and other wickednessess, we are said to be factious to seek to maintain our opinions in religion by force which we detest and abhor. I profess I could never satisfy myself of the justness of this War, but from the Authority of the Parliament to maintain itself in its rights: and in this Cause, I hope to approve myself an honest man and single-hearted.

It would seem that Cromwell was dissatisfied with Manchester and Crawford's leadership. He seems to have been opposed to the requests for money for the army and from a man who was known to pressurise parliament and the county committees for money to pay his troops, it must have seemed to him that the money was not required for the soldiers' wages. In turn, for objecting to this he himself was being attacked for his religious stance. Within months this would all become a very public argument and the sentiment of the last sentence quoted above, misplaced. The campaign which followed the assembly of the three armies did not meet with the success that the alliance in Yorkshire had met. The strategy was to pen the king into Oxford and encroach steadily upon the satellite garrisons around his capital. One target was Donnington Castle near Newbury, but the king was determined to furnish the satellites with supplies and ammunition and in late October he marched to Donnington with supplies. The king's army camped south of the castle: protected by Shaw House to the east, Speen Hill to the west, Donington to the north and Newbury itself to the south, the parliamentarians advanced from Basingstoke. A complex strategy was devised whereby Waller would march around the king's forces with most of the horse, including Cromwell and the Eastern Association horse regiments, during the night of 26–27 October. Then, as the Earl of Manchester attacked from the east, Waller would launch an attack on the king's rear from the west, crushing the 8,000 royalists in a pincer movement executed by around 19,000 parliamentarians.

The carefully planned attack failed. Waller's march took far longer than expected by which time Manchester's earlier attacks on Shaw House in the royalist centre had petered out. Waller approached what should have been the royalists' rear at Speen Hill only to find out that it had been fortified extensively during the night. Nevertheless, the royalists were pushed from the hill and Waller approached the rear centre of the royalist position. However, there was no renewed fighting around Shaw House where Manchester should have engaged the royalist centre from the front in a co-ordinated effort. Sir William Balfour with the Earl of Essex's horse and Oliver Cromwell with the Eastern Association horse advanced on the royalist horse stationed in-between the royalist rear at Speen and the royalist front at Shaw House, but as they completed the negotiation of the enclosed fields, Sir Humphrey Bennet and the Earl of Cleveland with the royalist horse attacked. It was opportune timing. Cromwell and Balfour were stopped in their tracks and, although the Earl of Cleveland was captured, the work of defeating the victor of Marston Moor was completed by the last general Cromwell had defeated back on 2 July, Lord Goring. The parliamentarian attack from the west collapsed, just as Manchester launched his belated attack on Shaw House. Fighting across the field died out as the autumn evening fell. It was a clear defeat for parliament's combined armies, but the wake of the battle was to be even more humiliating and would lead to a major crisis in the parliamentarian cause.

Over night the king slipped away, using subterfuge. His regiments lit fires and left slow matches burning in bushes and trees and slipped into the darkness. The artillery was put inside Donnington Castle and the royalists marched to Oxford. The late dawn of 28 October revealed the trick. Cromwell and Waller mounted the horse and set off after the king, but Manchester called them back, which they failed to do until it became clear that Manchester had no intention of following with the foot, allowing the king to reach Oxford on 30 October. Manchester made a brief attack on the castle: when this failed, he reluctantly followed the king towards Oxford on 2 November. It was not long before the earl began muttering about returning to East Anglia. The army promptly halted and then made its way back to Newbury. A week later the king returned to Donnington with a reorganised and reinforced army. Manchester ordered Cromwell to attack, but the horse was exhausted and underfed and he could not risk them in a fight. The king calmly took his artillery out of the castle and drew up in battle formation across the Shaw and Newbury open fields challenging his enemies, to the south across the River Kennet, to attack him. The whole of the combined parliamentarian army was in the same state as the Eastern Association horse, exhausted and underfed. The parliamentarian generals declined to fight and the king began to withdraw on 10 November and the generals again failed to attack. The Committee of Both Kingdoms ordered the army to stay in the field whilst the king was in the field, but because of its state it could not. The parliamentarian army began to withdraw from the area, and the king finally got the supplies into Basing House.

It was a debacle. The king had more or less made a mockery of the three chief parliamentarian generals and their armies. He had defeated a sophisticated battlefield strategy and achieved his own defensive strategic aim, bolstering Oxford's chain of defences in the face of an overwhelmingly large opposition. Parliament was angry at the conduct of the campaign, its generals had refused to cooperate with good grace, their armies had failed to work in a concerted manner. There would be an enquiry: worse, there would be an argument. Manchester, in charge after the battle during Essex's illness, and under pressure because of the failure to pursue and attack the king, turned on Cromwell.

Cromwell was accused of military failings: he had not had a good campaign. On the field he had been defeated by Bennet, Cleveland and Goring. On campaign he had failed to obey Manchester's order to attack the king when he returned to Donnington. The accusations went further and Cromwell's character was called into account. As commander in the field, Manchester would have felt the sting of criticism at the end of the Newbury campaign. In order to deflect this he tried to put the blame on Cromwell. The relationship between the two men had declined over the previous six months. Major General Crawford had played a part in this decline. Anthony Cotton in his seminal article on the quarrel dates the decline in the relationship to the affair of Lieutenant Packer and Cromwell's defence of him. The siege of York, which had seen Crawford fail in his attack on St Mary's precinct and Manchester's precipitous departure for Tadcaster during the battle of Marston Moor had coincided with Cromwell's coming into national prominence. Manchester compounded this apparent gulf in fortunes with two lacklustre periods in the field, the campaign in the Midlands and the Newbury debacle. All the while Cromwell's enemies had gathered information about alleged financial peculation and religious misconduct.

Parliament initially demanded an explanation of Newbury and MPs Cromwell and Sir William Waller returned to parliament to present their version. Cromwell on 25 November launched a scathing attack on Manchester's ability. Criticisms extended beyond Newbury and were set into a context: Manchester had, Cromwell argued, 'some principal unwillingness ... to have this war prosecuted to a full victory, and a design or desire to have it ended by accommodation (and that) on some terms to which it might be disadvantageous to bring the king so low'. This attack was a controversial move, Cromwell was targeting three things: Manchester as his commander; Manchester as an aristocrat; and Manchester as a member of the House of Lords: as such this was a grand scandal. The attack even went beyond Manchester for Cromwell also questioned the behaviour of the Earl of Essex. Traditionally historians view Manchester as Cromwell's main target, but Bulstrode Whitelock, who had the interests of the Lord General at heart, thought Essex was the main target of Cromwell's speech in the Commons. Cromwell 'seemed (but cautiously enough) to lay more blame on the officers of the lord-general's army than upon any other'.[12] A committee, under the Presbyterian MP Zouch Tate, was established to examine the accusations and counter-accusations and further evidence was called for.

It was Manchester who responded first. The Lords as a whole were angry that he and Essex had been attacked in the Commons, but it was Cromwell's commander who led the attack on 28 November. Coupled within it were counter-accusations about Cromwell's conduct at Newbury: his failure on the field and his failure to take the horse into the field to stop the king returning to Donnington. Behind this too was the evidence collected over the last year: the allowance paid to Elizabeth, the alleged misuse of funds collected for the defence of Ely. There was more to it than this: the lieutenant general, the earl argued, was a social revolutionary who wanted the end of the aristocracy and rejected Presbyterianism. The evidence for this had come from the same source, Manchester's informant had provided two pertinent instances.

After the defeat of royalists at Crowland, and being informed that several lords had been killed, he reported that Cromwell had said: 'God fought ag[ains]t them [lords] for god would have noe lording over his people & he verily believed that god would sweep away that lord in power out of this nation'. He also added that when some of Cromwell's officers had tried to get the informant to sign a petition in favour of freedom of worship he had replied 'if any nation in the world were in the ready way to heaven it was the Scots', Cromwell's officers had responded 'but now they perceive what I was & went away ever after Coll Cromwell did sleight me'. By adding for good measure that when Cromwell heard of the defeat of the Earl of Essex at the Battle of Lostwithiel the news was 'greeted with joy as if they had won a victory', the author portrayed Cromwell as a social radical.[13]

Essex turned on Cromwell too. On 3 December, Whitelock was summoned to Essex's home to discuss the lieutenant general. There he met the Lord General and the Lord Chancellor of Scotland, John Campbell, the Earl of Loudoun, along with five Presbyterian MPs, including Denzil Holles. The Scots had a plan to get rid of Cromwell about whom they asserted 'since the advance of our army into England he hath used all underhand and cunning means to take off from our honour and merit of this kingdom; an evil requital of all our hazards and services', and appended the accusation that 'he is no well-willer to his excellency'.[14] The point was to pick Whitelock and Sir John Maynard's legal brains to see if a charge of being an incendiary could be levelled at Cromwell – in effect accusing him of intending to provoke 'kindling of a fire of contention betwixt the two nations'. Whitelock poured cold water on the plan. He argued that the lords could not afford to fail in their attack on Cromwell because it would reflect upon their honour, and therefore they must prepare the ground perfectly, including assessing the support Cromwell could command. Whitelock suggested that Cromwell by that time had a lot of supporters: in the army 'some honourable persons here present, his excellency's officers are best able to inform your lordships' whilst Whitelock and Maynard could assess support in parliament:

I take lieutenant-general Cromwell to be a gentleman of quick and subtle parts, and one who hath (especially of late) gained no small interest in the house of commons, nor is he wanting of friends in the house of peers, nor of abilities in himself to manage his own part or defence to the best advantage.

Maynard added

Lieutenant-General Cromwell is a person of great favour and interest with the house of commons, and with some of the house of peers likewise, and therefore there must be proofs, and the more clear and evident against him, to prevail with the parliament to adjudge him to be an incendiary.[15]

Evidence was at that point lacking, even Manchester's informant could not provide sufficient proof of much other than Oliver's antipathy to Presbyterianism. Nevertheless Holles and Sir Philip Stapleton protested that Cromwell was not so popular in the Commons as Maynard and Whitelock had asserted and the Scots were more impressed by this latter assessment and they decided to assemble more evidence. Whitelock's comment about Cromwell's interest in the army was double edged, for he suspected that some of the men in Essex's house that night actually supported Cromwell and would tell the lieutenant general of the midnight meeting. It is clear that perceptions of Cromwell's political abilities had changed from 1640. He was now seen at least by Whitelock and Maynard, experienced lawyers and parliamentarians as a major player in parliament in his own right rather than as a bit-part actor working for his more experienced cousins.

Tate's enquiry proceeded. Waller and Cromwell and others presented evidence of Manchester's lack of motivation. The evidentiary statements included several versions of a conversation between Manchester and Cromwell at which the earl presented his seeming frustration with the straitjacket of a war against a lawful king: 'if we beat the King 99 times he would be King still, and his posterity, and we subjects still; but if he beats us but once we should be hanged, and our posterity undone.'[16] Cromwell responded 'My lord, if this be so, why did we take up arms at first? This is against fight ever hereafter'. Although there are minor differences in the versions of this conversation, held during the Newbury campaign, the essence is clear. It epitomises the argument between the developing 'parties' in parliament the war party and the peace party. One desired an all-out military victory, the other a negotiated peace that would secure the safety of endangered posterity. Cromwell wanted all-out victory, not as Manchester suggested, no victory at all if there would be a Presbyterian church established in England and Wales. It was as well, that if Whitelock and Maynard rather than Holles was correct, that Cromwell had important support in parliament, because the familial base which had got him into parliament and into the army in the first place was on the wane. Hampden was dead, and Oliver St John was now less important as the Middle Group was less and less able to hold the balance of power between the War Party and the Peace Party and in any case he was being overshadowed by Holles a man now clearly an opponent of Cromwell. The wider circle was still there, however, and Lord Saye and Sele would be crucial in the forthcoming struggle. The weight of the other evidence coming from army officers bore out Cromwell's charges, Manchester seemed unwilling to prosecute an all-out victory – even Major General Lawrence Crawford's evidence, whilst attacking Cromwell tended to support the main thrust of his enemy's case.

After seemingly successfully rebutting Manchester's charges on 4 December, suddenly, five days later, Cromwell stopped the attack, before Manchester's evidence was submitted to the committee. It is an almost perceptible drawing of breath, Oliver announced that the cause was more important than the individuals and their quarrels: 'The important occasion now is no less than to save a Nation out of a bleeding, nay almost dying, condition, which the long continuance of this War hath already brought it …', a position somewhat similar to his belief that the cause was greater than individual religiosity, but completely at odds with his most recent attacks on Manchester. 'I am far from reflecting on any', he said, but 'if the Army be not put into another method, and the War more vigorously prosecuted, the People can bear the War no longer, and will enforce you to a dishonourable Peace'. This solution was 'Members of either House will scruple to deny themselves, and their own private interests for the public good'.[17] The proposal honed by Zouch Tate, into the Self-Denying Ordinance, was that the members of either house should not hold military office. There has been considerable debate as to why Cromwell so suddenly backed off. Cotton actually traces Cromwell's change of heart to the rebuttal on 4 December, because he claimed privilege of parliament to try and halt the discussion there and then. Traditionally historians including W.C. Abbott (who claimed that his three speeches of 9 December were 'the first time Cromwell spoke in Parliament as a statesman') had seen Cromwell as backing off because of his commitment to the greater cause. Cotton instead argued that Cromwell was actually on the defensive, because his attack on Manchester back on the 25 November had been ill founded and easily rebutted, whereas Manchester's attack on Cromwell posed a threat to both Cromwell's military and his political career. Also it was true that sometime after Essex's midnight meeting, Oliver had got to know of the Scots' determination to charge him as an incendiary. Cotton's perspective is supported by Manchester's determination to continue the attack, despite Cromwell's withdrawal, suggesting that he believed the cause was going his way, prompting the Commons to continue their investigation into the charges made against him on 30 December.

The Lords as a whole rejected the Self Denying Ordinance on 13 January 1645 and a week later the Committee of Both Kingdoms was pressed, by the peers, to ensure that the case was continued. Cromwell was certainly in a weak position. For over a year his association with religious radicals had been a topic of discussion in ever widening circles. It may be true that when he dealt with the arrest of Lieutenant Packer in March 1644, Cromwell was not averse to Presbyterianism, but his biographer Peter Gaunt thinks that his contact with the Scots during the siege of York might have changed his open attitude. Certainly he had created enemies amongst the Scots, including Robert Baillie one of the representatives at the Westminster Assembly. This possibility has a lot to commend it, but it needs to be recalled that most of Manchester's informant's evidence about Cromwell's anti-Scottish or anti-Presbyterian remarks pre-dated the siege of York, so such a progress to a broader toleration, if such a progress were made, may have begun earlier. This still does not mean that Cromwell was exclusively an Independent seeking only a settlement that encompassed small associations of congregated churches, only that he did not want one that excluded others: an argument for his use of the word 'Godly' after Marston Moor and, as we shall see later after Naseby, as an inclusive term, embracing independents like Packer and Scots Presbyterians like Leslie and Crawford as well as English Presbyterians like Fairfax.

One other context needs to be referred to when discussing the Self Denying Ordinance. Cromwell has been depicted as taking a great risk when he supported the concept of self denial, as it should, if carried to its logical end have excluded him as well. It has already been argued that Cromwell had already decided to try and save his political career as a first priority, but there is an older argument that sees the Self Denying Ordinance and the creation of the New Model Army as a radicalisation of the parliamentarian cause. From such a perspective as this the 'neat trick' of the Self Denying Ordinance was that whereas MP officers could resign their seats in the Commons to stay in command of their seats, noble officers could not. This is somewhat undermined by the Commons' sop to the lords in 1645, when the possibility of reappointment (which had the effect of saving Cromwell's military career, but not that of Manchester or Essex) was added to the redrafted Self Denying Ordinance. J.S.A. Adamson raised interesting questions about this supposed radicalisation, suggesting that the reformation of the army was to remove Essex and therefore, by implication Manchester was 'collateral damage' even though Cromwell's attack on him provided the occasion. There was more than a hint of collusion when on 9 December the Self Denying Ordinance was presented in the Lords on the same day that Cromwell retreated from his attack on Manchester and Zouch Tate brought the ordinance to the attention of the Commons. The reformation of the cause was, Adamson argues, a struggle within a class rather than between classes. If so then Cromwell's role was again, as it was 1640–1642, as a dependable team member in a powerful political clique to which members of his extended family belonged, not as the deft politician capable of handling himself as Whitelock and Maynard had argued. It is probable that Whitelock's perception was nearer to the truth. Cromwell's disagreement was with single-church Presbyterianism but he did not question parliament's right to decide the issue. If he lost his position as either MP or officer Cromwell's ability to influence parliament would be wrecked and his fortunes probably similarly destroyed. To save his, and possibly Oliver St John and their allies' religious and political strategy, Oliver withdrew from an untenable position on 9 December.

The quarrel became a problem wider than the interests of Cromwell and Manchester and the two men and their supporters became subsumed in a wider context. The controversy threatened to create a division between the Commons and the Lords, for Cromwell's evidence was heard in the former and Manchester's in the latter. With negotiations between parliament and the king in the offing, and with less controversy over the need to remodel the army, the debate eventually fizzled out. The

Commons passed a bill for the creation of a new army on 21 January and a new Self Denying Ordinance was drafted, this time silent on the possibility that MPs could be reappointed to military command in the future.

The other aspect of the winter restructuring was the creation of one national army out of three of parliament's existing field armies. It must be recalled that this New Modelled Army was not the only parliamentarian army in the field, there remained that Western Association Army under Sir Edward Massey, the Northern Association Army under Sydenham Pointz and a smaller force in the Lancashire-Cheshire region commanded by Sir William Brereton and each of them played important roles in the rest of the war. Nevertheless, the Eastern Association Army, Essex's army and Waller's armies ceased to exist and their regiments reformed in the New Model. According to the ordinance of 11 February, the new army was to have eleven regiments of horse, each of 600 men, twelve regiments of foot, each of 1,200 men, one large regiment of 1,000 dragoons and a train of artillery. The imbalance in the existing army ensured that whilst there were enough troopers to create the horse regiments, and the same was true of the dragoons, there was a serious shortfall in the number of foot soldiers and conscription had to be employed to make up the numbers. The total numbers of foot in the three armies only amounted to 7,174 men and nearly 7,000 men had to be co-opted. There were too many officers however and a good number had to be cashiered or recruited as private soldiers. This offered the opportunity for the new commanders to pick and choose 'suitable' men.

Cromwell left Westminster on active service in March 1645, returning, eventually, to the south Midlands where he had been campaigning the previous spring. He was trying to complete the work undertaken in the autumn by attacking satellite Oxford's garrisons: he captured Bletchingdon House on 25 April, but failed to force Farringdon into surrender at the end of the month.[18] Meanwhile he was getting information about Lord Goring's forces in the west, which were about to move north to join the king at Oxford; all this information was passed on to the Committee of Both Kingdoms, and to Sir Thomas Fairfax.[19] It was realised that a conjunction of royalist forces was planned for the reopened campaign season. Cromwell was detailed to try and stop Prince Maurice joining the king, but as Goring approached, Cromwell had to withdraw from Farringdon to avoid being trapped. Fairfax and the New

Model moved from Windsor towards the West where they intended to relieve Taunton from Lord Goring's siege.

By this time the amended Self Denying Ordinance had come into effect. Fairfax had been appointed commander in chief – lord general – of the New Model Army and Sir Phillip Skippon was given the rank of sergeant major general and command of the foot, but the lieutenant general post, commander of the horse, was left empty. Cromwell should have surrendered his command by 12 May, but by then an emergency had arisen: the king had broken out of Oxford, and joined by Goring's forces and those of the brothers Princes Maurice and Rupert, headed north towards Chester. On 9 May Goring was sent back into the west. The king had intended to relieve the siege of the port, but Brereton abandoned the siege as the king approached and after 22 May the royalists sought a new target. Cromwell moved east from the south Midlands, via Warwick, to his home territory to ensure the security of Ely in case the Eastern Association was the target.[20] Fairfax returned from the west to besiege a weakened Oxford whilst the king's forces were shadowed by a detachment of horse under Vermuyden including Derbyshire and Nottinghamshire horse. The king decided against moving as far eastwards as Ely and instead attacked Leicester, storming the town in the early hours of May 31. Having appointed Lord Loughborough to rebuild Leicester's defences, the king then marched south with supplies to be sent into Oxford. Meanwhile Cromwell had been granted an extension to his commission allowing him to continue his work in Ely. As the king approached Oxford, Fairfax sought permission to advance upon the royalist army and eventually, shaken by the fall of Leicester, the Committee of Both Kingdoms allowed him to do so. Fairfax summoned Cromwell from East Anglia and on 10 June the Committee extended Oliver's commission. At the same time Fairfax demanded and got permission to appoint Cromwell to the vacant command of the horse. As Fairfax approached the king in Northamptonshire, the royalists began to retreat towards Market Harborough in south Leicestershire to where the king had recalled Goring's army. On 13 July Cromwell joined the New Model Army and took charge of the horse.

On the morning of 14 June, Fairfax, Cromwell and Skippon placed the New Model on an escarpment northeast of the village of Naseby across the road which led to Clipston and Market Harborough, from where the Royalist army was advancing towards them. This was a very strong position approached only by rough and boggy ground littered with furze and gorse. The royalist forces could not have hoped to attack across this ground and then uphill into the New Model. Both armies moved west. There is some dispute about which side moved first: in Naseby's most recent comprehensive history, Glenn Foard suggests that it was Rupert who moved first towards the almost parallel road between Sibbertoft and Naseby, rejecting the near contemporary assertion by Joshua Sprigge in *Anglia Rediviva* that Cromwell had 'as though he had received direction from God himselfe' inspired the move westwards.[21] Foard argued that Rupert would know that Fairfax would not move from such a strong position unless the advancing royalists moved first, Rupert's move west threatened a flanking attack and so the New Model shifted westward to face the royalists' new line of advance. This movement westwards resulted in the battle deployment of both armies.

The New Model Army redeployed on a ridge north west of Naseby on a forward slope. This was in Turmore field, one of Naseby's three fields. In June 1645 it was a fallow field with a ridge upon which the centre of the army stood looking down the slope towards the moors north of the village. The left wing rested near to the thick parish hedge between Naseby and Sulby. This wing comprised of two lines of horse under Henry Ireton. Skippon commanded the centre comprising two lines of foot regiments. Cromwell led three lines of horse on the right wing ranged along a fairly level plateau identified by Foard as being known as Closter. From Closter plateau the ground sloped downwards across Broad Moor, a moor partly divided into field strips, and there may have been some enclosed sections on the rising ground towards Dust Hill from where the royalists would advance upon the parliamentarians. Immediately opposite Cromwell's position was a set of rabbit warrens centred upon a warren house. The royalists moved onto the field within the confined space between the parish hedges of Naseby-Sulby and Naseby-Clipston.

As at Marston Moor Rupert arrived on Dust Hill with the horse first, and from there he summoned the rest of the army from the Clipston Road. The royalist forces arrived on Dust Hill around 8.30 to 9am, from there they began to advance down across the Broad Moor and the enclosed fields. At around the same time Fairfax withdrew his front line about 100 yards from the ridge to a position where they would be out of sight of the advancing royalists and somewhat out of danger from artillery fire, although the royalist artillery was still moving from Farndon Hills and therefore never actually posed a danger during the day. One effect of withdrawing the foot would be that the new recruits comprising a good part of the New Model foot would not be exposed to the dramatic sight of the royalist army expanding in size as it advanced southwards from the tight strictures imposed by the bottle neck on Dust Hill caused by the converging parish hedges. This manoeuvre would have over-emphasised the size of the royalist army, which was actually, at 7,500 around half the size of the New Model Army, which it attacked.

Cromwell oversaw Ireton's deployment on the left wing and ordered Okey forward to seize the Archwong enclosure abutting the Sulby parish hedge in front to the royalist right, commanded by Rupert in person placing them in front of Rupert's left wing. This resulted quickly in fighting as Rupert tried to stop the dragoons interfering with his line of attack. Cromwell then rode back to the right flank. The battle began between 10 and 11 o'clock, and Foard argues that Cromwell's flank was re-ordering itself to accommodate Colonel Edward Rossiter and the Lincolnshire horse that arrived suddenly, as the royalists advanced upon them possibly presenting the royalists with an apparent opportunity. On the New Model's left flank Ireton was faced with Rupert's attack. His wing met Rupert's advance, but because of small waterlogged hollows part of his line had failed to keep up and this weakened the counter attack, allowing Rupert to defeat an important portion of Ireton's line. However, this was a fight of mixed fortunes and some of Ireton's wing met with success and drove off part of Rupert's left flank and were able to turn on the exposed flank of the advancing royalist foot. The rest of Rupert's victorious regiments drove back the bulk of Ireton's foot and rushed southwards after the retreating parliamentarians.

Despite being outnumbered and advancing uphill the royalist foot was able to push back the Major General Phillip Skippon and the New Model foot, which had advanced against towards the ridge line. Two regiments in the centre, Colonel Montague's and Colonel Pickering's broke and ran, even before Ireton's wing had been defeated by Rupert. The success of the royalists began to wane once Ireton's remaining horse hit them in the flank, and in any case once Skippon led forward the reserve force, Colonels Hammond and Rainsborough's regiments. The royalist advance was slowed and then stopped in Turnmore field.

Cromwell on the other hand had undoubtedly begun to effect the complete defeat of the royalists. Using the technique with which he had defeated Sir Charles Cavendish at Gainsborough and with which he and David Leslie had defeated Byron and Rupert at Marston Moor, he attacked Sir Marmaduke Langdale and the royalist left with just a section of his wing: Edward Whalley's and his own regiment stove in the royalist front line in a very hard fight, but because Cromwell had used only a few of the regiments at his disposal, he had enough uncommitted troops to be able to outflank and overwhelm Langdale's front line and push it back towards the king and his reserves. Whalley's and Colonel Pye's regiments then reformed and continued following Langdale's defeated horse towards Leicester, ensuring that they could not reform and return to the fight. Cromwell was then able to use two regiments from the second line and the third line to attack the left flank of the royalist foot as it fought the New Model foot. Moreover, Cromwell was also able to turn on the royalist reserve – the third of Sir Jacob Astley's lines. Astley probably had to have committed both his first and second lines to defeat the parliamentarian front line. The lack of numbers on the royalist side was a major contribution to their failure to exploit the early success. Foard argues that we should not overestimate Cromwell's tactical foresight, suggesting that as Cromwell would not be able to see what had happened to Ireton as it was out of his line of sight and that his view of what was happening in the centre would also be limited and so it was probably Fairfax, whose overall grasp of what was happening was clearer, who suggested using the right wing reserve against the royalist foot. Nevertheless, it was only possible to do this because of the way Cromwell had disposed, and then used, his regiments: although he did of course have as many troops in his front line as Langdale had in his entire wing. It is also possible to add to the causes of victory the New Model's organisation. With a limited number of well structured regiments the army was able to be more responsive to tactical control, than the royalists' brigaded small regiments with too many officers and a multi-layered command structure. This was a problem that hampered parliamentarian forces too until the creation of the New Model Army.

Cromwell's letter to William Lenthall written on the day of the battle is brief and gives no detail about his own role. He seems to have had his helmet struck off in the fight with Langdale's horse and this personal experience, combined with what he had already gleaned about the rest of the field impinged upon his view of the 'three hours fight very doubtful'. He was clearly more impressed with the immediate outcome of the fight, in which about 1,000 royalists died as opposed to around 150 parliamentarian casualties, for he gave more detail of the rout which followed; 'we pursued the enemy from three miles short of [Market] Harborough to nine beyond, even to the sight of Leicester whither the king fled'. Cromwell gave all the credit in his letter, as was now common, to God, but the human agent that the lord had worked through was Fairfax whose feelings he felt fit to explain to Lenthall:

> ... the General served you with all faithfulness and honor; and the best commendation I can give him is, That I daresay he attributes all to God and would rather perish than assume to himself which is an honest and thriving way, and yet as much for bravery may be given to him in this action as to a man.[22]

It is almost a fatherly regard for the younger Fairfax. In his account, Fairfax referred to Skippon and Ireton but not to Cromwell. On the other hand, parliament's commissioners with the army, Lieutenant Colonel Harcourt Leighton and Colonel Thomas Herbert commented 'The general, Lieut. Gen. Cromwell, and Major Gen. Skippon did beyond expression gallantly; so did all the other commanders and soldiers'. Colonel John Okey's account of the battle suggests that he saw Cromwell's role as pivotal. Okey's position in a close sticking into Broad Moor from the line of Sulby Hedges seems to have enabled him to see across the battlefield towards the southeast and east where Cromwell defeated Langdale. He got a good view of this fight 'which I perceiving (after one houre's battail) caused all my men to mount and to charge into their Foot, which accordingly they did; and took all their Colours, and 500 foot ...' Like Cromwell, Okey perceived himself as part of a small minority 'a poore handfull of dispised men': the victory was due to God who had taken pity on this handful.[23] In *Anglia Rediviva*, Sprigge made an explicit and important point:

> The great share Lieutenant General Cromwell had in this action, who commanded the Right wing of Horse, (which did such service, carrying the field before them as they did at Marston Moor) is so well acknowledged, that envy itself can neither detract nor deny.

Cromwell's use of the landscape ahead of him was very similar to Marston Moor and his victory on the right flank at Naseby was similar but more emphatic than that on the left flank at Marston Moor. The two battles were tied together in the establishment of Cromwell's career, his failures in the later Newbury campaign were overlooked. The eleven months from July 1644 to June 1645 probably mark the 'point of take-off' for Cromwell's career, and it was his military successes that were largely responsible, although his familial and political connections had ensured that he had survived Manchester and Essex's attack upon him and subsequently secured him from the worst aspects of the Self Denying Ordinance. If Cromwell had not been so successful in the field, however, there would have been no point in doing so. Just as true is the case regarding Manchester's attack on Cromwell. For had not Oliver begun to urge toleration, then there would have been no grounds for much of the later criticism. In the letter to William Lenthall written after the battle which praised Fairfax, Cromwell has also referred to everyone else involved:

> Honest men served you faithfully in this action, Sir they are trusty, I beseech you in the name of God, not to discourage them, I wish this action may begat thankfulnesse and humility in all that are concerned in it he that ventures his life for the liberty of the country I wish he trust God for the liberty of his conscience, and you for the liberty he fights for...[24]

The House of Commons edited this section out of the first published version of the text as it was clearly in conflict with the ongoing movements towards establishing a Presbyterian system and would probably offend parliament's Scottish allies. Cromwell was arguing for religious toleration on the grounds that Presbyterians and other sects alike were blessed by God with victory at Marston Moor. God was evidently not singling out any of the separate groups fighting for parliament's cause: he rewarded all indiscriminately, so why should parliament? The House of Lords was less in thrall to Presbyterians and Lord Saye and Sele had the letter reprinted with Cromwell's call for toleration reinstated. Naseby distinguished Cromwell in more ways than one.

6

HE DID NOT OPENLY PROFESS
WHAT OPINION HE WAS OF
HIMSELF
1645–1647

Following the dramatic victory at Naseby, Fairfax did not follow the king's retreat into the west Midlands. After shadowing the remnants of the king's field army into Leicestershire and receiving the surrender of Leicester from Lord Loughborough, Fairfax chose to prioritise the southwest, to where he had been headed before the king's march from Oxford in early May. The first target was Lord Goring who had united the royalist forces in the south west and assembled an army of 7,000 with the aim of rejoining the king and rebuilding the main field army. The New Model Army moved through Wiltshire towards Goring who began to march towards Bridgewater to get to the king in the west Midlands. Goring sent Major General George Porter towards Taunton to distract Fairfax from the route to Bridgewater, and a detachment was duly sent in pursuit. Porter was caught and defeated at Ilchester, allowing Fairfax to concentrate on Goring. On June 10 the New Model pressed on through Somerton towards Goring's army at Langport. The royalists had a strong position on rising ground east of a brook: the Wagg Ryhne. Goring had displaced his men to cover the crossing point on the Wagg Ryhne and the marshy ground across which the New Model Army would have to cross to get at him, with only one narrow passage and bridge for any attacking army, the royalists were in a position to inflict serious damage upon an approaching army. The chief problems for Goring were lack of artillery and numbers: Fairfax's forces, if they could get across the brook, could overwhelm Goring.

The New Model opened the battle with heavy artillery fire that quickly silenced Goring's three guns covering the bridge. Musketeers approached Wagg Rhyne and opened fire on the royalist musketeers on the opposite bank, and again quickly silenced them. Clearing the royalists away from the approach to narrow crossing opened the route for Oliver Cromwell and the horse. Cromwell sent six troops of horse drawn from his old regiment, but now belonging to Fairfax's and Whalley's regiments. The bridge was only wide enough for two riders abreast, but two troops, Captain Slingsby Bethel's and Captain Evanson's got across before Goring's horse tried to stop them. These two troops drove back the royalists and almost came into contact with the main royalist force before withdrawing to the bridge to rejoin the other four troops. The reunited six troops then moved forward, but as they did the royalist army seemingly lost heart as a result of having lost control of the crossing and seeing the retreat of their horse: some units began to withdraw. In turn this precipitated a general retreat that caused Goring's army to disintegrate: half of his soldiers were killed as a result of the flight. Once again in a letter Cromwell, with his refined sense of providence, acknowledged the divine plan at work and the true cause of victory was 'through the goodness of God, who still appears with us'.[1] Cromwell was not alone in his interpretation, several officers and soldiers in the New Model believed that God was demonstrating his approval of the cause through the victories they achieved: the defeated too could interpret providence too, but they tended to see defeat as a test of their own behaviour, not usually as approbation for their enemies' actions and intentions. Within a fortnight Bridgewater fell to the New Model Army and Bath surrendered on 29 July. By this time, however, a new phenomenon had emerged in the west bringing Cromwell into contact with thousands of armed men.

Across southern England and Wales, in the south and west Midlands, the southwest and in the Home Counties, a series of protest movements developed, which brought together thousands of men and women united in their opposition to the war. Ironically the spark for some of these movements had begun in late 1644 when the king attempted to raise a 'popular army' under the banner 'One and All' to impose a settlement on parliament. This had not worked, but meetings of the sort of men

Charles was relying on to be the backbone of this new effort resulted in a drive to end the war by forcing peace on both sides. In Worcestershire, Herefordshire, Shropshire and Wiltshire in the southwest groups of men and women often labelled clubmen gathered together to draw up petitions to present to the king and or parliament and even to draft regulations governing their own behaviour. As Fairfax and the main body of the army besieged the royalist garrison at Sherborne, Cromwell marched towards Shaftsbury, on the way he stopped at the Iron Age fort of Hambledon Hill where a body of clubmen had gathered defiantly. The clubmen in this area had drawn up a series of rules which included peacetime precedents for raising the trained bands and a basis for creating their 'third force' and establishing watch and ward in each village to preserve Wiltshire and Dorset from 'plunder and all other unlawful violence'. All valid warrants from any army would be complied with as would orders for billeting, but a real care taken to ensure equity would be enforced. There was however no question about the response to unlawful acts for the clubmen would be armed at their own or wealthier members of the community's expense, just like the trained bands, and these men would arrest wrongdoers and return them to their units and resist force with force. The intention was to be strictly neutral, men demonstrating political affiliations to either side 'shall be accounted unworthy of our protection'. The association was expected to be universal for no one who was not associated would receive protection. Tellingly, neither would any Roman Catholic.[2]

Cromwell was perplexed. Both royalists and parliamentarians had difficulty fathoming the clubmen: royalists tended to negotiate with them until or unless they were in the ascendancy when they would turn on them; parliamentarians tended to state from the outset that they regarded the clubmen as rebels or perhaps covert royalists, but proved over time that they could work with the clubmen if there was a chance of using them to drive out the local royalists. Fairfax had met some of the Dorset clubmen a week before the Battle of Langport: he treated them with respect, partly because of their numbers and the threat Goring still posed, but he refused to let them have passes to travel to parliament with peace petitions. Cromwell met a party of men on 4 August, after Goring's defeat, and he could afford to be less accommodating, and Fairfax had already arrested some clubmen on putative charges of raising a 'Third Party in the Kingdom' but initially he was outwardly respectful, although he did not really think they merited it. When Mr Newman, who had met Fairfax at Dorchester asked for information regarding the arrested men, Cromwell told them: 'no account was due to them'. Nevertheless, perhaps because he believed that, as Newman had explained to him, that the clubmen could raise 10,000 in Wiltshire and Dorset, he did give them the information they asked for. Moreover Cromwell promised to deal with the issue of plunder that Newman raised. Within the region Goring's presence had thrown the regular taxation system out of kilter and rogue royalists were subverting the system by taking goods straight from local communities rather than using the normal collection methods. Cromwell promised to deal with any plunderers if the clubmen brought them into the army. This seemed to mollify Newman and his colleagues and they departed peacefully.

However, when Cromwell arrived at Shaftsbury he was informed of a gathering of 2,000 clubmen at Hambledon Hill and he took a party of horse to meet them. This group according to Cromwell's account were not willing to negotiate; Cromwell's advance party was fired upon. One of the clubmen, a Mr Lee, did come down the hill to talk to Cromwell, but the lieutenant general was unequivocal in his demands of them: 'To desire them to peaceableness, and to submit to Parliament'. The clubmen rejected Cromwell's demand and fired upon his men again. A second attempt to negotiate was made in which Cromwell explained that by peaceableness he meant them laying down their arms, but stressed that they would come to no harm. Again they refused: this time Cromwell sent part of Fairfax's regiment of horse up the hill to hopefully outface them. Still, so Cromwell reported, he urged restraint asking the captain lieutenant commanding Fairfax's own troop to accept their surrender if they lay down their arms when he engaged them. But the clubmen fired upon the troopers and killed two of them. It was difficult to cross the embankments of the fort and the entrance way could only accommodate three abreast, but Desborough manoeuvred some troops into the rear of the fort and the clubmen were dispersed, leaving about twelve dead. Three hundred were rounded up. Most of these promised to go home quietly, but Cromwell did find a hard core who were clearly covert royalists:

> bragging They hoped to see Lord Hopton, and that he is to command them. They expected from Wilts great store; and gave out they meant to raise the siege of Sherbourne, once they were all met ...[3]

Perplexed Cromwell might have been, but his attitude to the Clubmen was grounded in his belief in authority. Cromwell would only accept the traditional forms of authority. He recognised the power of the king insofar as it was encompassed within king and parliament and so like many of his contemporaries he ignored civil titles and sometimes the military ranks of royalist soldiers granted since 1642: parliament's temporarily assumed authority was the only source of power he truly recognised during the war. Power derived from non-parliamentary democracy, such as the associations of clubmen had no place in Oliver's political world and demanded no real respect or compliance. This attitude would be severely tested in the next two years as Cromwell had to deal with diverse political groups – it would be stretched and altered substantially over the years, but never truly broken.

Following the defeat of the clubmen, Cromwell returned to join Fairfax at Sherborne. Once the castle fell into their hands on 14 August, the New Model commanders held a council of war on the future plans, discussing the prospects for a march into Cornwall or an attack on Prince Rupert ensconced in Bristol. They decided upon Bristol, the country's second port that had been in royalist hands since July 1643. They may also have discussed a broader strategy for the west, for Cromwell on 8 September wrote to the High Sheriff of the county urging him to reject the royalists currently occupying his county, promising to treat the county fairly, offering to regard past taxes paid to royalists as having been taken by force: a pretty generous offer in some respects. Underlying the encouraging tone was naturally the threat that the army would, if necessary, enter the county by force.[4] One other issue was discussed at the meeting: Scotland. By the end of August the king's commanders in Scotland, James Graham, Marquis of Montrose and Alasdair MacColla had defeated the home army in a string of battles, culminating at Kilsyth on 15 August, and had forced the Covenanter leadership to call a parliament to meet at Glasgow. It was a potential catastrophe that would lead to parliament's ally withdrawing from the conflict. The news of Kilsyth had clearly reached southwest England, for Cromwell and the army leaders wrote to Alexander Leslie, Lord Leven, their ally at the Battle of Marston. They expressed their sorrow at 'how far God, for his best and secret ends hath been pleased to suffer the enemy to prevail there'. 'Our Bowels do yearn toward you' wrote the officers and followed it with the practical suggestion that once the war in England and Wales was over, and if parliament was willing, to 'help you faithfully in your own kingdom' and to 'engage ourselves to suppress the enemy there'.[5] At this point Cromwell still considered the Presbyterian Scots as brothers in Christ, allies in the cause.

The decision to attack Bristol, currently the base of Prince Rupert, was taken probably because it would have been dangerous to leave such an important port in the rear of the army had it advanced into the southwest. Reinforcements and ammunition could have been landed behind the New Model. Within a week of taking Sherborne the New Model was approaching Bristol, Cromwell and Fairfax went to look at the defences. On 3 September the decision was taken to storm the town one week later after encircling Bristol and conduct negotiations in the hope of gaining the port without a fight. According to Patrick McGrath[6] Rupert also bought time, hoping to defeat an initial assault so successfully that it prevented another before the onset of winter.

Sometime between 1 and 2am on 10 September the New Model Army attacked Bristol. The main attack took place on the south and east of the town's ring of earthworks: with Colonel Thomas Rainborough leading the northernmost attack, on Priors Hill Fort, Colonel Edward Montagu to his left and over the River Frome attacking Lawford's Gate and over the river Avon, attacking Temple Gate and Redcliffe Gate from the south, Colonel Weldon's brigade. In the hard night-fighting Rainborough and Montagu were successful, by daylight they had captured the defence line and pressed in upon the town walls and gates between Prior's hill Fort and the Avon. Weldon had made little headway, but the attack petered out as several outlying areas of the town caught fire and Fairfax and Cromwell grew fearful for the town: 'fearing to see so famous a City burnt to ashes before our faces'. However the royalists had had enough. With the defences rendered useless, Rupert sued for peace and at 2pm on 11 September he and his army marched out with full military honours.

The praise as always was granted only to God; Cromwell wrote:

> It may be thought that some praises are due to those gallant men of whose valour so much mention is made: – their humble suit is to you and all that have an interest in this blessing, is, That in remembrance of God's praises they be forgotten. It's their joy that they are instruments of God's glory, and their country's good. It is their honour that God vouchsafes to use them.

Cromwell had already carefully outlined the valiant actions and named the gallant men; anonymity was not a prerequisite of being one of God's servants and Cromwell ensured that earthly rewards could be given to the successful officers by a fully informed parliament. Cromwell was still being even handed: God's party was multifaceted:

> Sir, they that have been in this service know, that faith and prayer obtained this city for you: I do not say ours only, but of the people of God with you and all England over, who have wrestled with God for a blessing in this very thing. Our desires are that God may be glorified by the same spirit of faith by which we ask all our sufficiency, and have received it. It is meet that He have all the praise. Presbyterians, Independents, all have here that same spirit of faith and prayer; the same presence and answer; they agree here, have no names of difference; pity it should be otherwise anywhere! All that believe, have the real unity, which is most glorious because inward, and spiritual, in the Body, and to the Head. For being united in forms commonly called Uniformity, every Christian will for peace-sake study and do, as far as conscience will allow. And for brethren, in things of the mind we look for no compulsion, but that of light and reason.[7]

Cromwell was clearly arguing for a broadly tolerant state church that could encompass Presbyterians and Independents in one body or church. Intolerance, such as some historians have argued he became associated was not desirable, and the proof of this was God's granting victory to an assembly of Presbyterians and Independents who respected each other, and did not label each other whilst about God's work. Parliament ignored this plea, just as it had ignored the tone of his letter after Naseby and edited it from the published version. Parliament likewise also edited out Cromwell's plea for toleration in the letter about Bristol.

Richard Baxter's view of Oliver Cromwell's religiosity was completely different and more closely resembled parliament's dominant Presbyterian attitude: he had arrived in the army as a chaplain just after the battle of Naseby. Looking back on the experience during the 1660s Baxter recalled the army in 1645 as craven in its attitude to Cromwell. He was invited by Captain William Evanson, one of Cromwell's captains, now in Whalley's regiment to be regimental chaplain. In Baxter's opinion Evanson and Whalley were orthodox and they and men willing to be swayed by orthodox teaching were in the majority. However, the one in twenty soldiers who were 'hot-headed sectaries' held the important commands and 'bore down the rest or carried them along with them'. His description of Major Thomas Harrison's reaction to the victory at Langport was that of a man surprised by Harrison's 'loud voice break forth into the praises of God with fluent expressions, as if he had been in rapture'.[8] Baxter suggested that he had gone to the army with an open mind, having rejected claims about the army's sectarianism as malicious rumour but the experience changed his mind. Yet this memoir needs to be regarded with some suspicion, he quickly decided that Cromwell was filling all vacant posts with sectaries ('when an place fell void, it was twenty to one a sectary had it'), and suggested that Fairfax left all such matters to Cromwell. Nevertheless, Baxter was as pressed as historians are to define Cromwell's own faith 'yet he did not openly profess what opinion he was of himself; but the most that he said for any was for Anabaptism and Antinomianism, which he usually seemed to own'.[9] Baxter was clearly demonstrating through the device of being an impartial observer turned convert to the negative assessment of sectarianism in the army and the other accusations he had apparently rejected, but he claimed to be convinced that the army was plotting to overthrow the monarchy, because it saw the king as a tyrant. As such Baxter's work fits into the genre of work that accused Cromwell of a 'grand design' in the 1640s all with the benefit of knowing that Cromwell had been head of state in the 1650s. Several commentators began to 'see' this 'truth' in Cromwell's actions during the period 1645–1648.

Having captured Bristol, Fairfax and Cromwell continued to hound the royalists in the west. Fairfax marched towards Cornwall, but Cromwell took a detachment to Basing House which had been under protracted siege since 20 August. En route Cromwell captured Winchester Castle having turned heavy artillery on it. He took the same guns to the Marquis of Winchester's family seat at Basing. Cromwell arrived on 8 October and battered the house walls until 14 October when he stormed the house. Winchester was a leading Roman Catholic and the latter stages of the attack witnessed sectarian violence on a scale common in Ireland but not in England. Cromwell was not as forthcoming as he would be in later descriptions of the killing of Roman Catholics in sieges, but nevertheless stated 'many of the Enemy our men put to the sword, and some officers of quality'. At least one woman was killed and an actor also died in the last minutes of the fighting. The marquis and many of his party, including Inigo Jones and perhaps Wenceslas Hollar survived possibly saved, as Richard Baxter asserted, by the actions of Cromwell's distant relative Colonel Richard Hammond who had been captured by the garrison shortly after arriving with Cromwell's detachment.

Cromwell rejoined Fairfax near Exeter as the royalist cause went into terminal decline. Scotland was saved from the threat of a royalist government when David Leslie defeated Montrose's forces at Philliphaugh on 13 September. The king's small but experienced field army was beaten at Rowton Heath near Chester on 24 September. The recruiting grounds of south Wales were denied Charles when the gentry of the region went into revolt against his army and administrators. The king's attempts to march towards Scotland had come to nothing because of Philliphaugh and an attempt to send much needed horse to Montrose failed at Carlisle Sands on 24 October. The king's defeat was staved off by winter, but attempts to hurry a treaty in Ireland through secret negotiations conducted by the Earl of Glamorgan also failed. The king was hemmed into looking for an English solution to impending defeat and there was none to be had. Lord Hopton was called out of retirement to try and hold off Fairfax and Cromwell, veteran Lord Astley tried to forge an army in the Midlands. On 16 February the New Model crushed western royalist resistance at the Battle of Torrington and on 12 March Hopton surrendered. Nine days later Astley's last army was defeated at Stow on the Wold. The war, bar skirmishes and hopeless sieges was over in England and Wales, although fighting continued in Scotland and reignited with intense vigour in Ireland. The king, hoping to create a political split amongst the allies whose military alliance he had failed to break, escaped the tightening net around Oxford and surrendered to the Scottish army jointly besieging Newark with Lord Fairfax's Northern Association forces. The Scots escorted the king northwards with them as they pulled back to Northumberland and the battle to win the peace began.

Cromwell had been away from parliament and London for about a year by the late spring of 1646 and when he did return, the life of him and his family changed dramatically. The New Model Army moved into the south Midlands and resumed its siege of Oxford, receiving its surrender on 20 June. During the siege, Cromwell's daughter Bridget married Henry Ireton at Lady Whorwood's house at Holton near to the besieging army and possibly Cromwell's headquarters on 15 June. At least Cromwell was present at this wedding, he missed that of his youngest and favourite daughter Bettie who had married John Claypole at Ely on 13 January as the New Model moved in on Lord Hopton. The core of the Cromwell family now moved from Ely to King Street, Westminster when Oliver resumed his seat in parliament on a more permanent basis following the surrender of the king's capital and the end of the most recent six-month extension to his exemption from the Self Denying Ordinance: the Claypoles remained at Ely. Fairfax appointed Oliver, his son-in-law Ireton, Charles Fleetwood, John Lambert and MP Bulstrode Whitelock to form a committee to decide how the army should be best used to defeat the pockets of royalist resistance. Cromwell's position in parliament itself was less secure than this appointment. His pleas for toleration, voiced in his letters to the speaker had not only been ignored, they had consistently been struck from the public record by the Commons. Cromwell was a very different MP to that who had taken the captain's commission in 1642. He was a successful soldier with powerful friends; he had been able to circumvent the Self Denying Ordinance and other MPs recognised his support as crucial. Cromwell was also now well-known in the country as a whole, through the newspaper accounts of his activities. Nevertheless, despite being part of the same political circle when war broke out, Cromwell had enemies. The Middle Group, once led by John Pym and embracing Cromwell's relatives, Hampden and St John, was now led by Denzil Holles, a Presbyterian who had discussed impeaching Cromwell during the argument with Manchester. Moreover, Hampden and Pym were now dead. Even so there was a support network there: in the Lords, there were Wharton and Saye and Sele, and around him in the Commons were still Oliver St John and MPs Sir John Evelyn, representing a Wiltshire seat, and Sir Henry Vane the younger, treasurer of the navy. The divisions over the proposed religious settlement were at the core of Cromwell's difficulties in 1646; parliament had put in place the groundwork of a Presbyterian settlement earlier in the year, the outcome of the Westminster Assembly, although one which the Scots Presbyterians regarded as weak: it was essentially intolerant, and this intolerance was endemic. One of the few surviving letters written by Cromwell in 1646 deals with intolerance in a Norfolk village in response to a plea from Sir Thomas Knyvett a royalist Cromwell had captured when he stormed Lowestoft in 1643. It seems that Knyvett's community was being forced into Presbyterian conformity and that he had knowledge of Cromwell's pleas for toleration. In his letter, Cromwell bemoaned the state of the times, and whilst ostensibly referring to the village of Hapton, he could have been discussing the Commons;

> I not ashamed to solicit for such as are anywhere under pressure of this kind; doing even as I would be done by. Sir, this is a quarrelsome age; and the anger seems to me to be the worse, where the ground is difference of opinion.[10]

There were other issues springing from religion and politics that Cromwell would have to deal with. In the background was of course the problem of winning the peace. The king was at Newcastle, and as the next few months would show had little interest in simply accepting the consequences of defeat and negotiating a settlement based on the treaties offered him.

Nearer to Cromwell's interests in some respects was the issue of the army. The New Model Army had been established with a firm financial organisation to pay for it; but by 1646 the soldiers' pay was slipping into arrears. At the same time the high taxation that had been collected since the beginning of the war was resented; all the more so now that war had apparently ended. The New Model Army was blamed for the high taxes and in the areas where the army was based, this resentment was redoubled. Criticism of the army was grist to the Presbyterians' mill: they perceived the army, as Baxter did, as the haven of sectarians – enemies of the religious settlement. This negative attitude towards the army was chiefly directed at the New Model, although there were three other large armies in existence; the Army of the Solemn League and Covenant was still in Northumberland based around Newcastle; the Western Army, under Edward Massey was still in its home territory, as was the Northern Association Army of Sydenham Pointz. Numerous garrisons still occupied castles and strongholds around the country, and for a while there were still long running sieges, like that at Harlech that continued into March 1647, all drawing upon the hard-stretched resources of the people.

Against this background negotiations with the king were conducted at Newcastle: the first set of proposals, known as the Newcastle propositions, were presented to the king there in July 1646. Cromwell's attitude to these negotiations is unknown, in surviving writings, he referred only once to the negotiations, suggesting to Fairfax that the Scots were willing to leave the northeast and that with Montrose still active that 'Things are not well in Scotland' adding 'would they were in England. We are full of faction and worse'. The king, he told his commander, 'gave a very general answer'.[11] Historians such as Peter Gaunt, are left to speculate that with regards the king, as with regards to parliament's role in religious affairs, Oliver was fairly conservative: just as parliament should retain the role of establishing the nature of religious worship, the state should remain a mixed monarchy with a king at the heart of government.

In other sectors, however, this axiom was under threat. During the war soldiers had been enlisted physically and mentally for the war-effort. Having secured their bodies for its armies, parliament sought to secure their minds by targeting them with political tracts, including a pocket bible and a catechism, each of which promoted the godliness and political necessity of the cause, but also which sought to get the soldiers to identify with the cause. The effect was to create a substantial body of soldiers who expected their views of the political settlement should be taken into account and a greater number who expected that parliament should ensure that they would be paid their arrears, indemnified against malicious royalist-inspired prosecutions and that it owed compensation to the widows and orphans of men who had died in its cause. Outside the army too there was the parallel development of radical politics that was based upon humanist and proto-democratic principles. Over the ensuing months, these two strands of radical politics developed and occasionally intertwined creating a powerful pressure for radical change that fed into the eventual post-war political change. Cromwell was essentially antipathetic to such wide-scale change as the radical movements proposed, and was unconvinced of the claims for political authority made by military and civilian political radicals. He regarded such claims as just as invalid as those made by the clubmen at Hambledon Hill: unless authority was granted by a legal body such as parliament, but preferably king and parliament, then it was no authority at all. Shifting him from this political stance would prove hard and for some radicals, impossible to effect. Cromwell would always remain uncomfortable with aspects of the revolution he was party to. Even so in 1646–1647 Cromwell had to shift his position as parliament and the army drifted apart.

The attack on the army intensified at the end of 1646, and Cromwell in a letter to Fairfax complained of a petition coming from London which 'strikes at the army'. On 11 March 1647 he again wrote to his commander, 'There want not in all places men who have so much malice against the army as besots them: the late petition which suggested a dangerous design upon the parliament in your coming to those quarters doth sufficiently evidence the same'.[12] The deepening political crisis was about to thrust Fairfax and Cromwell to the fore, but over the winter Cromwell had been ill and had feared for his life. However, his recovery was interpreted as God's singular care for him, because the illness had brought him so low, 'it exercised the bowels of a father toward me': it was what would now be called a life-affirming experience, 'I received in myself a sentence of death; that I might learn to trust in him that raiseth from the dead' he told Fairfax on 3 March.[13] This certainty would soon be very necessary.

The army had encamped on the fringes of the Eastern Association in the spring of 1647 where opposition to it was manifest; the constable of Linton in Cambridge was arrested by the civil superiors when he tried to allocate billets for the army. It was this relocation which had caused the anger Cromwell had referred to in his 11 March letter. Parliament had decided in February to reduce the field army to being a mobile force of 5,400 horse and 1,000 dragoons to supplement the foot soldiers in the garrisons. The New Model's foot would be disbanded and some of its soldiers would be conscripted for service in Ireland.

Attempts to replace Fairfax as commander failed, but there was a continuing effort by Presbyterians in parliament to exclude Cromwell, Ireton and other suspected sectaries from their commands. Simultaneously the army rank and file began to collect signatures for petitions setting wider political demands alongside demands for back-pay and compensation for widows and orphans. Even though officers stripped the petitions of much of their political content the House of Commons was furious when it received the petitions and ordered Fairfax to suppress petitioning. It ignored the army's anger by pressing on with creating the new army for Ireland. This inflamed anger even more at a time when the political radical movement the Levellers, centred upon Lieutenant Colonel John Lilburne, Robert Overton, John Wildman and William Walwyn, was also collecting signatures for massive petitions in London demanding real political change, and which began to incorporate some of the army's demands. The Levellers would develop into a relatively sophisticated political movement capable of mobilising large scale support in London and the army and of articulating a mature proposal for radical constitutional change based on humanist and democratic bases. The Leveller movement was at its strongest when it incorporated soldiers' demands in their programme, and this was to bring them into conflict with Cromwell's political perspective.

The projected army for Ireland failed to materialise due to a lack of military supporters and in the wake of this failure parliament voted to disband the New Model with just a token payment of six weeks' back pay. To soldiers with arrears dating back over forty weeks in some cases, this suggestion was insulting. The insult permeated the ranks. Fairfax was reluctant to suppress the petitioning of the soldiers and Cromwell too was sympathetic to the soldiers' non-political demands. This conflict put him into a difficult position for Cromwell was trying to balance his roles as lieutenant general of an angry army and MP, in a determined House of Commons as the victors of the First Civil War drifted apart.

The rank and file of the horse regiments led the way in electing representatives, known as agitators, to press their case to the officers. As the movement spread throughout the army Cromwell, Skippon and Ireton contacted the field officers of each regiment and got them to visit every troop and company to assess the 'present temper and disposition'.[14] The army leaders wanted the agitators to be shadowed by officers, but the representatives' authority was recognised to some extent and by July 1647 they were welcomed onto the General Council of the Army. In the meantime Denzil Holles MP had tried to get three of the agitators arrested, and although parliament as a whole disagreed with him, the men were interrogated. This treatment inflamed anger in the army even further and the agitators appealed to Fairfax for help.

Parliament felt so threatened by the army's unity that it reorganised the city Trained Bands. Independent officers were replaced with disbanded Presbyterian officers congregating in the city trying to secure their own arrears of pay. On 23 May parliament ordered the New Model to begin disbanding on 1 June with eight weeks back pay. Instead Fairfax ordered the army to rendezvous at Newmarket. At the time Cromwell was at his London residence on Drury Lane where on 31 May he was visited by George Joyce.

George Joyce was a cornet of horse (in Fairfax's lifeguard), the lowest ranking commissioned officer in a regiment of horse, carrying the cornet (or standard) of one of the six troops. A meeting between the army's second in command and such a low ranking officer has attracted a great deal of speculation, the more so because Joyce was also an agitator and because of what he did immediately after the meeting at Drury Lane. Cromwell and Joyce apparently discussed the king's current situation. At the end of January, after receiving some of the back-pay owed for service in the first civil war, the Scots had released the king into English custody, even though no peace deal had been agreed. By May the king had been lodged at Holdenby House in Northamptonshire, but there were rumours that parliament was going to have him brought closer to London and the suspicion was that the Presbyterian MPs hoped to negotiate a quick peace treaty with him. When Fairfax ordered a rendezvous of the army at Newmarket in Cambridgeshire Joyce had gathered about 500 troopers from three regiments that had been appointed to guard the king and set off from Bury St Edmunds towards Holdenby, whilst Joyce himself took a detour to Cromwell's home in London. At the same time Thomas Rainborough's regiment of foot, in league with Joyce, marched to Oxford to take control of the artillery train left there after the siege. Critics of Cromwell maintained that he either ordered Joyce to go to Holdenby or at least colluded in it, but Oliver always denied it, long after there was reason to do so. Austin Woolrych thinks that Cromwell and Joyce discussed the undesirability of parliament taking charge of the king, but that Cromwell did not order Joyce to do so. Joyce left Cromwell and rode to Holdenby, sending orders for his troopers to meet him there. Joyce and his men took over guard duty at Holdenby on 2 June, but alarmed by the prospect of an attempt by forces more immediately loyal to parliament to recover him, Joyce and his men took the king towards Newmarket on 3 June. The authority Joyce cited was the troopers 'behind me' when the king asked him where his commission was. Neither Cromwell nor Fairfax, who was aghast when he heard that the king was on his way, had ordered action. Both men may have given tacit backing to Joyce's expedition. The visit to Cromwell had been unorthodox but logical: when the soldiers took it upon themselves to effect negotiations, they still showed deference to their senior officers whom they trusted. Joyce, an officer in the horse empowered by troopers sought out Cromwell as his most senior 'line manager'. Whilst their preferred course of actions may have differed from their soldiers' both Cromwell and Fairfax knew that action was necessary, and Joyce's summit with Cromwell would confirm this. Nevertheless it was Joyce and his constituents who drove on the action. Cromwell was on his way to Newmarket too.

Oliver Cromwell was both in a dangerous position and at an important crossroads. He had been in London for almost a year, trying to work within parliament in the army's interest, and latterly attempting to ameliorate the Presbyterians' attacks on it. He tried to assure the army of parliament's good intent on 16 May informing the army, alongside new MPs Henry Ireton, Phillip Skippon and Charles Fleetwood, at Saffron Walden, that parliament had promised another two weeks arrears on top of the six weeks already promised.[15] This dual policy had been fairly low key, especially in parliament, in recent months due to his illness, but some historians, including Peter Gaunt, think that he and his political ally Sir Henry Vane were avoiding the house, because they could not now influence its activities.

Under a growing shadow of suspicion that he was directly involved in the growing militancy of the army, Cromwell did make a couple of speeches assuring the house of the army's loyalty. It would, he argued, disband when ordered. Whilst there remains a possibility that Cromwell was actually encouraging or not really attempting to abate the hostility of parliament knowing that it would provoke the army into taking action against it, recent scholarship suggests that Cromwell was being consistent in his belief in parliament as the real arbiter of power and authority. He was in effect walking a tightrope, genuinely holding two ideas: belief in parliament and a commitment to upholding the army's interests. But now he was in danger, the Presbyterian group, led by Denzil Holles in the Commons was able to out manoeuvre and outvote the army's supporters, and was confident that it could muster an armed response to the New Model Army with the remodelled city forces under their chosen Presbyterian and loyal commanders. With the seizure of the king Cromwell became vulnerable because of the rumours surrounding him and he probably in reality fled the city and joined the army at Newmarket. Freed of his double role Cromwell now threw his weight behind the army and joined with Fairfax and other senior officers in accusing eleven MPs, including Cromwell's enemies Denzil Holles and Sir Phillip Stapleton, but also former general William Waller, alongside Major General Edward Massey of fomenting all the difficulties between parliament and the army. These were serious charges made against the very body that has called together the army in the first place communicated in a letter to the city of London.[16] This was a dramatic step, but it was in accord with Cromwell's belief in parliament, for the problem lay not with the form of government, but with individuals within it, and the letter concluded by assuring the Londoners that despite what parliament was saying to it, there was no intention to bring the army into the city.

Cromwell was still able to work within his overarching belief in the nature of government for alongside the other senior officers he met the king and negotiated with him during the next few months. There is no real reason to doubt, as his critics and enemies so volubly did, that Cromwell had any other desire than to see the restoration of traditional civil government of king and parliament to bring about the political and religious changes necessary to move the nation beyond the catastrophe of the early 1640s. The solution to this problem would be the drafting of a treaty to be presented to the king by the army command, but in the end the solution to the problem of the relationship between parliament and the army would involve direct intervention by the army but targeted, in accordance with Cromwell's views, at the eleven MPs not the institution itself. However, Cromwell was not completely in tune with the background to this political pressure. Some soldiers were convinced now that they should have a say in the political solution to the crisis and that MPs should earn rather than command respect. Parliament had made a further conciliatory gesture by sending money to St Albans for the army's pay, but it was too late.

When the MPs did not respond to the army's declaration about the eleven MPs the army moved to Uxbridge. Parliament took notice, rejecting the charges against the MPs but wisely the eleven men voluntarily withdrew from the House of Commons. Things cooled down and the army withdrew to Bedford and Fairfax began to disperse the regiments around the Midlands, thus minimising the apparent threat to London. However, the Northern Association Army then arrested its commander Sydenham Pointz and sent him under large escort to Fairfax at Bedford. Fairfax had him released quickly but parliament responded by appointing Fairfax commander of all forces in England and Wales. This apparent surrender to the New Model Army prompted another crisis when Londoners rose in anger and physically reinstalled the eleven MPs in parliament. This was a direct challenge to the New Model Army by sections of the London population so crucial to the propagation of the revolution of 1640–1642, which the Presbyterians took as a vindication of their cause. Massey was put in charge of the London defences, despite now falling within the remit of the Self Denying Ordinance. The rioting Londoners wanted the New Model disbanded so as to reduce the tax burden and to offer the king a generous peace treaty. Fairfax drew the army together again and marched on London. This time it was independent MPs who fled Westminster and along with the speakers of both houses joined Fairfax in his march upon the city. In the midst of this turmoil Ireton presented his proposed peace treaty, the *Heads of the Proposals*, to the king. The treaty accorded with what Ireton's father-in-law held axiomatic, it was constructed in the framework of a mixed monarchy. Parliament would meet at least every two years, with a minimum session of 120 days, a step beyond the Triennial Act of 1641, ensuring that it would remain an essential and permanent part of governance.

The proposed religious settlement was essentially tolerant: there would be no single over-arching church and Anglicans, Presbyterians and Independents could be encompassed within this broad settlement. In so many ways it was what Cromwell had been campaigning for at least since he had gained a public voice, it echoed his letters from Marston Moor and Naseby fields. For Cromwell, there was to be no compulsion, other than the internalised compulsion of rational faith. Parliament would not compel anyone into a particular form of Protestant faith, but by using a negative voice against Roman Catholicism and Unitarianism, it would remove the perceived irrational from consideration. This argument is something of a compromise between the rival perspectives of Cromwell as a tolerant man and Cromwell as an intolerant puritan.

The king it has been argued by several historians, most recently by Austin Woolrych, was never to receive better terms and Sir John Berkeley former royalist commander in the west had been sent by the queen to urge the king into coming to terms with the army. Berkeley thought the terms acceptable and worked with Ireton and Cromwell to gain concessions from them during negotiations with the king. But the king was still not prepared to compromise on what he saw as some personal and political fundamentals; including the rights of kingship such as control of the armed forces and his position as head of the church: he also refused to abandon loyal servants to a vindictive parliament. In maintaining these remnants of his political position he could not see beyond his own plan to disarticulate his enemies: he saw the Scots as his potential saviours, especially as they were not happy with the *Heads of the Proposals*, because of its failure to establish a Presbyterian state church. He also overestimated the importance of the London counter rebellion. Together these misreadings of the runes led Charles to refuse to agree to the treaty and he only grudgingly and belatedly sent an encouraging letter to the army. In the meantime Fairfax led the New Model into London, and with the authority of the MPs, Lords and Speakers who had fled to his side, declared parliament to be 'unfree'.

Fairfax and Cromwell led the army to Westminster to restore the fugitive MPs on 5 August and despite the tumults of the last weeks of July, the army was received enthusiastically by some of the citizens at least. Cromwell and Ireton took up their seats in the Commons again and made headway in securing the rejection of the business conducted in the absence of Speaker Lenthall, but it was hard work. The Commons submitted a revised version of the Newcastle Propositions as a proposed settlement rather than the *Heads of the Proposals*, because the large Presbyterian presence still wanted a treaty that encompassed both the Scots and a Presbyterian state church. Cromwell and Ireton worked on the king to persuade him to set aside the Commons' treaty in favour of the *Heads of the Proposals* and the king did so confident that he was directing events by buying time and driving the wedges between the army and parliament and between parliament and the Scots deeper.

There was another wedge, as yet unseen by many: this one was between the army high command and the rank and file and their agitators. Persisting on a treaty with the king the army commanders were alienating the soldiers who thought a solution should be imposed on the king. There was a small number of radical elements in the army who thought that the king should be held accountable for the war and tried. This group was influenced at least partly by the Levellers, but it also had its own internal political motivation. Earlier in the year as the soldiers elected agitators its petitions to the army commanders and parliament had contained a mixture of elements, one set of demands focussed on immediate issues, the need for back pay and indemnity from prosecutions for acts carried whilst under orders and pensions for the widows and orphans of soldiers killed during the war. These demands had been considered to be legitimate by the army leaders even if parliament regarded them as presumptuous: the incorporation of agitators into an expanded army council had legitimised the process of making such requests. The other element was not so welcome and the commanding officers discouraged it. Some soldiers saw the issues of pay and pensions to be a symptom, rather than the illness itself and sought to participate in the creation of a settlement. Their support for the *Heads of the Proposals* when Ireton first presented it to the Army Council had been lukewarm because they were not enamoured with negotiating with the king: instead they were thinking of an end to the monarchy and a broader basis for the democratic element within parliament.

When, despite the king's failure to accept the *Heads of the Proposals*, they saw their commanders, hitherto allies in the struggle for soldiers rights, continue to work with Charles, even to side with him against the House of Commons, they were less than happy. There had been little consultation with the agitators before the *Heads of the Proposals* were presented to the council, and even less now. Moreover Fairfax, Cromwell and Ireton had bound the army in an engagement with parliament back at Newmarket, which meant that despite the difficulties with the Presbyterian group, the soldiers had committed themselves to supporting the institution of parliament. This was of course in keeping with Cromwell's need for a legitimated process. If the rank and file and the army were to be allowed a say in the peace settlement and whatever came after, then it would be at the behest of parliament and through its auspices and not otherwise. Essentially, whilst Cromwell had genuine sympathy with the army-centred demands, he considered the soldiers as almost as politically illegitimate as the clubmen on Hambledon Hill. Cromwell had been heavily involved in heading off the radical suggestions at a Council of War in Reading on 16–17 July for an immediate march on London and a forcible purging of parliament's Presbyterians, and instead had been involved in the council's acceptance of Ireton's proposed treaty. He would be similarly involved in curbing radical enthusiasms later in the year.

The soldiers were however a force to be reckoned with and for Cromwell hopefully to be turned to work towards the legitimate purposes of parliament: the incorporation of agitators on the council was part of this design. Cromwell spent August and September in parliament, 'I scarce miss a day' he told Fairfax on 13 October, although he was frequently to be found at the army headquarters outside London at Putney.[17] There was still a dual purpose, whilst Cromwell and Fairfax were engaged in the attempts to persuade the king to come to an agreement with the

Heads of the Proposal., the radical elements in the army were drafting their document for a settlement *The Case of the Army Truly Stated* and the Levellers worked on their constitutional proposal *The Agreement of the People for a firme and present peace.* These two documents were ready by October, and they were sent to the General Council of the Army late in the month. Both would entail abandoning the engagement with parliament and the *Heads of the Proposals* and the adoption of a far more radical constitutional settlement.

Army agitators from five horse regiments with unclear and perhaps dubious claims to a mandate from all the soldiers themselves, drafted *The Case of the Army Truly Stated.* The proposals in *Case of the Army* were incredibly radical, proposing that power arose from the people unequivocally and that any authority for government could only be derived from that source. In other words they were arguing that government should be a democracy with no place for monarchy or aristocracy. Parliament would dissolve within a year and in the ensuing elections all men over twenty-one would have a vote, unless disqualified by their royalism. Cromwell quickly and publicly disassociated himself from the document, speaking in parliament on 20 October. It is not surprising that he should do it, for it bore none of the hallmarks that Cromwell would understand or accept: the basic structure of the mixed monarchy was swept away and legitimacy conferred by parliamentary succession or continuity. The present parliament would be ordered to dissolve by the virtue of *Case of the Army* not through its own decision, and Cromwell said as much in the Commons. A day later the General Council discussed the document and because there was some disquiet at the accusations that the council was being manipulated by the generals the reaction was distinctly cool.

A sub-committee, set up to investigate the authors of *Case of the Army* instead referred the document back to the next week's meeting and invited them to attend. But on 27 October the second document, *An Agreement of the People for a Present Peace*, a finely worked constitutional proposal which contained the same premise about the origins of power as *Case of the Army* also appeared. Both documents would be discussed the next day. Fairfax was ill and Cromwell chaired the enlarged army council that discussed the two proposed settlements with invited civilian Levellers present. The sessions were held at Putney, where the army's headquarters were based, in the church by the side of the Thames.

Ireton spoke most of all the army commanders present, and he was already regarded by some soldiers, prompted by the Levellers, as the man who had corrupted Cromwell and led him into being party to the *Heads of the Proposals*: thereby abandoning the soldiers who depended upon him. The army commanders were being labelled 'grandees': Cromwell's and Ireton's opposition to a proposal to end negotiations with the king added to the distrust and the belief that the army commanders were determined to strike a deal with the Charles without consulting the soldiers. The new document was a bombshell, for in comparison with *The Case of the Army* the *Agreement* had in Austin Woolrych's phrase 'dealt in first principles', the very nature of the political system was to be recreated from the bottom up by the people who had defeated the most recent of William the Conqueror's descendants. The people of England it asserted had lived in the bondage of the Norman Yoke imposed upon the free people of England in 1066. Cromwell and Ireton were determined to prevent either of the two documents being adopted by the army and Woolrych amongst others suggests that they probably expected the general council to castigate the authors at the meeting on Thursday 28 October. Instead it quickly became clear that council wanted to debate both the documents and on the first day the *Agreement* was read, but Cromwell and Ireton tried to head off more prolonged discussion by questioning whether or not the council could even receive the documents at all, because the army had of course engaged itself loyally to the present parliament, back at Newmarket. Discussion should centre they argued upon the obligation of this engagement. The veracity of this was not clear and there were several discussions of who was obliged by the engagement: the civilians present of course were not, and Cromwell sought to gain time by postponing further discussion until the following day after a morning of prayer. Discussions would follow in the afternoon. On realising that the first day was descending into acrimony, he did make a plea for a less confrontational approach on the second day: 'they should not meet as two contrary parties, but as some desirous to satisfy or convince one another'.[18]

On day two, Cromwell returned to the obligations on the army and set about directing discussions to consider whether there 'be nothing, or if it be weak'. When this seemed to fail because Colonel Thomas Rainborough suggested that they could spend ten days on discussing the engagements without getting to the papers, he switched tack citing imminent danger as a reason: 'that's above law'. Quickly the discussion moved beyond Cromwell's attempts to hold on to the engagements and after reading the whole *Agreement* they concentrated on Clause One, the distribution of parliamentary seats. Rather than Cromwell, it was Ireton who responded to the suggestion that there had been a more equal distribution of voting rights before the Norman Conquest and more importantly the right to vote. Ireton knew the *Agreement* would profoundly alter the nature of political power and representation. Hitherto representation in parliament was based upon very largely property ownership, the realm of civil right or entitlement that the Levellers were suggesting was a natural right or entitlement. In other words in a Leveller world a person voted because he had the right to do so at birth, and if he had not sacrificed his rights through criminal activity (or in the context of 1647 having been a royalist) at twenty-one he could vote. There was as yet little formulated as to women's rights to vote, but certainly some people were beginning to think of that too, but at Putney the context was male. Ireton came from a south Nottinghamshire family that had been part of a system of civil right: as a gentry land-owning family the Iretons had voted in elections, but only recently, in the recruiter elections held to fill vacant seats in parliament in 1645, had Henry become an MP. Now he was listening to men who wanted to remove the whole system that had put him there. Thomas Rainborough a New Model colonel influenced by what he had heard had read in recent months argued that there were indisputable reasons for the *Agreement's* argument:

> I do think that that the main cause why Almighty God gave men reason, it was that they should improve it for the end and purpose that God gave it them... I think there is nothing that God hath given a man that any can take from him. And therefore I say, that either it must be the Law of God or the law of man that must prohibit the meanest man in the kingdom to have this benefit as well as the greatest. I do not find anything in the Law of God, that a lord shall choose twenty burgesses, and a gentleman but two, or a poor man shall choose none: I find no such thing in the Law of Nature, nor in the Law of Nations. But I do find that all Englishmen must be subject to English laws, and I do verily believe that there is no man but will say that the foundation of all laws lies in the people ...[19]

Ireton saw anarchy in this: 'He that is here to-day, and gone to-morrow, I do not see that he hath such a fixed interest'.[20] By 'fixed interest' Ireton meant property and the relationship between it and law making: as much of the law related to property in many ways laws on ownership, land sale and transfer, taxation and theft, for example, meant to Ireton that property owners had the most interest in making and operating the laws. If the propertyless could vote and perhaps even sit in parliament, might they not vote away property ownership or at least fail to understand the requirements of property owners?

Cromwell played a mediating role in this heated exchange, for Rainborough interpreted Ireton's position as accusing the radicals of wanting anarchy: a state without government structures. Cromwell tried to assure him that this was not what Ireton was saying: 'No man says you have a mind to anarchy, but the consequences of this rule tends to anarchy'.[21] Soothing words, but revealing that Cromwell held essentially the same position as Ireton. Cromwell's opinion was neatly encapsulated in one of his few interventions. He was aware that the distribution of seats in parliament and the uniform application of voting rights were inadequate. Moreover he was prepared to accept that the *Heads of the Proposals* 'offered' a solution to these problems 'too weakly'.[22] That was as far as he was prepared to go, in effect a readjustment of the system that he and his family would be familiar with and beneficiaries of. Cromwell did offer to withdraw from the proceedings if he were perceived as a hindrance, because he could not 'go so far as these gentlemen that bring this paper (*The Agreement*)', but he was probably confident that the army would not want him to stand aside. He was angered by the accusation made by agitator Edward Sexby that the soldiers had been deceived by parliament and its officers.

> There are many thousands of soldiers that have ventured our lives; we have had little propriety in the kingdom as to our estates, yet we have had a birthright. But it seems now, except a man hath a fixed estate in this kingdom, he hath no right in this kingdom. I wonder we were so much deceived. If we had not a right to the kingdom, we were mercenary soldiers.

Sexby implied that the soldiers would not stand idly by whilst their recently regained birthright were stolen from them.[23] This Cromwell could not abide and it marked a clear division between him and radicals like Sexby. Cromwell like Ireton did not regard democratic participation as a birthright. At the close of that Friday's debates, Cromwell's proposal for a committee to discuss the inequalities within the parliamentary system was adopted. This can be seen either as a block to further debate on the *Agreement* or as a genuine attempt to build upon points upon which they had all agreed: the present system was inadequate and renewed discussions would start with looking at the common ground between the *Agreement* and the *Heads* ....

Over the next few days the discussions continued and drifted further from the parameters of political power as Cromwell understood them and even became directed towards proposing that the king be tried and executed. On 1 November Cromwell chaired a new session and according to Austin Woolrych made a mistake by asking for anyone who had received divine guidance over the weekend to speak out. Unfortunately for the conservative family alliance of Ireton and Cromwell they were faced with accusations that God had deserted the army because the grandees were negotiating with the king. Moreover God had judged against the king and the army should do so too; the king was a man of blood, responsible for all the blood shed during the war. In this kind of biblical analogy, only the death of the man of blood could expiate the guilt. The argument that ensued prevented any practical discussions on common ground. On 5 November Fairfax chaired a meeting that directly accused Cromwell and Ireton of misleading the House of Commons when they claimed that the army wished to negotiate with the king. The lord general stormed out of the meeting when a letter to the Speaker of the Commons making this accusation was being drafted. Four days later the letter was abandoned at the last meeting of the General Council on 9 November as Cromwell and Fairfax, alarmed at the manipulation of the council by radical agitators sought to bring it back under control, if necessary by not holding any more meetings. At the same time announcing that the army would rendezvous at three separate places between 15 and 18 November. This angered the Levellers who had wanted the whole army to assemble at once where it would, they hoped and expected, approve the *Agreement of the People*.

The king thwarted all his opponents' plans by escaping from captivity at Hampton Court on 11 November, forcing a change of plan. The king had not only been discussing treaties with the army, but he had been also negotiating with the Scots, who were angered by the *Heads'* failure to establish a Presbyterian regime in England or to deal clearly with bi-national issues. The Scots were authorised to prompt a rising in Ireland and the king's former lieutenant, the Marquis of Ormond, had returned to forge an alliance with the Kilkenny government. The Scots tried to persuade the king to flee Hampton Court and go to Scotland, but Charles had no wish to throw his hand in with any one faction and so instead went southwards, crossed the Solent and went to Carisbrooke Castle, perhaps as a first step towards fleeing abroad. The governor at Carisbrooke was Robert Hammond a relative of Cromwell and this fact formed part of the two developing myths of Cromwell: firstly royalist enemies saw this as part of Cromwell's plan for seizing power, a myth which would only reach a fully rounded state as Cromwell became head of state; secondly, radical critics saw this as Cromwell's way of stopping the progress of radical debate. Certainly the king's escape worked to Cromwell's advantage, but it was of course also to Fairfax's and Ireton's advantage too; all three agreed to call off the three rendezvous. This was a reaction to a situation that had suddenly become dangerous, but it was resented and seen as a ruse to prevent discussion. It is highly unlikely that Cromwell or his colleagues engineered this dangerous situation, but there is no doubt that they took advantage of the situation.

Charles I did not get far. Any plan to get to the continent came to nought and his decision not to head for Scotland did not please the Scots commissioners who had tried to persuade him to escape the army and parliament's captivity. However, in ways that no one yet foresaw, it would finally bring the king and the Scots together. Moreover, Cromwell would be thrust back into the glare of those who we would now call 'conspiracy theorists', because Charles's brief flight ended at Carisbrooke Castle on the Isle of Wight: based there was the governor of the isle Colonel Robert Hammond, Oliver's relative and Edward Whalley another cousin of Cromwell was the commander of the guards at Hampton Court. Cromwell had written to Whalley warning him of rumoured attempts on the king's life but was soon being accused of collusion in the king's escape. Some critics of Cromwell suggested that he had engineered the whole escape to Cousin Hammond so that he could have private negotiations with Charles. Richard Baxter wrote that most people thought that the rumoured plot to murder the king 'was contrived by Cromwell to affright the king out of the land or into some desperate course which might give them advantage over him'.[24]

It may have seemed that the escape was convenient for Cromwell: negotiations with the king had stalled and continued communications between army leaders and Charles was driving a wedge between the generals and the rank and file. Moreover, the demand for bringing the king to a trial was leading the army in a direction that Cromwell had no intention of going. With the clear and present danger posed by the king the army could be brought back into line and Fairfax and Cromwell achieved just that at Corkbush. Several regiments refused to accept the order to not meet and several turned up at Corkbush Field near Ware on 15 November, with copies of the *Agreement* in their hat bands. Cromwell and Fairfax turned up at the meeting and harangued the soldiers reminding them of their primary duties in the time of danger. The two men rode amongst the ranks, pulling the papers from their hats. Prominent radicals were arrested and one chosen by lot for execution. With the death of one of their comrades at the hands of their leaders and a firing squad of their colleagues, the army was brought dramatically under order. Suppressing army radicalism heralded a period of general repression: some of the Levellers were already imprisoned: John Lilburne had already accused Cromwell of having a hand in the king's escape from Hampton Court, one of the Leveller supporters had been shot at Corkbush by his erstwhile comrades, prominent speakers at Putney, Major Scot and Colonel Rainborough were ordered to account for their actions and the authors of *The Agreement* were arrested. Radical debate was stilled for a while and Cromwell returned to dealing with the political situation in the environment in which he felt more comfortable: parliament.

7

I NEVER IN ALL MY LIFE SAW MORE DEEP SENSE
1647–1649

When he escaped from Hampton Court on 11 November, Charles apparently had no idea where he was going. He was prompted to flee by allegations of an attempt on his life: a letter received on 9 November signed by E.R. claimed that eight or nine agitators were planning to kill him, but the plans for escape were probably set before the letter arrived. Charles escaped with two advisors, Sir John Ashburnham and Sir John Berkeley, who had opposed plans for joining the Scots, and they were against the northern flight; Berkeley had proposed London, but changed his mind, Ashburnham remembered meeting Colonel Hammond who had given up his regiment of foot because he was disaffected with the army's role in politics. Asburnham claimed that Hammond had told him that he had wanted no part in 'such perfidious actions'. Ashburnham proposed that the king make for Sir John Oglander's house on the Isle of Wight from where they could make contact with Hammond to see if he was willing to help or get a boat for the continent. Hammond proved not to be the instrument that Charles and Ashburnham had wished. The governor quickly secured the royal party and the king was back in captivity as close as that at Hampton Court causing Ashburnham subsequently to refer to Hammond as 'that detestable villaine (the Governour)'.[1] Hammond lodged the king in Carisbrooke Castle and contacted parliament immediately. The governor's letter to parliament was read in the Commons on 15 November informing MPs that he had thought it his duty to take the king to Carisbrooke to preserve him from the apparent threats to his life and ensure the continuation of negotiations. Hammond also thought it necessary to make abundantly clear 'his own fidelity and care' in order to offset any damage to his reputation should it be discovered that the royalists had thought it worth making approaches to him.[2] Parliament was quick to assure Hammond that he would be supported with new troops and he was equally quick in ensuring parliament that he was working with the gentry of the isle to raise sufficient guards.

Another factor that impinges upon the credibility of the argument for Cromwell's collusion in the king's escape is the hopes that he and his allies had of a new simplified negotiation process, being prepared in parliament as the king escaped. Four Bills were being prepared by allies of Cromwell in the House of Lords that would form the opening stages of a full peace deal. Once the king's location was known the completion of the four proposals continued, and the Scots commissioners also quickly made their way to the king and continued their negotiations in parallel to those of parliament. Charles felt besieged by the two increasingly forceful groups of negotiators and tried to get the army on his side by contacting Fairfax who was unsurprisingly cool, reminding him that the army he commanded belonged to parliament. The House of Commons had three competing factions, serving to slow down the peace proposals: the Independents wanted the king to agree to the four proposals before any other negotiations; Presbyterians were inclined to be more lenient; but a radical but still small faction wanted no treaty with the king at all. In the end after passing the Commons by just nine votes, the four proposals became the Four Bills: the first gave control of the armed forces to parliament for the next twenty years, the second annulled all the king's proclamations made against parliament during the war; the third cancelled all peerages established since May 1642, and the fourth extended parliament's control over its own structures and procedures. The bills were presented to the king on 24 December with a four-day time limit imposed on him to try and curtail instability. The Scots commissioners were concerned by the Four Bills which reduced religion to a supplementary negotiation and did not really refer to Scotland at all, and it is possible that they were driven into offering their peace solution by panic, because on 26 December they had got the king to agree to an Engagement. However, to get the king's agreement quickly they had had to trespass upon the very foundations of Scotland's war aims, actions that would lead to major political ructions in Scotland once the truth about the terms of The Engagement became known.

Although the king on the Isle of Wight was not 'a pinfold,... more secure of him than before' as Baxter argued, Cromwell's attitudes to the king were changing. In the Commons he argued that the king was 'a man of great parts and a great understanding, but that he was so great a dissembler and so false a man that he was not to be trusted'.[3] Parliament, upon discussion of The Engagement, decided not to negotiate with the king further. Cromwell reported the outcome to Hammond

> The house of Commons is very sensible of the King's dealings, and of our bretheren's, in this late transaction You should do well if you have anything that may discover juggling to search it out and let us know it. It may be of admirable use at this time because we shall I hope instantly go upon business in relation to them to prevent danger.
>
> The house of Commons has this day voted as follows: 1st They will make no more addresses to the king; 2nd None shall apply to him without leave of the two houses upon pain of being guilty of high treason; 3rd they will receive nothing from the King, nor shall any other bring to them from him, nor receive anything from the king.

On the same day the Commons effectively dissolved the Solemn League and Covenant established in 1643 and created a new executive from the English members of the Committee of Both Kingdoms. In the letter Cromwell referred to having clarity of vision, 'I never saw in my life more deep sense'. It may be possible that this was something of an epiphany for Cromwell, for the king had exposed his duplicity directly to a man who had negotiated with him and for whom monarchy had remained a cornerstone of government. It had also exposed the essential weakness of Cromwell's own intentions to critics who had been pressing for a more radical political solution against Cromwell's belief in a monarchical system. It may be that the evident anger in Cromwell's voice, noted by many observers at the 3 January speech may have been partly an act in the face of such opposition and his projected clarity could have been to bolster Hammond who remained loyal but had evidently been placed in the way of temptation. The certainty of vision was of course given to Cromwell by God and thus to him would have been unarguable: Hammond would know him well enough to understand that Cromwell was passing on this undeniable argument. Cromwell's clarity was probably less than 20:20 for he had not yet turned his back on monarchy: attempts to draw him on the subject failed to get a straight answer. Edmund Ludlow was assaulted by flying cushions in private and by obfuscation in public when he asked Cromwell outright about his attitude to a monarchy. There are, perhaps not surprisingly, several Cromwells in this period: some saw in him one who sided with the militants and others one who wanted a peace settlement within existing structures. Parliament, now more finely balanced than in the wake of the army's occupation of London, voted on 28 April that government should remain a mixed monarchy but two days later the army, having decided that the *Heads of the Proposals* marked the point when the army had strayed from God's path, decided to bring the king to account for his deeds. Cromwell's whereabouts are unclear. Peter Gaunt dismissed the idea that Oliver along with Lord Saye and Sele went to negotiate with the king or with Hammond in late March and April, saying that Cromwell's trip out of London was related to marriage negotiations, on behalf of his son Richard, to Dorothy Maijor of Hampshire. J.S.A. Adamson on the other hand cites Lord Cottington's letter to Richard Browne of 19 April referring to Cromwell's return from the Isle of Wight empty handed. Certainly Saye and Sele had broken the edict of the Vote of No Addresses, but Cromwell may have been erroneously tied into this by the proximity of the Maijor family to the Isle of Wight and his close association with Saye and Sele: but it is not impossible that Oliver had had a hand in the negotiations. It is likewise unclear if Cromwell participated in the officer's vote on 30 April, at Windsor, that threatened a harder line with the king. William Allen's account, published after Oliver's death, recorded Cromwell's involvement in the debate there on 29 April suggesting that he had encouraged the officers to take a radical position by pressing them to 'a thorough considerations of our actions as an army'.[4] Despite the belief of Blair Worden and others that Allen's account is probably accurate; having been presented with two opportunities to contravene the orders of parliament Cromwell might have avoided doing so. If he had been organising Richard's marriage, it would not be the last time in 1648 that Cromwell seemed to have kept his head down.

Outside parliament events in 1648 had taken several dramatic turns. In Scotland selling The Engagement had led to an uncomfortable but briefly potent alliance of moderate covenanters and royalists that drove harder line covenanters from power. This led to the creation of an army to support the obligations placed upon the Scots to use military force to restore the king to his lawful powers if negotiations with Westminster failed. The army however was a shadow of the past armies raised in Scotland and many of the experienced commanders refused to take command, leaving the inexperienced Marquis of Hamilton. Because of the political struggle and the resulting difficulty in creating the army, Scotland's efforts on behalf of the king were overtaken by events in Wales and England.

On 22 February 1648 the Pembroke Castle garrison commander Colonel John Poyer refused an order to hand over the castle to a detachment of the New Model Army. His reasons were partly based upon his paranoiac fears that the local gentry intended to oust him: they had already accused him of malfeasance. Poyer's soldiers were unhappy that the arrears of the New Model Army had been repaid with relative alacrity whilst their own remained unpaid. Poyer's refusal to hand over the town was supported by the soldiers and together they drove Adjutant General Fleming and his soldiers from the town. Parliament over-reacted and declared Poyer a traitor, thus leaving little room for negotiation. Conservative Presbyterian Welshmen began to see Poyer's stance as a blow against the Independents of the New Model Army, furthermore local royalists began to treat Poyer as a defender of the king's rights. Poyer's brother-in-law Rowland Laugherne was hitherto a parliamentarian hero in south Wales, only the previous year he had put down a serious anti-parliamentarian rebellion in the region: however he too was dissatisfied with the political dominance of the New Model in Westminster. Laugherne had been forced to attend an enquiry in London but whilst he was there Poyer's rising led to a change of heart. When parliament began to disband Laugherne's own army in south Wales the soldiers began to drift towards Pembroke. Bolstered by a mixed bag of recruits, the old garrison, disgruntled Presbyterians and opportunistic royalists, Poyer took control of a series of regional towns. Laugherne and his second Rice Powell left London and joined the Poyer. Parliament quickly dispatched another section of the army under Colonel Thomas Horton to replace Fleming who had been killed in preliminary fighting.

Horton ended the expansion of the rebellion across south Wales by defeating Laugherne at the Battle of St Fagins near Llandaff on 8 May and drove the rebels back into Pembrokeshire. In Horton's wake came Oliver Cromwell.

The rebellion in south Wales had clearly offered hope and opportunities to the royalists, and more importantly it was not the only one. In April royalist forces seized Carlisle gateway into England for Hamilton and the Scottish army, and in the same month rebellion broke out in the south east and East Anglia. Over Christmastide 1647–1648 the Presbyterian prohibition of celebrations had caused riots in urban areas across the country, notably in Ipswich, Bury St Edmunds, Canterbury, London and Norwich. In many places the Christmas riots reflected a deeper unease at the process of parliamentarian government: higher taxes and the dominance of the New Model Army. The riots were generally short lived and only that at Norwich led to serious loss of life. Principal rioters were imprisoned to await the Easter Assizes. It was when these courts sat against the backdrop of the Welsh rebellion that trouble began in Kent and Essex. Christmas rioters were generally acquitted and new riots broke out. Petitions were sent to Westminster calling for the disbanding of the army. By 12 May, two days after Cromwell entered south Wales the southeast of England appeared to be engulfed by counter-revolution. However, Cromwell led only a detachment of the army, Fairfax had remained in London with most of the New Model.

Cromwell entered Wales with about 6,500 men, including local forces assembled on the way. Once across the border Cromwell sent a detachment to attack the royalist forces in Chepstow castle, whilst he followed up Horton's defeat of Laugherne and pressed on towards Pembroke. Chepstow and Tenby had fallen to parliament by the end of May, but Pembroke was a much stronger garrison and Cromwell needed heavy artillery; but his train of artillery, which was coming by sea, had run aground in the Severn Estuary in heavy storms. They were not available for a month. Horton joined Cromwell at Pembroke after capturing Tenby, bringing Cromwell's numbers to around 8,000. Inside the castle Poyer had 2,000 men and good stores: without heavy guns there was little to be done. Westminster kept sending requests to Cromwell asking him to send troops to join Colonel John Lambert. Lambert had been dispatched into the north to watch for a Scottish invasion. Cromwell did send Colonel Isaac Ewer and the forces which had captured Chepstow and then over the next weeks of inaction sent a total of six troops of horse and two of dragoons. In the meantime, Cromwell's attacks on the castle were low key. One attack in early June failed because of inadequate artillery support and the ladders proved too small for the breach, but Cromwell wrote optimistically on 14 June of plans to destroy two mills in the town and of an attempt to block off the water supply. Whilst waiting for the heavy guns to arrive Cromwell organised the rounding up of royalist supporters around south Wales and threatened to burn Sir Richard Herbert's 'royalist nest' around his ears.[5]

It was 4 July before the guns were pulled from the estuary mud but Cromwell made quick use of them, setting them to batter down the town and castle walls. By 10 July Cromwell believed that Poyer's situation was impossible and told him so: '[if] this offer be refused... I know where to charge the blood you spill'; he enclosed the fairly generous terms. On the day following Poyer took the hint and surrendered the castle. Cromwell wrote to Speaker Lenthall telling him of the victory, and even before the surrender commissioners had returned with a list of the spoils.[6] Cromwell's speed was to enable a rapid march out of the country towards northern England because on 8 July Hamilton crossed the border into northwest England.

In the southeast of the country Fairfax had led the New Model into Kent where 10,000 assorted Presbyterians, discontented opponents of parliament's county committee and royalists had been moulded into a makeshift army by royalist appointed commander the Earl of Norwich. On 30 May Fairfax attacked the rebels with just 4,000 men, captured a thousand after a brief scrap at Burnham Heath and pursued the rest to Maidstone. On the following day the New Model forced its way into the town. With the fall of the town the Kentish rebellion collapsed. The leaders and diehard followers headed for London, but unable to force their way into the city, crossed the Thames estuary and joined the Essex rebels at Chelmsford. As the briefly garrisoned Kent towns began to surrender, Fairfax followed the fleeing rebels. The threats to parliament must not be underestimated, despite the seeming ease of defeats inflicted in May by Horton and Fairfax. A war seemed to be breaking out on four fronts: Wales, the southeast of England, the border with Scotland and at sea. The fleet, which had been a firm supporter of parliament in the first civil war, had rebelled on 10 June. Parliament dealt relatively sensitively with the sailors' discontent, removing the unpopular Thomas Rainborough from his command and sending the old commander the Earl of Warwick to negotiate with the angry sailors. The rebellion was largely contained within the southeastern ships, but in the end ten ships did sail to the United Provinces where they became the basis of a royalist fleet. Fairfax's pursuit of the Kentish rebels took him across the Thames estuary where his march on Chelmsford forced the assembled royalists to flee towards Colchester. With Fairfax in close pursuit the royalists reached the town but had to fight their way through the suburbs as the New Model began to catch them up. As the doors of Colchester slammed 100 royalists were left outside the gates and 1,000 parliamentarians lay dead. Fairfax, like Cromwell at Pembroke settled down for a long siege: by 20 June he had the town surrounded by earthworks and on 1 July the town was so closely enclosed that the garrison could not conduct foraging raids outside the walls. The rebels' choice of Colchester had not been a good one. If the Scots made slow or insignificant progress then the garrison would remain isolated. There was hope that the royalist fleet might reach Colchester, but once the Earl of Warwick eased tensions at sea, the small fleet of deserters were unable to make it to the Essex coast.

Fortunately for parliament, the Scots' advance was painfully slow. Having entered England on 8 July, Hamilton stayed in Carlisle for six days awaiting reinforcements. He then moved south to Penrith but slowed again waiting at Kendal for a further week later in the month. This would prove fatal. John Lambert's progress toward the north in the days before Hamilton's invasion had been hampered somewhat when the royalist Marmaduke Langdale captured Pontefract castle in Yorkshire, however the castle remained isolated even if inconvenient in terms of communications links, and Lambert's forces grew. Cromwell's detachments arrived, 1,500 men were raised in Lancashire and Fairfax spared what he could for the beginning of July. By the time Hamilton crossed the border, Lambert had prevented the outbreak of any royalist risings in the north that could have been coordinated with the invasion. Lambert crossed the Pennines and placed himself close to Penrith but withdrew as Hamilton's forces grew in size to over 16,000. Langdale expected Hamilton to cross the Pennines after him to march south via the royalist stronghold of Pontefract and on 17 July a small force did approach his base at Appleby but withdrew after a brief fight. Lambert still withdrew, in the expectation that Hamilton would follow en masse.

The Engager government also wanted Hamilton to cross to the east of England so it could be supplied by the royalist fleet, link up with Pontefract and bring some relief to Colchester; but Hamilton decided to stick to the west and maintained slow progress. In complete contrast, Cromwell marched quickly from south Wales, thirty troops of horse taking only a fortnight to reach Lambert at Barnard Castle. Hamilton was still only at Hornby in Lancashire. Lambert now shadowed him, closing off routes into Yorkshire and placed his forces between Knaresborough and Leeds. Cromwell himself marched via Warwick and onto Leicester, picking up new boots and shoes for his men, and also taking command of recruits from the north Midlands; these however, he left behind in south Yorkshire when experienced men spared from duty at the Colchester leaguer joined him there. The artillery made a better journey by sea than when on the way to Pembroke, arriving this time at Hull. The guns were hauled to Cromwell's command at Doncaster on 11 August. Two days later in the vicinity of Ripon Cromwell and Lambert's armies joined.

Having amassed an army at least comparable in numbers but vastly superior in experience to the majority of Hamilton's scratch Engager Army, Cromwell could contemplate confronting the Scots. He took the decisive course of forcing battle. Cromwell could, as Ian Gentles pointed out, allow Hamilton the possibility of retreat to Scotland by placing his forces in south Lancashire ahead of the Scots' advance. Instead Cromwell crossed the Pennines on 16 August camping at Stonyhurst, north of Preston that night. He was only three miles away from the Engager Army's camp. By the next morning Marmaduke Langdale belatedly realised Cromwell was close behind, having earlier dismissed information that he was at Stonyhurst and began to prepare to defend the northern approaches to Preston. Hamilton's army was stretched out over twenty miles, with Langdale at the rear, north east of Preston, and the advance guard of horse approaching Wigan. Langdale probably hoped to hold off Cromwell until Hamilton's army could be reassembled. He had the advantage of the dreadful state of the ground north of Preston, weeks of summer rain had turned the fields into bogs, and that should have offset Langdale's shortage of horse. It did not, Cromwell prepared a sledgehammer of an attack, putting three regiments of horse on the road leading to Langdale's centre flanked by, and interspersed with, foot. In front was a forlorn hope of dragoons and foot. About six miles northeast of Preston the two sides clashed. Langdale began a fighting retreat towards the town ready to join the main army where a counter attack or at least a more structured defence could be made.

Langdale reached the town and posted his regiments with a frontage of about three quarters of a mile on Ribbleton Moor with a forlorn hope north of the river holding the steep cut of Eaves Brook. In total, Langdale had about 3,000 men in the rearguard. When Cromwell's forces reached this defensive line from down the Longridge Road, they debouched into battle lines: the five foot regiments arranged on either side of the road, two regiments of horse moved to the right flank and another 1,000, including the Lancashire horse on the left, but two others, including Cromwell's own regiment continued advancing down the road. Langdale was outnumbered and now outflanked and desperately in need of support. To his rear, however, confusion reigned: some of the Scots were crossing the town bridge in a southerly direction; for there was the belief that the fighting was only a distraction and that the main priority was to reassemble the Scottish army which was strung out between Preston and Wigan.

Hamilton had sent some of his horse to join Langdale's left flank, but the main body was still marching towards the Ribble Bridge southeast of the town. But as the noise of the battle grew louder, General Baillie stopped the march on the bridge causing an argument over interpretations of Hamilton's orders when Langdale rode over to find out what was going on. Langdale had wanted the Scots to attack Cromwell's left flank at Ribbleton, but only belatedly did Hamilton realise that he had misunderstood Cromwell's intentions. Suggestions that Hamilton abandoned Langdale deliberately has been dismissed by the battle's authoritative historians, Stephen Bull and Mike Seed, who argue that lack of military intelligence about Cromwell's intentions and confusion on the field was the real cause of Hamilton's failure to support Langdale's defence of north Preston. It would make no sense to abandon Langdale's men and the damage to the Scots' case for invasion would be immense if the English force had been betrayed. Troops began to be fed back onto the moor, but it was now too late and in any case Hamilton still considered regrouping to the south to be an important objective that could still be tried. Langdale had done well with the resources available, he had slowed Cromwell's advance; but confusion had ruined any chance of long term resistance: the initiative was now firmly with Oliver's army.

Cromwell moved the foot regiments forward through the hedge lines north of Preston and began to press Langdale's line back towards Preston. At the same time he began to send Lancashire units down Watery Lane, a small sunken lane that led from his left flank, southwestwards towards the bridge. At that time there was only one major crossing of the Ribble, the Walton Bridge southeast of Preston. The Scots were using it to filter troops to the battlefield, Langdale would need it to retreat and Cromwell would need it to march southwards after the main Scottish forces. The foot regiments passed down the sunken lane, remaining hidden from view and then emerged close to the bridge and behind Langdale's right flank. They began an attack on the bridge, over which the Scottish foot was still passing northwards. In its attempt to break through towards the south, Cromwell's right wing of horse attacked the few sections of Scottish horse that had joined Langdale's left and drove them back. As Langdale retreated towards the town his front shifted eastwards to try and hold off the developing attack on the bridge and hold open the Ribble crossing, which was now rapidly becoming his line of retreat rather than anything else. At around five o'clock Cromwell sent the two regiments of horse in his centre to pound Langdale's crumbling centre. This new attack split the royalist line and pushed into Preston itself down Church Lane. The continued attack on Walton Bridge forced the Scots to accelerate sending troops into the field and Hamilton himself sought out the ford over the river and launched a series of attacks to push the parliamentarians back. After the collapse of the centre, Langdale also crossed the river. Soon however, the Scots were driven from the north side of the bridge and Cromwell crossed on to the south bank in their wake. The fighting stopped as evening drew on, but the battle was in a lull not at an end. Cromwell reported the day's business to the Committee at Manchester saying as much: 'it pleased God to enable us to give them a defeat which I hope we shall improve by Gods assistance to their utter ruin', acknowledging also that the full details were not available and casualty statistics had not been compiled. Cromwell was not sure of Hamilton's intentions and he told the committee that he was posting units on his flanks to prevent the Scots making a dash for the north. The Manchester Committee were asked to raise more county troops to guard against any southward march. He was determined to bring about the Engagers' 'utter ruin' rather than simply drive them out of England.[7]

Hamilton was not thinking of going north at all and used the cover of darkness to withdraw from the Ribble and set off southwards towards the horse under Lieutenant General Middleton's command. Cromwell quickly realised what Hamilton was up to and the Scots only made three miles before they were attacked again, by Francis Thornhaugh's regiment of horse. Meanwhile, the Scottish horse had turned around and were marching northwards on the Chorley Road. Unfortunately Hamilton was on the parallel Standish road to the east of him. Middleton ran into Cromwell's army without making contact with Hamilton and began a covering action to protect his own withdrawal, in which Thornhaugh was killed. Nevertheless the pressure was too great for the Scots and retreat continued throughout the next day 18 August. Late that day, the Scots reformed their army north of Wigan, but when Cromwell arrived with the New Model they retreated into the town, but they stayed there only briefly. Cromwell pushed through the abandoned town the following day and approached Warrington, where the Scottish army had stopped again. This time the Scots did not retreat but the ensuing fight at Winwick was brief and once Cromwell, with the help of local information, filtered troops through the woods on the Scots' flank, panic spread through the Scottish army which fled towards Warrington Bridge. At Warrington the commander of the Scots' horse, Baillie, found that his superiors had abandoned him, leaving behind a letter asking him to surrender. Cromwell met him on the bridge.

Cromwell's terms were not harsh because the Warrington bridge was the only crossing on the Mersey from some distance around: he demanded complete surrender of the forces still under Baillie's command with all officers as prisoners of war, but with security for their lives and goods. Unusually these troops were chiefly foot soldiers; because as many as 3,000 horse had escaped along with Hamilton. Cromwell's officers began to assess their achievement: in the running battle from Preston to Warrington, 7,000 sets of arms and 8,000 prisoners had been taken. Despite Hamilton's escape with the horse, the Engager invasion was over: Hamilton was captured a few days later at Uttoxeter, Langdale and Callander both eventually escaped, although Langdale was briefly held prisoner at Nottingham.

Following the running battle through Lancashire Cromwell left the clearing-up operations to others; his horse were exhausted:

> if I had a thousand horse that could but trot thirty miles I should not
> doubt but to give a very good account of them but truly we are so

> harassed and haggled out in this business that we are not able to do
> more than walk an easy pace after them.[8]

Cromwell was ordered to go north by parliament where his first objectives were to secure the borders and drive any remaining Scottish forces back into Scotland. Cromwell then was to cross the border and assist the anti-Engagers in establishing themselves in government. The Engagement had riven both the Scottish political establishment and the Kirk, as well as provoking regional opposition. There had been a rising against the Engager movement in the southwest earlier in the summer, but this had been quelled by the government. News of Hamilton's defeat reinvigorated this opposition and inspired a new revolt against the Engagers. This time the rising known as the Whiggamore Raid was joined by leading anti-Engagers, the Marquis of Argyll, Lord Leven, and David Leslie and even one of the men who had secured the king's agreement to the Engagement, Lord Loudoun. It was to be a short-lived military challenge: the government used George Monro's forces that had crossed the North Channel from Ulster to defeat the raiders on 12 September at Linlithgow, just as Cromwell reached the northeast border. As Austin Woolrych so perceptively reminded us, the Whiggamore Raiders whilst opposed to the Engagers, were not natural allies of Cromwell and the New Model Army. In fact Cromwell's presence near the border drove the two Scottish factions into negotiations: with both sides declaring themselves to be supporters of the king and covenant. Cromwell's soldiers were described as sectarians with questionable intentions towards the king. Argyll tried to keep Cromwell out of Scotland by returning Berwick and Carlisle, but Cromwell still advanced into Scotland. Cromwell was not convinced that Argyll and his anti-Engagers were capable of either defeating or controlling Monro or the other scattered Engager forces. Cromwell did write a letter commending Argyll's allies for their concern to secure the unity of the two kingdoms but even as he did so he was aware that Monro's army at Stirling was opposed by Lord Leven with only a small army between it and Edinburgh. Cromwell rightly was not convinced that the anti-Engagers were in control of the situation:

> the governor of Berwick [is] also daily victualling his garrison from
> Scotland side and the enemy yet in so considerable a posture... still

prosecuting their former design having gotten advantage of Stirling Bridge and so much of Scotland at their backs to enable them thereunto and your lordships condition not being such at present as may compel them to submit.[9]

Cromwell moved north towards Edinburgh and Lambert was camped within six miles of the capital by the end of the month. In the first few days of October Cromwell went to Edinburgh. The purpose of this visit was to press his advantage. Whilst welcoming the new face of Scottish government, Cromwell was not shy of apportioning blame:

the Kingdom of England hath lately received so great damage by the failing of the Kingdom of Scotland in not suppressing malignants and incendiaries as they ought to have done and in suffering persons to be put in places of great trust in the kingdom.

Scotland had to redress this: the 'least security I can demand' was that the Scots debarred anyone involved in the Engagement from holding office.[10] The result of this would be the Act of Classes that categorised the level of involvement with the engagement and prescribed the level of punishment due to each category. By 9 October Cromwell was satisfied with the outcome of his discussions with Argyll and his allies who had finally established themselves in government as the Kirk Party. Predicting to William Lenthall that Scotland would be a better neighbour, Cromwell returned to England leaving two regiments of horse and two troops of dragoons behind at the request of Argyll to guard the country whilst a new army was raised in Scotland. Whilst Cromwell's relations with Argyll and the Kirk Party were friendly enough, it was not a close relationship. From the tone of his letters, Cromwell clearly regarded the Scots as brothers in Christ. Yet in their turn the Kirk Party was far less welcoming of Cromwell's sectarianism. From outside this relationship was however open to very different interpretations. Former bishop of Stirling Henry Guthrie recorded rumours of the discussions between Cromwell and the Kirk Party:

While Cromwell remained in the Canongate those that haunted them most, were, besides the marquis of Argyll, Loudoun the chancellor, the earl of Lothian, the Lords Arbuthnot, Elcho, and Burleigh, and of ministers, Mr David Dickson, Mr. Robert Blair, and Mr James Guthry. What passed amongst them, came not to be known infallibly; but it was talked very loud, that he did communicate to them his design in reference to the king, and had their assent thereto.

It would be difficult to support any assertion that Cromwell and Argyll could have agreed upon the death of the king, given the Scot's reaction to the events of early 1649, but it fitted closely with the expectations of hostile observers in England.

The second civil war in England, Wales and Scotland had a profound effect upon Cromwell and many of the others involved in it. It was clear that it had hardened the hearts of some. At the conclusion of the siege at Colchester at the end of August after the defeat of the Scots and royalists in Lancashire, Fairfax executed two of the royalist defenders, George Lisle and Sir Charles Lucas, using the excuse that they had broken parole terms imposed at the end of the first civil war. Cromwell too showed that he too expected the royalists to face condign punishment when he criticised the lax terms imposed upon Sir John Owen captured during the summer's campaign alongside Sir Marmaduke Langdale. On the other hand, parliament had moved in the opposite way, repealing the Vote of No Addresses before the end of August, perhaps to head off more radical solutions proposed within the army.

Radical solutions were being discussed; some soldiers were openly calling Charles I a 'Man of Blood'; some, like Colonel Harrison, had done so back at Putney. There is a debate over Cromwell's precise attitude to the king and to monarchy at this point centred upon whether or not Cromwell favoured the removal of the king and the end of monarchy or whether he just wanted to get rid of Charles I. Some historians are not even sure that Cromwell had decided to get rid of Charles I at all. Cromwell's words and actions are open to a variety of meanings and interpretations. At Putney he had rejected any notion of republicanism, but it has been argued he did not explicitly suggest that Charles I was the only possible monarch. In January during the debate on the Vote of No Addresses he had even referred to the king as a man against whom the heart of God had hardened. It remains doubtful that Oliver Cromwell was present at the April meeting of the army that argued for bringing the king to trial. As both John Morrill and Philip Baker have argued, Cromwell did not endorse the Man of Blood accusations. There is of

Plate 1   Oliver Cromwell aged 2

Plate 2   Cromwell's school, Huntingdon

Plate 3 Cromwell's home in Ely

Plate 4 Cromwell by Robert Walker

Plate 5   Parliament during Commonwealth

Plate 6   Cromwell dissolving parliament

Plate 7   Equestrian portrait

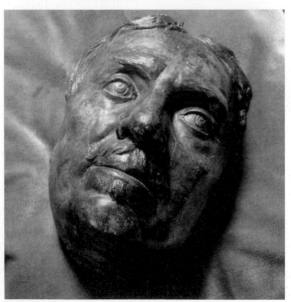

Plate 8   Cromwell's death mask

course Cromwell's behaviour after his return from Scotland to add into the equation.

Cromwell left Scotland after his letter to William Lenthall on 9 October. By 15 October he was at Carlisle, ensuring the town's security after its return to English hands. On 29 October, as he progressed south royalists at besieged at Pontefract apparently bungled an attempt to kidnap the commander of their besiegers, the much loved Colonel Thomas Rainborough. Cromwell marched to Pontefract and took over. There was no need for him to do so. Pontefract had a high profile, but militarily it was not truly significant: there was no hope of relief and no chance that the bold stand of the garrison could ignite a royalist rebellion. The nearest, and indeed only other, royalist garrison was at Scarborough and similarly beleaguered. Any other commander could have taken over from Rainborough. Cromwell, it appears had other reasons for staying away from London and historians have speculated that it was during this period, which lasted until early December when Cromwell left off command of the leaguer, without having secured the surrender of the castle, and returned to London. Whilst, Cromwell remained in south Yorkshire the radical impetus gained momentum and by the time he returned to London the means by which the army would bring about the trial of the king were in motion. The range of interpretations of Cromwell's attitudes is varied. At one end of the scale is the idea that Cromwell decided only in late 1648, perhaps even later than his stay at Pontefract, that the king should be tried. In opposition to this interpretation is the possibility that Cromwell had decided that Charles was unacceptable late in 1647, after the king's flight from Hampton Court, but that he retained a belief in a monarchical system. The third possibility is that he had decided that both the system and the person should go at an earlier date. Of course within each of these options lay various possibilities about timing.

Cromwell was essentially conservative, a country gentleman with his social and political position confirmed by the existing political system and the church. His family position had been enhanced by the Reformation which had brought with it position in parliament and court for several generations of Cromwells. The disestablishment of church or state would not be something to be taken lightly. To shake Cromwell's essential faith would require a great shock; but a revolution in Scotland, a Catholic rebellion in Ireland and two civil wars in England and Wales could be argued to be a great shock to Cromwell's system. Moreover his participation in the two wars and in the failed negotiations with the king gave him a greater insight into the catastrophes that befell the British Isles.

Cromwell's changing attitudes can be seen through his contributions to the debate at Putney and the letters he wrote during 1648. At Putney he and the other generals had rejected the calls for bringing the king to justice and afterwards he had conjoined with them in shutting down news coverage of the debates. After the king's flight from Hampton Court, Cromwell quickly saw the hand of God at work: he himself also saw more clearly what was happening because God revealed it to him. 'Now Blessed be God I can write and thou receive freely. I never in my life saw more deep sense... How good God has been to dispose all to mercy And all though is was trouble for the present yet glory has come of it...' he wrote to Robert Hammond on 3 January in the wake of discovery of the king's dealings with the Scots. After his winter illness, he wrote to Fairfax that he had been blessed by God, who had raised him from death and treated him as a son. The workings of God are manifest in the letters Cromwell wrote to many correspondents: to Richard Norton in a letter about the marriage treaty between Dorothy Maijor and son Richard he inferred that God was not concerned by 'ill reports, and will in his own time vindicate me'. To Lenthall he inferred that God rather than Fairfax had won the victory in Kent: to Fairfax himself in late June Cromwell wrote that he hoped that they would all discern God's will that surely involved removing the yoke of bondage from the godly. When Pembroke surrendered he exempted from terms those men who had recently sided with the royalists and rebels: their 'iniquity' was 'double' because they had 'sinned against so much light and against so many evidences of Divine Providence' by taking up arms against the parliamentarians to whom God had granted victory in the first war.

After Preston, Cromwell clearly called the Engagers and royalists enemies of God: he also reminded Lenthall and the Commons that God would reprove kings in defence of his people. His heart hardened towards the foot soldiers of the enemies of God. Following the battle at Winwick, Cromwell also gave orders to massacre prisoners being held in north Lancashire if there was any chance that Monro would counter attack.[11] His anger at the lax treatment of Sir John Owen was entirely in character with Cromwell's mood at this time: the enemies of God would be punished, and it is probable that Cromwell understood that to include the king. There was one snag; Cromwell remained a parliamentarian in the broad sense: the army alone could not effect such change and for some reason Cromwell seems to have doubted that he should play any role in parliament's move towards such a radical step. He therefore stayed out of the way at Pontefract and left the revolution to others. Cromwell's involvement in the most dramatic weeks was an attempt with Saye and Sele to get the king to agree terms, possibly even agreeing to abdication in favour of his youngest son, Henry.

Several historians, including Barry Coward, have pointed out that Cromwell was displaying inconsistency in his letters during the period: he also began to use nicknames for himself and for other close political allies, calling Sir Henry Vane the younger as 'Heron' and referring to himself as 'Heron's brother' or even 'Brother Fontayne'. Whether this was more than the employment of casual references is difficult to fathom, but it adds to the obfuscation that Cromwell used during late 1648. For all his parliamentarian background he was clearly exposed to his son-in-law's drift towards a more radical solution; an army inspired purging of parliament to bring about the end of formal negotiations with the king and a trial, and W.C. Abbott suggested that Cromwell was even in sympathy with elements of Leveller politics at this point. In a letter to Robert Hammond Cromwell seemed almost to muse upon following the recent example set by Argyll's Kirk Party and the Estates 'a lesser party of a parliament hath made it lawful to declare the greater part a faction, and the Parliament null, and call a new one, and to do this by force … Think of the example …'.[12] On the other hand Cromwell was aware that the Levellers were involved in the post war politics. In a later letter to Hammond, Cromwell argued that the Levellers were not to be feared and acknowledged that their radical politics had driven some people into unwise negotiations with the king.

By this time Oliver's son-in-law, Henry Ireton was involved in discussions with the radicals meeting them at the Nag's Head on the Strand to discuss radical solutions to the post war impasse. Ireton's own regiment was proposing a radical solution, demanding that impartial and speedy justice be executed upon 'all criminal persons', and his soldiers demanded that this include 'the person of the king or lord as is the person of the lowest commoner'. Everyone who helped Charles should be regarded as traitors unless 'he be acquitted of the guilt of shedding innocent blood'.[13] Ireton had earlier attempted to control the army's progress by guiding the creation of the *Remonstrance of the Army*. Twenty five thousand words long, the remonstrance called for the end of negotiations: with an irrefutable logic based on the king's attitude to the series of treaties presented to him during the past decade, Ireton argued that no treaty with Charles could ever bring peace: the king must be brought to trial. Furthermore the document suggested that in future monarchs would be 'elected' by the reformed parliament or representative, in itself elected by a reformed electorate and should be bound by a new *Agreement of the People* which would be drafted shortly. On 7 November Fairfax called the army General Council to meet at St Albans to discuss the *Remonstrance*. For four days the officers debated the proposals, but in the end rejected them as too radical. Ireton in disappointment turned to the Levellers whose own proposed solution he had rejected a year before. There was no firm common ground; the Levellers rejected the notion of a trial driven by the army: John Lilburne's argument was that removing the king in a hurried way would simply replace one unelected tyrant with another. The negotiations ended with a compromise that would establish a new government structure before any trial – a committee was established to draft a new *Agreement of the People*. After the rejection of the *Remonstrance*, the army leaders had been thrown back on making a personal appeal to the king. This met the same response as Cromwell and Saye and Sele's discussions. The king was now looking to Ireland, where a new alliance was being forged by the Marquis of Ormond with the Catholic Confederation, and so rejected Fairfax's approaches. The commanders were thus bounced back once more on the *Remonstrance* this time accepting it on 18 November.

The lord general called Cromwell to London. By this time there had been a petition drafted in the north calling for the end of negotiations with the king and 'impartial justice done upon offenders' along the same lines as that drafted by Ireton's regiment. The officers asked Cromwell to send the petition to Fairfax, which he did along with his commendation: 'and I verily think and am persuaded they are things which God puts into our hearts'.[14] Just over a week later, as Cromwell prepared to leave Pontefract, the same officers had received and read the *Remonstrance* and unlike Fairfax's officers, they approved of it: Cromwell informed Fairfax that they 'see nothing but what is honest and becoming good Christians and honest men to say', somewhat unrealistically adding that he hoped the Kirk Party would agree to the proposals too.[15] The *Remonstrance* was sent to the House of Commons who baulked at the radicalism of the proposals and set it aside for a week preferring to deal with another message from the king. Their inaction quickly became irrelevant; Fairfax, having earlier ordered the arrest of Hammond who was still suspected of being too sympathetic to Charles, now ordered that the king himself be brought from the Isle of Wight to London. Parliament reacted swiftly enough this time and declared his action illegal and voted down the *Remonstrance*, but these acts were the last gasp of the unreformed house, which still seemed to be unable to see the crisis into which its continued negotiations with Charles I had led it and the country. On 5 December the Commons concurred with the Lord's assessment that the king's communiqué on the Newport negotiations provided a way forward: two days later the troops moved in.

Cromwell had probably received his orders to join Fairfax on 30 November, but he only reacted slowly. Both lord general and lieutenant general, experienced MPs, avoided close involvement with the purge of parliament leaving the direction of the matter to Ireton, an MP of only three year's standing; and even he avoided personal contact with the mechanics of the purge. Although Ireton and others tried to persuade some MPs to try and get the house to dissolve itself before the army needed to act, military action became inevitable. On 7 December 1648 Fairfax and the General Council of the officers printed their proposals, they demanded the impeachment of the eleven chief Presbyterian opponents of the army and the sheriff of London, Major General Richard Browne. It also proposed that there were others in parliament 'to the number of ninety and odde' who were not to be trusted as they were responsible for repealing the Vote of No Addresses, reopening negotiations with the king and the leniency with which the authors and actors in last summer's war were being treated: they should be arrested. This would result in a house comprised of those 'who retained their trust', allowing the house to 'take order for the execution of justice' and call a new reformed parliament as demanded by the *Remonstrance*.[16] On the same day former major general, Thomas, Lord Grey of Groby and New Model Army Colonel Thomas Pride stood at the door of the House of Commons and regulated entry to the chamber. Over the next five days a total of 186 MPs were excluded by them; 56 more stayed away when they heard what was happening and 41 were arrested at the door. Just

156 MPs were left sitting in the house: it was a very large 'odde' that had been added to the ninety expulsions called for in *The Humble Proposals and Desires*.... The necessary legislation for the trial could now then be introduced into the house as Fairfax and the officers had demanded. Only then did Cromwell appear in the capital, although he had perhaps arrived on the eve of 'Pride's Purge'. His reception in parliament seems to have been a positive one: being thanked by the Commons for his work in the north.

Ascertaining Cromwell's precise attitude to what had happened in Westminster is not easy, perhaps he hoped that because he was not associated directly with purging parliament he could now sit as a member, once again adopting his almost unique place as a mediator between the Commons and the New Model Army: this is what J.S.A. Adamson has argued and he is probably right. If this was his aim it would be unlikely that he would be allowed to do so, he was already portrayed on royalist satirical playing cards as a piper playing a tune to which Fairfax danced. Cromwell's comment on the ill reports circulating about him in his letter to Richard Norton back in March 1648, that 'God will in His own time vindicate me', would prove too complacent.[17] Accusations that Cromwell was playing the tune in late 1648 would reverberate through time, reinvigorated by the attempt at the Restoration to apportion as much blame to the dead Oliver as possible to facilitate settlement. There was little at first for him to do publicly: parliament adjourned for five days until 12 December, and parliamentary activity during this period centred upon drafting the new Agreement of the People, which was completed by the committee of Levellers, soldiers and MPs by 11 December and then passed it onto the General Council of Officers. There it remained for five weeks.

Cromwell began to play an active role in the arrangements for the king's trial, attempting to get evidence from the Scots to add to the material charges to be levelled at the king. But historians are still unconvinced of Cromwell's readiness to completely accept the need for the king's death at the end of a trial. Back in London and in the vicinity of parliament Cromwell seemed to eschew the consequences of the sentiments he had expressed in Pontefract. There were alternative strategies, despite parliament's re-adoption of the Vote of No Addresses and the ban on private treaties. Discussions with the king still happened based on a couple of ideas: leaving Charles in place as a constitutional monarch – a plan emanating from the House of Lords or getting Charles to abdicate in favour of his youngest son Henry, Duke of Gloucester – the one prince untainted by military service with the king. Cromwell considered both these proposals probably in the series of discussions he had with other MPs such as Bulstrode Whitelock, but the king's intransigence obliterated both proposals.

Cromwell's speech in parliament, on 23 December 1648, during the first debate on the establishment of a court to try the king, explained his position. He argued that any man who had pursued a design to put the king on trial and depose him would be the greatest traitor in the world; but this was the work and will of God who had 'cast it upon them'.[18] Although Cromwell seems not to have actually offered a solution, it can be inferred from this belief that the prospective trial was what God had brought them to. It was also the day that the army officer MPs including Cromwell, saw off the attempt of the Commons to put full responsibility for the trial upon the army. Civilian MPs argued that there was nothing in history or law that would allow for a king to be tried by his people: 'irregular and unheard of business' should be 'done in an irregular way by such irregular men'.[19] The officer MPs 'were subtle enough to see and avoid that' but found 'many… strangely forward to engage in it'. In other words Cromwell and the officers argued that dramatic change to the constitution had to be undertaken by constitutional elements from within the existing state and polity. This fits entirely with Cromwell's essential constitutionalism and could be seen in the light of this as an extension of the 'functional radicalism' that Gerald Aylmer has outlined for the actions of parliament throughout the war when faced with the necessity of taking radical constitution-changing steps to defeat the king. Only through parliamentary process could any legitimacy at all be brought to the proposed trial. It may seem Cromwell's indecision came to an end at the end of 1648; however it can be argued that rather than indecision we may perhaps interpret this as a period in which he made an important personal and political decision. Others made the decision more quickly; some people had arrived at the solution over a year before Cromwell. Many of these men had far less invested in the traditional state than Cromwell: some may well have voted in parliamentary elections, but others would have been excluded from even this role in the political process. Any agreement with the king by either the grandees or MPs without consulting the junior officers and Agitators would have the effect of leaving them still excluded. Within the context of the argument set out in Chapter 1, Oliver and his family network, the cocoon into which he had been born, were intimately associated with the post reformation political state, Oliver's grandfather had been a star of Charles I's father's court: Cromwell could not be expected to acquiesce in the destruction of the monarchy from which the Cromwells had gained so much without a great deal of thought.

The king was brought from the Isle of Wight during December and was lodged at Windsor Castle on 23 December the same day as the debate on his trial. As he lodged at the castle over Christmas a committee of 38 (although some including Whitelock did not attend) began to set out the process of bringing the king to trial. The high court was to consist of 150 members led by the two chief justices, of the king's bench and the court of common pleas, and the chief baron of the exchequer court. Cromwell's cousin Oliver St John was the chief justice of common pleas, however he declined to preside over the trial as did his two counterparts leaving the Chief Justice of Cheshire, and John Bradshaw was prevailed upon to preside. Many nominees, like Cromwell's close associate Henry Vane did not attend, and his commander, Fairfax attended only one session of the court's preliminary meetings. Colleague in arms Major General Skippon also declined. Many of these men would benefit from and serve the regime that was put in place after the execution of the king, but they were not prepared to participate in the event itself: their attitude reflecting somewhat Cromwell's avoidance of the purging of parliament a month earlier but their absence serves to underline Cromwell's commitment. By contrast Cromwell, now convinced of God's intentions, took up his place in the scaled down court. The trial consisted of four open sessions commencing with the king in attendance and a closed session on 24 January when the evidence of witnesses was heard in court. On 25 January the evidence was read in open court and a verdict reached by the commissioners. On 27 January the king was sentenced to death. He was executed on 30 January on a scaffold erected beside the Banqueting Hall of Whitehall Palace. Cromwell's role in the trial was somewhat greater than that of a member of the commission: he missed only two of the 23 sessions, but it is one of the areas of his life clouded by the post-Restoration attempt by several regicides to escape blame. His association with the trial was underlined on 27 January when as court president Bradshaw began to announce the sentence in the name of the people. A masked woman stood up in the balcony and shouted 'Not half, not a quarter of the people of England. Oliver Cromwell is a traitor'. What made this particularly embarrassing was that Cromwell probably recognised immediately that this was the wife of his commander Fairfax. No doubt that Oliver knew that Anne Fairfax, a Presbyterian, opposed the action being taken against the king and that she was perhaps putting pressure on her husband influencing his decision to avoid public sessions of the court. Lady Fairfax was hustled out of Westminster Hall by her friends just as the guards levelled their muskets at her: but Cromwell had been clearly shoved into the limelight by being accused of being responsible for the trial.

On 27 January Cromwell was angered by the belated attempt by John Downes to persuade his fellow commissioners to listen to any proposal the king should make. Downes caused the commissioners to withdraw in to the Court of Wards where Cromwell was said to have bullied Downes and other waverers back into line and marshalled them back into the chamber where the court continued and the king was sentenced to death. Moreover, on 29 January when the signing of the king's death warrant was completed by 59 of the commissioners Cromwell was reportedly in a jocular mood, signing third after Bradshaw and Lord Grey of Groby, flicking ink at other signatories, presumably in sheer relief at the end of such a dramatic period of his life. Many accusations were made about his role in the signing, by effectively searching out MPs commissioners who appeared to be avoiding signing the death warrant and allegedly physically forcing some men, including that of Richard Ingoldsby to put their name on the paper. There is not much to support the claims made by regicides about him forcing them to sign the warrant, but some historians have nevertheless argued that Cromwell was able to compel some of the waverers into supporting the death sentence.

On 30 January 1649 Charles I was executed in front of an audience agog at the temerity of such an action. As if the death of the head of state was not dramatic enough, it was underlined by its staging: it was conducted outside the Whitehall Palace Banqueting House, architectural symbol of early modern monarchy. Charles's death was preceded by a declaration that anyone proclaiming the succession of any of the king's children would be charged with high treason, which effectively suspended rather than ended the monarchy. With the king dead it was time to establish a new regime. The House of Lords was in limbo: back in early

January it had refused to pass the bill setting up the High Court. In response to this blocking action the Commons had declared itself to be the supreme authority and proceeded to set up the court. Final decisions were not to be made for several weeks but the drift from a monarchy seemed to have been confirmed by the time the Commons opened its doors to some of the secluded members. There were only about seventy still attending the house during January and there were often far fewer in the house for debates. On 1 February some MPs removed at Pride's Purge were allowed in if they abjured the vote to support the Newport Treaty negotiations on 5 December, the effective spark for the purge: about seventy or so returned that month and fifty or so in later weeks. Cromwell, Blair Worden has argued, was important in persuading the absentees to return. It was part of his belief in the authority and centrality of parliament and went hand in hand with his determination to ensure the supremacy of civil not military authority.

On 7 February a Council of State was established with forty-one members, five of whom were peers, but only three of whom were soldiers – Fairfax, Cromwell and Skippon, and only one of them was a regicide. Even so for the first month or so that one regicide, Cromwell, was the chair or president of the council. On the same day that the council was established, decisions were taken to dispose of the monarchy and the House of Lords properly. The legislation was prepared over the next month and on 17 and 19 March the bills were passed. Two of the fundamental parts of the constitution that Cromwell had grown up with and participated in had been swept away. In mid-May England and Wales was declared to be a 'Commonwealth and free state'. The political revolutions of Scotland (1639–1640) and England (1641–1642) had been taken a step further. The earlier revolutions had altered radically the balance of power within the political system; that in England in 1648–1649 had swept away huge sections of the political state.

More radical solutions to the political crisis had been shelved: the *Agreement of the People* drafted by the committee set up in December, had been presented to parliament on 20 January whilst it was busy with setting up the king's trial. The House of Commons and the Council of State were both fairly conservative and not inclined to take a radical path but Austin Woolrych has argued that the Levellers, led by John Lilburne, undermined the *Agreement* by claiming, with little truth, that the officers had altered it and rendered it of 'no value'. This set them on a collision course with the very group who had brought the Levellers into the revolution in November 1648. Henry Ireton had been party to the Leveller involvement and as Cromwell's son-in-law could be expected to have an input to Council of State, even if parliament had rejected his nomination. By alienating Ireton the Levellers were also alienating Cromwell, thereby ensuring that they stopped being an essential element within the creation of the republic. Rapidly the Levellers became identified as one of the state's enemies, of which there was a growing number.

The Scottish political nation angrily repudiated the execution of its head of state and proclaimed his eldest son king of Great Britain. By doing so Scotland challenged England and Wales's sovereignty and put itself onto a collision course with the republic. In Ireland the Marquis of Ormond who had been sent there to negotiate a settlement with the Confederation of Kilkenny, was creating a reorganised military effort aimed at taking control of the country. At a meeting of the army General Council on 23 March 1649, Cromwell made what was perhaps his first important speech as a statesman, and reported on it to the Council of State. At this point the country was facing a series of enemies, each of which threatened the republic's existence. It was Cromwell who set the agenda for the next two years by prioritising the state's response to the threats:

> I had rather be over-run by a Cavalierish interest than a Scotch interest;
> I had rather be over-run with a Scotch interest than an Irish interest;
> and I think of all, this is the most dangerous, and if they shall be able
> to carry on with this work they will make this the most miserable
> people on earth.[20]

This prioritisation did not embrace the Levellers with whom Cromwell was to tangle within weeks, but included the current legal dealings with the representatives of the 'Cavalierish interest' captured the previous year. Five principal royalists were brought before the High Court of Justice in early March and Lord Capel, the Earl of Holland and the Duke of Hamilton were executed.

On 29 March, the day after he and colleagues were arrested by no less than two regiments of foot, John Lilburne was examined by the Council of State. Lilburne's own account suggests that his former saviour Cromwell had by this point rejected the radicalism of the Levellers. He and William Walwyn had been summoned to answer charges that they had encouraged mutiny in the army in the newly issued pamphlet, a second part of the tract *England's New Chains Discovered*. This pamphlet suggested that the new government was as bad as, or even worse than, that of the king. The declaration of supremacy by the commons, censorship, the creation of the High Court of Justice and the Council of State were all evidence of a new tyranny. It was more the implications of the pamphlet that concerned the Council for there was a call to action that could be read as directed at parliament, urging it to prevent the army from dominating politics. However, the Council of State could read it another way: as an exhortation to soldiers and others to overthrow it and parliament. Lilburne and Walwyn were committed to the Tower of London, but parliament was careful to ensure that the men would be tried under Common Law, thus avoiding adding grist to Lilburne's mill.

The dysfunction of the times was indeed throwing up a series of rejections of the revolutionary settlement. At the end of the month a small group of radicals set up an alternative lifestyle on St George's Common near London. These Diggers set up a colony on wasteland and declared the earth to be a common treasury whose resources were to be shared by all mankind. Because they called themselves True levellers there was a fear that this was somehow a dangerous precedent, so Lord Fairfax and parliament set about investigating the colony during April. To the lord general, they appeared largely harmless. The fall of these radicals owed far more to the local landowners who resented their new neighbours and the insinuation that property ownership contravened God's intentions at the creation. Far more threatening were the events closer to the heart of politics in the wake of the second part of *England's New Chains...* and the arrest of Lilburne and Walwyn. In late April a scrap outside the Bull Inn on the Strand seems to have been deliberately blown out of all proportion and declared a mutiny by the army leadership. The supposed ringleader, a Leveller soldier Robert Lockyer was court martialled and executed by firing squad. His funeral provided a rallying point for radicals. Petitions were drafted across the city, including two womens' petitions presented to parliament on 25 April and 5 May. On 1 May a third draft of *The Agreement of the People* was published and in this heady atmosphere sections of the army declared their support for the Levellers.

Regiments of horse heading towards the coast to embark for Ireland stopped at Salisbury and mutinied. Other radical soldiers gathered around dissident William Thompson at Banbury. By mid-May the threat to stability was serious. Cromwell and Fairfax gathered loyal regiments to them and on 14 May marched towards Burford in Oxfordshire where the Leveller soldiers had gathered. The army covered fifty miles that day, travelling so quickly that the rebels were caught in their beds. Negotiators were swept aside and after a brief fight Cromwell and Fairfax took control of the town and the rebels surrendered. Of the 400 prisoners, four were tried and found guilty: three, known to history as the Burford martyrs, were shot. This ended the mutiny and was the beginning of the end for the Levellers as a powerful political lobby: it symbolised too the regime's defeat of its internal enemies, begun six weeks earlier with the trials of the defeated royalist generals. The republic could now turn its attention elsewhere. In Essex John Clopton, a diarist who had political and familial connections to the parliamentary cause, noted the day of thanksgiving for the defeat of the state's internal enemy (21 June): it was 'kept of very few'.[21]

8

EVERYONE MUST STAND OR FALL BY HIS OWN CONSCIENCE
1649–1651

A few months after the less than enthusiastic response to the Thanksgiving for Burford, there was a fast for the success of the army in the forthcoming campaign in Ireland. John Clopton noted in his diary:

> Some hereabouts called it Crumwell's fast. few hereabouts present, but Mr Burwell his text for let thine enemies perish oh god: text he first made use of at the foaregoing thanksgivinge for ye Armies victory against ye levellers.[1]

In March Cromwell had set out his principles to the Council of State and later to the General Council: it was the Irish who inspired the greatest fear in him. Their Catholicism singled them out. Cromwell like the rest of his country – men and women – had been bombarded with propaganda depicting the Irish Rebellion as a mono-causal war aimed at the extirpation of Protestants and Protestantism. This publicity campaign originated in the large scale enquiry into the rebellion begun on 22 October 1641. The enquiry sought interrelated information: the names of rebels and the acts that they had committed; the losses that the Protestants had incurred; and a narrative of the rebellion. The method of enquiry involved assembling a collection of depositions taken from fleeing refugees at Dublin and elsewhere. The names of the rebels were important as the depositions were intended to provide the main evidence for prosecutions once the rebellion had been defeated. Such evidence would also provide grounds for the confiscations of property that would fund the repayment of the investors (adventurers) who gave money to parliament to counter the rebellion. Parts of this information made its way into the public sphere, via parliament. A report on the rebellion was presented to the House of Commons by Dr Henry Jones, Vice-Chancellor of Trinity College, Dublin on 16 March 1642. This eighty-two page report was accompanied by a transcript of eighty-five edited depositions, selected to provoke anger and a desire for retribution in the readers and listeners. Parliament was impressed by the content and ordered the report and the depositions to be published.[2] In 1646 as fighting drew to a close in England and Wales's war, more of the content of depositions made its way into the public sphere. Sir John Temple produced *The Irish Rebellion*, which would act as a justification for and a spur to parliament's attempt to launch a new campaign to re-conquer Ireland after the first civil war in England and Wales had ended. Due to the anger these intentions caused in the New Model Army and their contribution to the political impasse that led to the army occupying London and driving its chief opponents from parliament, these plans had not been developed far.

Nevertheless, these two publications, amongst others, carried a vivid picture of the rebellion into England and Wales, which worked: Cromwell was amongst the many MPs who provided money out of his own pocket to defeat the rebels; he lent £300 in August 1642. Later, on 11 September 1643 he estimated that 'the business of Ireland and England, hath had of me, between eleven and twelve hundred pounds – therefore my private can do little to help the public'.[3] It also worked in a different sense, for Cromwell was convinced that Roman Catholics in Wales presented a threat too: there could be an 'Ireland there'.[4] This attitude pervaded the first civil war, the Irish, either real or imagined, were considered as a special case and singled out in the press and on the field of battle during the war for distinctive treatment.

The publications were however, only one means of spreading the stories of the rebellion into the rest of the British Isles. The deponents were part of a rebellion-inspired counter migration. Their statements were taken at ports of embarkation. The deponents then sailed for Britain. They landed at the major ports such as Bristol and London, as well as smaller ports at Chester, Liverpool and Boston and made their way inland to relatives. Few communities in Britain would be isolated from the incomers, who with licences from JPs could claim hospitality from the communities through which they passed during the 1640s, in family groups or as part of convoys of tens of refugees. In some cases their numbers were so large as to inspire fear of invasion. It is clear that hundreds of returning colonists passed through Cromwell's home region, each of them carrying a tale of rebellion and fear.

The campaign in Ireland would be the first real point at which Cromwell became directly embroiled with Catholics on a large scale. His storm of Basing House had been the only time that he had fought against an enemy primarily defined as Catholic. His ferocity of attack was a marked difference from any of his other actions in the first civil war, although it was not entirely out of keeping with some other attacks on garrisons suspected of harbouring Irish or Catholic royalists by other parliamentarians. Cromwell's attitude to Catholicism is fairly hard to define precisely: his pronouncements up until this point fit general English anti-Catholic patterns rather than any particular personal position. For Cromwell, as for many English men and women, Catholics were a combination of two things: a few individuals in their own town or parish, with whom they did business sometimes but with whom they did not worship – tangential members of the community; and a dark menacing evil empire based on the continent and in Ireland, which had agents in England – perhaps even amongst those few Catholics with whom they did business. Going to Ireland would be for Cromwell and for many of his officers and men their first contact with the 'evil empire' aspect of Catholicism. It is probable that such close contact had a profound effect on Oliver – Catholics were suddenly real and at close hand – they were not an isolated minority, but the majority and this presented problems Cromwell had not had to face before: attitudes and postures would have to be developed to deal with this new reality. It remains possible that Cromwell, like many other men and women was still seeking to comprehend fully his own religiosity during this period. It is clear that Cromwell was always more confident of his religion within the presence of 'the other'. 'The other' was generally Roman Catholics and in these circumstances he became simply a Protestant. In the Irish sphere, following the rebellion and the well-publicised murder of Protestant settlers, Protestant equated with victim: something Cromwell acknowledged.

Preparations for the campaign took place on both sides of the Irish Sea. New Model Army soldiers began moving to major west coast ports, in particular Bristol in England and Haverfordwest in Wales. In Ireland the situation had undergone dramatic changes in the last eight years. For much of the 1640s the Catholic Confederation of Kilkenny had dominated much of Ireland. Enclaves loyal to England remained ensconced in Dublin and Cork and a few other ports around the coast, and Scottish forces held Antrim and Down. A cessation was agreed in September 1643, which halted much of the fighting but when the Scots and the English and Welsh parliament agreed the Solemn League and Covenant, Ulster remained an important battleground. However, as the tide of civil war in England began to turn against Charles I, Murrough O'Brien, Lord Inchiquin, frustrated candidate for lord president of Munster, changed sides and took his province's forces into the parliamentarian camp, reopening war in the southwest. After the end of the civil war over the Irish Sea, the king's Lord Lieutenant, the Marquis of Ormond handed Dublin to parliament. Ironically parliament's failure to support Inchiquin's forces during the second civil war in England and Wales led to him changing sides again and siding with the Confederation. However, the Confederation was now divided within itself, with more conservative forces within it challenging the radical clerical party, backed by the papal nuncio Cardinal Rinuccini and led in the field by Owen Roe O'Neill. These divisions, which by 1648 constituted a virtual civil war within the confederation, prevented a concerted attack on Dublin's new governor, Michael Jones who was able to extend parliament's authority beyond the city into Leinster. The return of Ormond into Ireland changed things again, as he began to assemble a broad coalition in support of Charles I during late 1648. Formed in the very last days of 1648, and thus too late to intervene and save the king's life, the coalition soon embraced most factions in Ireland with the exception of forces in Leinster and Ulster under the authority of parliament and some of the Scots that had not agreed with the Engagement with the king. On paper it was a powerful force, but it contained too many factions to be harmonious, and Owen Roe O'Neill remained aloof (and sometimes cooperated with parliamentarian forces in Ulster) until it was too late.

Ormond determined to capture Dublin and as the summer of 1649 began, coalition forces moved towards the city. Dublin was the most likely place that parliament would land its forces so capturing it would be a major blow to the Commonwealth's pretensions to govern Ireland. Dublin was indeed the principal target: the Commonwealth had resolved to send 12,000 men under Cromwell, although his son-in-law Ireton would initially consider a secondary landing on the south coast. Cromwell arrived at Bristol in mid-July where he found the soldiers restless: parliament was sorting out problems with current pay, but it had needed £1,300,000 for back pay, and £1,200,000 annually thereafter for its standing army of 44,000 men.

Cromwell's presence backed by the sale of the dead king's property brought the army under control and preparations for embarkation could begin. The threat to Dublin was brought to an end on 2 August. As Ormond moved his armies closer to Dublin, trying to sever links between the garrison and the deepwater port at Ringsend where Cromwell would have to dock his ships, Michael Jones seized on the opportunity caused by dislocation within the attacking forces near Baggotrath and attacked the coalition forces. The fight, through the Rathmines area south of Dublin resulted in the complete defeat of the coalition forces and their withdrawal from the area. In a letter to his daughter-in-law Dorothy new wife of Richard, and her father Richard Maijor Cromwell described the victory as 'an astonishing mercy' and a 'late great mercy'. It was proof to Cromwell that the invasion of Ireland was part of God's plan and he asked Maijor to pray for him 'that I may walk worthy of the Lord in all that he hath called me to unto'.[5]

With Dublin and Ringsend safe, Cromwell could prepare to depart England and Wales, and he embarked at Haverfordwest on 13 August aboard the ship *John*. Ireton sailed for the southwest two days later hoping to persuade English garrisons on the Irish south coast to change sides. A third flotilla followed a day after Ireton. In all 123 ships sailed to Ireland. Cromwell arrived at Ringsend on 15 August where Ireton would join him on 23 August having failed to gain access to any Munster port. Cromwell set about reorganising the forces under Jones's command and created a field army of eight regiments of foot and six regiments of horse. On 31 August the army set off north. On 3 September the advance guard arrived at Drogheda, a town captured for the coalition at the beginning of July 1649 by Inchiquin where a new, largely Protestant garrison, was installed. Cromwell used the next week to ring the town with his forces and establish a series of gun batteries. He summoned the governor, Sir

Arthur Aston, a royalist from England. Aston refused to surrender and Cromwell's guns opened fire, on 11 September 1649.

The town was divided by the River Boyne, the major part of the settlement to the north, with a smaller settlement gathered round Mill Mount on the south side of the town bridge, on top of which were defence works. The primary assault would take place on this section of the town. Cromwell had placed two batteries of artillery to the south east of the town to batter the walls at the town's southeast corner. These batteries fired 200–300 cannon balls at the walls and the tower of St Mary's church during the morning. It was devastating fire: the church spire was destroyed and breaches made in both the south and east walls. Two regiments attacked the southern breaches and Hewson's attacked across the ravine to the east of the town late in the afternoon. The fighting inside the walls was hardest where Aston had constructed two trenches cutting off the southeast corner. Hewson's men were driven back, but Cromwell reinforced them with two more regiments and they pushed their way back into the town. As Hewson forced his way in the troops on his left were also assaulted by a vicious counter-attack and likewise ejected from the town. This time Cromwell himself led the parliamentarian response. Both Hewson's and Cromwell's renewed attacks were successful and the two waves of attackers pushed northwards into the town. The governor, Aston, had been leading the counter-attack on Hewson's left and was thus caught in the southern sector when Cromwell and his reinforcements overcame the defenders. Whilst some of the defeated soldiers sought safety across the river, via the drawbridge, Aston was swept into an alternative tide headed for the defence works atop the mount.

Once into the town Cromwell ordered that no quarter be given to the defenders and Aston, caught on the mount fell prey to the order, along with 250 defenders, possibly after he had been offered and had accepted quarter. The rest of the troops from the southern sector made for the bridge, but they were now in a race with the New Model and proved unable to pull up the drawbridge quickly enough. The New Model regiments were able to force their way over the Boyne and into the northern part of the town. The fighting continued uphill through the town and into the vicinity of St Peter's church and the towers along the north wall. Cromwell continued the policy of no quarter and even had soldiers set fire to the church pews under the St Peter's steeple to force trapped defenders out: fifty escapees were murdered as they got out. Soldiers caught in the towers were subjected to decimation – one in ten were killed after surrender.

The pursuit through the town was bloody and large scale killings had taken place. Some of the blame for the killing which took place could be passed onto the nature of the fighting. The garrison had refused to surrender when probably beyond all means, internal and external, of recovery or rescue. Theoretically then, the soldiers could expect no mercy. Moreover, the fighting had been very hard and the casualties suffered by the New Model whilst entering the town had been very high. This ensured that the soldiers had been acting in 'hot blood' when the killings had taken place. Indeed there was little immediate criticism of, or even reference to, the events at Drogheda. Cromwell himself ensured that this would change.

In a letter to his successor as the Lord President of the Council, John Bradshaw, Cromwell took personal responsibility for the killings: 'we refused them quarter ... I believe we put to the sword the whole number of the defendants '.[6] He elaborated on these assertions in his letter to the speaker of parliament William Lenthall, describing the killing of officers commanding the defence of Drogheda, the burning to death of soldiers holding out in St Peter's Church and the decimation of common soldiers captured during the siege, Cromwell confirmed that he had empowered his men to take such actions in a series of statements: the soldiers 'were ordered by me to put them to the sword'; 'I forebade them to spare any that were in the town'; 'I ordered the steeple of St Peter's Church to be fired'; 'When they submitted, their officers were knocked on the head; and every tenth man of the soldiers killed and the rest shipped of to the Barbadoes'; 'I believe all their friars were knocked on the head'.[7] These letters were written almost a week after the storm. It was not a series of claims simply made on the spur of the moment or in 'hot blood'.

Cromwell clearly felt that he needed to explain himself, but he did not seek to excuse his actions. It was a manner very different to his almost careless comment about the death of royalists in the aftermath of the storming of Basing House in October 1645. Of Basing he had simply stated 'many of the Enemy our men put to the sword; and some officers of quality ...'.[8] Even though Cromwell regarded Basing House as a 'nest of papists', he felt no need to fully associate himself with the bloodshed.

In Ireland there was no ambiguity, for Cromwell he and the soldiers were fully justified by the mission upon which he was engaged:

> I am persuaded that this is a righteous judgement of God upon these barbarous wretches who have imbrued their hands in so much innocent blood ...[9]

In military terms the massacres at Drogheda met with success, for while there was at the time little suggestion that Cromwell had done anything wrong during the attack, many garrisons in the vicinity, including Trim and Dundalk surrendered without a fight in the wake of Drogheda and the loss of the town was a major blow, Drogheda being a very useful port and an important link between Ulster and Leinster. The deaths of 2,000 soldiers, Protestant royalists and Irish Catholics was also a critical blow, especially following the catastrophic defeat at Rathmines; Ormond was in no condition to face Cromwell in the field. Confederate and Royalist Ulster was opened to renewed assault, whilst parliamentarian north Leinster and Dublin were simultaneously covered from attack. Ormond drew back to Kilkenny, but at last Owen Roe O'Neill was persuaded to join the coalition. Cromwell himself returned to Dublin to prepare for a march into south Leinster and Munster.

The New Model Army marched southwards along the coastal roads towards Wexford in late September. Some Royalist or Confederation garrisons along its route surrendered without a fight, and others were abandoned before the army arrived. Only one serious attempt was made to impede the New Model was made: an attack was launched by Brian O'Byrne in the hills south of Arklow, but the last barrier to Cromwell's progress, the garrison at Enniscorthy surrendered after being threatened with bombardment. Wexford with its large enclosed bay and important harbour would be a useful asset for parliament in supplying campaigns in the south. Denying its use to Ormond and to Prince Rupert and the small royalist fleet assembled during England and Wales's Second Civil War was also important to Cromwell's aims. On 1 October Cromwell arrived at Wexford and, with a republican fleet in attendance off the coast, he positioned his army southeast of the town and on the southern side of the harbour. Rosslare fort, guarding the entrance to the bay, was surrendered on the following day, allowing the fleet to enter the bay and land the heavy artillery. Negotiations began with the garrison on 3

October as Cromwell continued to assemble his forces outside Wexford. Unlike the five other garrisons en-route, Wexford did not surrender immediately and Cromwell faced some defiance because the new governor David Sinnott had freshly arrived in the town with reinforcements and Ormond had moved his army to New Ross just twenty miles away. Sinnott played for time allowing further reinforcements to arrive.

Cromwell's artillery was positioned not far from where it had been landed, south of the town and place so as to direct fire on the castle to the southeast of the town's own defence works. The town's walls had been backed internally with earthworks that would deaden the effectiveness of roundshot which had been so devastating to the walls of Drogheda. It had not been possible to take such precautions within the castle and so it remained weaker. Capturing the castle, which because it overlooked the rest of the town, would be advantageous as then Cromwell's men could fire down into the town defences too. Cromwell wanted the town intact for winter quarters and also to retain its importance as a trading port, so he allowed negotiations to continue for more than just military concerns. Sinnott's instinct was to continue to play for time because Ormond wanted Wexford to hold out until winter, but on 10 October as Cromwell's bombardment began he sent two officers and two Aldermen as guarantors during reinvigorated negotiations. It was clear now that Ormond could not or would not rescue them and so the governor and the townsmen had agreed to accept the terms Cromwell had offered them. However almost spontaneously during the latter stages of negotiations English troops gained access to the town through the castle. The artillery had continued to batter away during the negotiations and two holes had appeared in the castle's unstrengthened walls. The castle's commander prematurely accepted surrender terms as English troops poured in to the breaches and then began an assault on the town itself.

The attack on the town's southern walls took Cromwell by surprise, and he quickly lost control of his troops. The fighting was vicious and confused and because negotiations were underway and with gunfire restricted to the vicinity of the castle, the townspeople had not sought cover. Initially they were caught in the crossfire and then beset by panic and many died as they tried to escape across the river Slaney. About 1,500 soldiers and civilians were killed during the storming of the town. Cromwell's letter to Lenthall following the siege of Wexford was markedly different to his response to Drogheda. Here, there was no reference to his orders, for at Wexford he had not empowered the killings in cold blood, God alone was given the credit for the fight in the market place where:

> ... our forces brake them; and then put all to the sword that came in their way. Two boatfuls of the enemy attempting to escape, being overprest with numbers, sank; whereby all were drowned near three hundred of them. I believe in all there were lost of the Enemy not less than Two thousand...[10]

Cromwell indicated that this killing and the attendant destruction of the town had not been planned by God having seen providential signs in the narrative of the attack:

> ... yet God would not have it so; but by and unexpected providence, in His righteousness justice brought a judgement upon them; causing *them* to become a prey to the soldier who in their piracies had made preys of so many families, and now with their bloods to answer the cruelties had exercised upon so many poor Protestants! Two instances of which I have been lately acquainted with. About seven or eight score poor Protestants were by them put into an old vessel; which being as some say, bulged by them, the vessel sunk and they were presently drowned in the Harbour. The other 'instance' was thus; They put divers poor Protestants into a chapel (which since they have used for a Mass house and in which one or more of their priests were now killed), where they were famished to death.[11]

There is evident symmetry in these judgements, the murderers of poor Protestants being killed by poor Protestants the drowners, drowned, and the site of the murder of Protestants being the site of the murder of priests in an implied cleansing ritual.

For Cromwell Protestants and the Godly in particular were always the 'poor' and the 'weak' and such revelations of Providence underlined that. At the skirmish near Grantham back in early 1643 he described his men as a 'handful' with which 'it pleased God to cast the scale': often he would play up the strength of the enemy, as he did after the Battle of Preston (17 August 1648), after Dunbar (3 September 1650) he related how his army was weak in flesh, faith and numbers in the face of his enemies. Such language has in the past, by Cromwell's enemies, and in the recent present by historians, been described as a disingenuous rhetoric, but it is more likely that as with the Scots in 1650–51, Cromwell was bearing in mind the example of Gideon and his small army of godly soldiers, even if his numbers were not really small at all. Cromwell held an image of himself and the Godly as being small, something like David, battling Goliath, facing insuperable odds, with only God to support them.[12]

In the meantime there was the question of the invasion of Munster. On 17 October Cromwell arrived at New Ross. Ormond had already abandoned the town leaving a garrison there under Lord Taffe. Cromwell threatened Taffe:

> Since my coming into Ireland I have this witness for myself That I have endeavoured to avoid effusion of blood having been before no place to which such terms have not been first sent as might have turned to the good and preservation of those to whom they were offered this being my principle, that the people and places where I come may not suffer, except through their own wilfulness.[13]

However, after the disastrous unplanned destruction of Wexford, Cromwell needed a secure base for the winter and wished to do as little damage as possible. Although he put heavy artillery in place and began a bombardment on 19 October, Taffe's bargaining was useful for his request for 'liberty of conscience' for those who chose to stay in the town after surrender met with a firm response.

> As for that which you mention concerning liberty of conscience, I shall meddle not with any man's conscience. But if by liberty of conscience you mean a liberty to exercise the Mass, I judge it best to use plain dealing and to let you know Where the Parliament of England have power that will not be allowed of.[14]

Taffe accepted Cromwell's otherwise generous terms and part of his garrison, troops from Lord Inchiquin's regiment changed sides.

Waterford had been one of the ports of embarkation for fleeing Protestants at the beginning of the rebellion, but had been in confederation hands throughout the war. It was a substantial port on Ireland's south coast and would need to be captured if Cromwell was to progress along the south coast to Youghal and Cork and the royalist fleet base at Kinsale, but the port was important in its own right. The estuary leading to Waterford was guarded by two outposts, Passage Fort and Duncannon Fort on the east and western sides of the waterway. Cromwell sent Ireton to deal with Duncannon whilst he was dealing with New Ross. Ormond strengthened the garrison at Duncannon and replaced the governor. Cromwell was held back, the governor Colonel Edward Wogan led an aggressive defence, attacking Ireton's construction works and not only held out when Michael Jones arrived with more troops, but was undaunted when Cromwell himself arrived following the fall of New Ross. With Duncannon denied him, Cromwell could not get the fleet into the estuary to land the siege guns that had been so devastating at Drogheda and Wexford. In the face of this failure, Cromwell regrouped at New Ross and began an alternative approach, sending Jones and Ireton towards Kilkenny to seek and destroy Ormond's field army. Again Cromwell failed as Ormond withdrew north and destroyed the bridge over the River Nore at Thomastown, thus saving himself and the confederate capital at Kilkenny. On the other hand Cromwell's capture of Carrick allowed for an approach towards the west of Waterford and Jones captured Passage Fort which surrendered precipitously:

> ... what can be said of these things? Is it an arm of flesh that hath done these things? Is it the wisdom and counsel or strength of men? It is the Lord only. God will curse that man and his house that dares to think otherwise. Sir you will see the work is done by divine leading...

More realistically it was Ormond's initial failure to follow up his success against Ireton with a suitable defensive strategy for Waterford, and the lack of courage at Passage fort, for as Cromwell acknowledged:

> ... considerable part of your army is fitter for a hospital than the field: if the enemy did not know it I would have held it impolitic to have writ this. They know it yet they know not what to do.[15]

Ormond did not remain ineffective for long, with troops from O'Neill's Ulster army to reinforce him, the marquis was able to push more troops towards Waterford. Cromwell realised that a major siege was needed, but the wet weather was making it unlikely that the siege artillery could be moved across country. Waterford was saved and Cromwell withdrew, sending his men into winter quarters across Munster. Whilst the last few days of the 1649 campaign might have been frustrating for Cromwell, he had undertaken, according to James Scott Wheeler, the most sustained and successful campaign during the war in Ireland: now he was ill. Much of the hard work had been done by Ireton and Jones, whilst the commander remained at New Ross, but in early December, Michael Jones died, and he would be the first of two members of the trio of commanders responsible for the victory in Ireland to die. One of Cromwell's own family died about the same time, the illness sweeping through the shrinking army was claiming a high toll. Cromwell tried hard to understand why God had brought about this mayhap: Jones had never been ill to Oliver's knowledge; his 'finger, to our knowledge, never ached in all these expeditions'. Cromwell likened it to what we might refer to as a cocktail, with bitter contents mixed with 'sweet' in the bottom of the cup, in this case fending off an attack on the Passage Fort launched by Henry O'Neill and Ulster forces, along with heavy artillery. Nevertheless the tone of the letter from the sick Cromwell to William Lenthall seems almost one of bewilderment and he ended not on the triumphal note of a month ago, but searching for an end to the melancholic campaign: 'And who knows or rather who has not cause to hope that He may in His goodness put a short period to your whole charge'.[16] God did not put a short period to it, but a month later when William Lenthall read the letter to the Commons, parliament did – it ordered Cromwell home. There would be some time before the 'crazy company' as Cromwell referred to his army, would be ready to give up its commander. Cromwell had also to confront his own prejudices too.

At the beginning of 1650 Cromwell responded to a published accusation that he was there to destroy the Irish people. On 4 December 1649 twenty bishops gathered at Clonmacnoise had issued a manifesto accusing arliament, Cromwell and the army of intending to extirpate the Catholic religion. The people of Ireland and their religion would be killed or transported to 'the tobacco islands': the West Indies.

From Youghal Cromwell responded to the declaration angrily. He returned to the issue of guilt:

> You, unprovoked, put the English to the most unheard of and most barbarous Massacre (without respect to sex or age) that ever sun beheld.[17]

Cromwell's perception of Irish history informed this response. Because of this the basis of his response was extremely flawed. He picked up on the use of the word 'extirpate', alleging that it referred particularly to the destruction of something which was 'rooted and established'. Cromwell suggested that the word was inappropriate, because the Roman Catholic Church was not rooted in Ireland, but was a recent intrusion. This is almost breath-taking in its naivety. Cromwell seemed to believe that the Ireland he knew had been a Protestant nation for eighty years. On two levels this is a belief with no foundation. Eighty years would effectively refer to the reestablishment of the Roman Catholic Church during Queen Elizabeth's reign, would assume that all four provinces were incorporated into English rule, which they were not. Only the flight of the earls in 1607 effectively secured the complete Anglicisation of Ireland in terms of government structures. But complete governance did not mean a successful religious imposition. In recent years Patrick Corish has shown that by 1641 the Catholic Church in Ireland had ceased to be a missionary church: a post-Tridentine parochial structure had been established with resident priests and bishops shadowing their Protestant counterparts. In fact this existent structure was responsible for the rapid spread of the rebellion, the Oath of Association and corresponding structure of administration imposed upon rebel Ireland. Nevertheless, to Cromwell the Catholics were '*intruders*' who had raised a rebellion and war which had entailed a massacre of Protestant settlers. Cromwell was explicit on the reasons why, therefore, he and the army had come into Ireland:

> We are come to ask an account of the innocent blood that hath been shed and to endeavour to bring to an account – by the blessing and presence of the Almighty, in whom alone is our hope and strength, – all who, by appearing in arms, seek to justify the same. We come to break the power of a company of lawless rebels, who having cast-off the Authority of England, live as enemies to Human Society; whose principles, the world hath experience, are, To destroy and subjugate all men not complying with them.[18]

For Oliver Cromwell, Ireland provided a series of certainties. His imperfect knowledge of Irish history offered him a simple view of the rebellion: it was perpetrated by a group of outsiders who had seduced the people of Ireland into secular and religious rebellion (he would also accuse them of having external loyalties on both religious and secular grounds; to the pope and to the king of Spain). The religious element also offered him a comforting scenario. The presence of 'the other', the Roman Catholic intruders, gave him a clear position of his own: a Protestant. That the Protestants he was identifying with had a variety of interpretations of Protestantism: Scots Presbyterians, adherents of the church of England Cromwell had been so keen to see disestablished, and 'probably' a group of others interests too, did not matter. In 1649 the victims of 1641 were Protestants like Cromwell. In England Cromwell had a range of 'Protestantisms' to deal with, and his own beliefs were perhaps still fluid in reflection of this. In Ireland certainty was offered. Even by 1649, Cromwell may not have been firmly of the mind that he was a particular sort of 'godly', other than anti-formalist, and that whilst in Ireland he saw himself as a Protestant acting on God's behalf to revenge the murder of Protestant brethren is undoubted. Being in the presence of 'the other', in Ireland and a year later in Scotland honed his mind and would confirm in his mind in the Erastian strategy seen in the protectorate church, which was in itself no more than a development of his aims since 1640.

Cromwell, the little Englander or East Anglian could also become something else in Ireland. For the only time in his life, he was identified with the only group of people within the British Isles consciously referred to as British. However, the fact of their Britishness is less important than the fact of their innocence and of their (multifarious) Protestantism. Cromwell in 1649 identified with them because of these two factors. By doing so he defined himself clearly as part of that battered small or pitiful 'company' against whom the 'other' was always larger and more threatening whenever they were described in the rhetoric of the Godly. Cromwell has been accused in the past and more recently of being a 'canting hypocrite' capable of de-humanising his enemies. His most famous letter, that written after the battle of Marston Moor, likened human beings to 'stubble' as they were cut down by the swords of pursuing troopers.[19] In Ireland he painted his enemies in very human, if not flattering, terms. It was the Protestants who were left vague in his accounts of Ireland. It would be a vagueness that he would perpetuate in relation to his own nationality during the Protectorate when he would strive to be God's Briton.

The reason for the recall was Cromwell's own success, rather than his melancholy. The campaign of 1649 had convinced the royalists that

Ireland would not be a secure base for the would-be king, Charles Stuart, and forced the young man to switch his attention to Scotland. This was a tough political decision, for it would mean that he would have to accede to the demands of the hard-line Presbyterian Kirk Party that had been in government since Cromwell had helped it overcome the Engagers. It was in response to this threat that parliament wanted Cromwell home to discuss: it was not secret that should there be a war with Scotland, then the commander in chief, Fairfax, would be a reluctant leader. In Ireland, though the 'British' problem had a more immediate feel and Cromwell, suspecting his recall was imminent, set about a renewed campaign once reinforcements arrived in late January. Cromwell pushed into north and central Munster with Lord Broghill and troops from the English garrisons on the south coast, Cork and Youghal that had changed sides after Wexford covering the west flank by capturing a string of minor garrisons. Cromwell, with an only lightly equipped army also captured some minor garrisons before concentrating on larger targets, Fethard surrendered without a fight when Cromwell bluffed the commander into thinking he had a larger army in his wake on 3 February, Cashel was abandoned by the Ulster forces stationed there and surrendered within days: all without the need for using the siege train which would follow when Broghill opened the roadways to the west. Cromwell's speed mesmerised the allies. Riddled by plague and dispersed into winter quarters, Ormond could not bring his forces together despite apparently suspecting what Cromwell was up to. Before the end of the month Cahir was surrendered to Cromwell after his preliminary actions undermined the confidence of the governor. Cromwell made a fairly uncharacteristic earthly military boast in his letter to Bradshaw, referring to the Earl of Essex's campaign in the Nine Years War:

> It cost the Earl of Essex, as I am informed, about eight weeks siege with his army and artillery. It is now yours without the loss of one man. So also is the castle of Kiltinan; a very large and strong castle of the Lord of Dunboyne's; this latter I took in with my cannon, without the loss of one man.[20]

This success left the southern approaches to Kilkenny open and isolated the garrison in Clonmel. John Hewson, governor of Dublin, meanwhile conducted a campaign northeast of Kilkenny capturing a string of small garrisons south of Dublin that had cramped the garrison's operations.

By mid-March Cromwell and Hewson's two campaigns had been amalgamated with the capture of Gowran east of Kilkenny. For the past eight years Kilkenny had been the capital of Confederate Ireland, housing the General Assembly and the Supreme Council in the centre of the High Town, and would over the course of time give its name posthumously to the independent government itself. Moreover, and with no small irony it was the home of the Marquis of Ormond whose family castle was on the southern edge of the town: the mediaeval 'Old English' market town may not have been a serious rival to Dublin, but its capture would have symbolic as well as strategic impact. When Cromwell approached the town it was in dire straits, plague had drastically reduced the garrison strength, and the defence in any case was based on divided responsibility. The civil (and Catholic) administration was responsible for defending Irish Town to the north, with the military administration defending the High Town and the castle to the south.

Cromwell summoned governor Sir Walter Butler on 22 March, but Butler decided to hold out. Cromwell suggested that he was there for several reasons – 'the reduction of the City of Kilkenny to its obedience to the State of England', backed by God who 'hath begun to judge you with His sore plagues' because of the 'unheard-of Massacre of the innocent English'.[21] The following weekend was taken up with assembling batteries and forces around the town, and a vain attempt to rush Irish Town with a cavalry force on Saturday morning. The main bombardment began on Monday morning, and after a hundred shot there was a hole in the south wall. Three attacks followed, one from the east across the river at St John's Bridge, one towards the breach in the south wall and the third at the Irish Town Gate again. The latter was a spectacular success. Cromwell thought that only three or four of Colonel Hewson's men died in the attack. The attack on the east, however, stalled after initial success, and the attempt on the south wall 'was not performed with the usual courage nor success', and it failed completely as Butler had built a series of palisades inside the breach. Even so, with the Irish Town in his hands and the St John's suburb was also occupied during the following day. Butler offered to treat, and Cromwell restated his generous terms from the end of the previous week. As James Scott Wheeler points out Cromwell had adopted a far more liberal approach to offering terms, they were now generous and offered the opportunity to leave the towns unmolested to priests as well as soldiers and civilians.

Compared with the sparse terms offered the previous year, such conditions were a real encouragement to civil populations in towns to press the military authorities into surrender. They clearly worked, as town after town accepted them. This run of success was about to end, for once Butler agreed to Cromwell's offer on 27 March, the matter of Clonmel, back in Munster and behind Cromwell's army had to be tackled. This was something Cromwell referred to in his letter to Lenthall on 2 April. He knew of the desire to have him return to England and the votes in parliament to that end. But he used the excuse that the official letter had not yet come to stay put until it actually arrived. Cromwell actually got the communiqué on the day he summoned Butler at Kilkenny. Despite being in possession of the command, he used its lateness as an excuse to remain put. Circumstances had changed: he wrote asking for 'a more clear expression of your command and pleasure' knowing that this had bought him more time.[22]

Cromwell's lenient terms contrasted with Lord Broghill's massacre of captured officers in the wake of his defeat of Lord Inchiquin's forces near Mallow. This had a major political effect. The confederation Catholics decided that there was little point in paying the wages for Protestant forces when they appeared to be so ineffective, and forced the beleaguered Ormond to disband royalist Protestant units. Cromwell saw an opportunity to further enhance this split and offered generous terms, including protection and safe passage 'without any violence, injury or molestation' to England to Inchiquin, his family and other newly disbanded Protestants. Cromwell took the opportunity on May 7 to also draft a safe passage for Ormond himself, to drive a wedge between him and the confederation.[23]

Following the political and military success in dismantling the alliance, Cromwell moved on Clonmel. This town had been isolated, but the garrison led by Hugh O'Neill since December, was well prepared, despite plague and food shortages. Following the capture of Kilkenny Cromwell was able to despatch increasing numbers of troops to Clonmel: he himself arrived on 27 April. O'Neil was an aggressive governor, seeking to disrupt the establishment of the leaguer; so much so that Wheeler maintains that Cromwell considered besieging the town at a distance: but time was pressing. Cromwell knew that a second summons to return to England would be on its way: indeed it was, in duplicate just to make sure he got it. Attempts to attain the town through treachery were tried but the discovery was costly and some of Cromwell's men were lured into a murderous trap. Similarly bombardment with light artillery failed. It took until 16 May to get the heavy siege guns into place, and then because of the terrain around the town they could only be established in one place, opposite the wall west of the North Gate. Nevertheless it was a good position as the gate led directly to Clonmel's main street, useful as Wheeler argues for manoeuvring horse. Nevertheless, this did mean that there would be only one breach to attack and of course, only one attack to repel.

On 16 May as Cromwell's guns battered an increasingly wide hole in the wall, the townspeople built a new fortification inside: they created a v-shaped work with a firing step behind the breach, effectively creating a killing ground between it and the breached wall. Cromwell was unaware of the scale of this internal work and launched his attack at 8am on 17 May. The foot regiments poured into the breach where they were to be confronted by ranks of musketeers behind the new wall and more musketeers in the surrounding buildings. As the musketeers volleyed into soldiers packing into the enclosure, pikemen attacked the besiegers in both flanks near the inside of the wall. Log-wielding contraptions were loosed to further batter the trapped soldiers and on top of all this, artillery fired into the mass of milling bodies. It was a disaster.

Bizarrely, in the face of this defeat Cromwell remained single minded and unreceptive to the lessons inflicted upon him. At 3pm an identical attack to that of the morning's attempt was launched, this time with dismounted troopers backing up the foot soldiers. The attack was furious and determined, but for once the New Model had met its match: experienced soldiers, a talented commander and determined townspeople who joined in the slaughter with the weapons of the field labourer, proved that Cromwell's men were not the only force in Ireland possessed of a single purpose. Over 2,000 of Cromwell's soldiers died, including large numbers of the officers who had led the determined assault. If this humiliation were not enough having lost this little war, Cromwell lost the little peace that followed. The mayor of Clonmel offered to surrender the town that evening. O'Neill knew that there could be no second day's fighting ammunition and supplies were exhausted, and he removed his forces under cover of darkness as negotiations opened. Cromwell was thoroughly tricked, he marched into town ready to accept the surrender of the garrison only to find it had gone. The losses were immense, nearly ten per cent of the army killed and O'Neill had escaped. Ten days later Cromwell was on his way home: his greatest humiliation shrouded in a forgetful mist. There must have been no escaping from the knowledge that the catastrophe had been his doing. A single point of attack could have worked quite easily but the scale of losses in the first assault should have prompted an alternative approach to a single-minded rush for the breach. Diversionary attacks pressed with enough vigour to put a scintilla of doubt into O'Neill's mind would have drawn Irish troops and townsmen and women from the new work. It was a grave tactical error.

Generally the evidence is that Cromwell matured in Ireland. The war there confirmed his ability to lead an independent force and that he could coordinate the actions of dispersed forces in a concerted campaign, such as the drive for Kilkenny. He had proved a master of siege warfare, notwithstanding Clonmel. Moreover, his behaviour after the surrender of the town showed a statesmanlike maturity. There probably would have been sufficient motivation for an aggressive attitude towards the town because Cromwell had clearly been deceived by the mayor; no doubt the soldiers would be feeling vindictive after their mauling by soldiers and civilians alike in the town, but Cromwell stuck to the terms and the soldiers were reined in. This was not the Cromwell of Drogheda or Wexford. The Irish were not to be regarded as incorrigible and irredeemable reprobates upon whom God's wrath was to be visited. It is hard to imagine Inchiquin, Broghill, Coote or even son-in-law Ireton behaving the same way.

Cromwell was needed elsewhere. Jitters had set in at home. After the defeat of the royalist confederation alliance in Ireland, Charles Stuart, eldest son of the executed King Charles I, had reconsidered his position vis-à-vis Scotland. Having considered the Scots to be out of the reckoning because of the Kirk Party's commitment to hard line Presbyterianism, Charles was now thrown back on recognising their rejection of the execution of their king by the English and Welsh revolutionaries. The thought of an alliance with the Marquis of Argyll and the Kirk Party was really not appetising, and Charles had even sent the Marquis of Montrose into the northern isles with a view to leading an assault on Scotland. The Covenanters' insistence that their king sign the covenant was a major problem for Charles Stuart, but in the end he had little choice, English and Welsh royalists and anti-parliamentarians had failed to defeat parliament in 1648 and Ireland failed to deliver victory in 1649–1650. Negotiations were naturally protracted: the Scots were determined to deprive Charles of his trusted, but religiously dubious, supporters and sought to isolate him from outside influence, even ensuring that he travelled to Scotland in a Scottish boat, and even then hardened their terms whilst he was at sea. In the meantime the putative king (the Scots would delay the 'coronation' for some time) abandoned the loyal Montrose who was captured and executed by the king's new allies. These latter stages of negotiation between Charles and the Scots in early 1650 caused parliament's insistence upon Cromwell's return to England because there was also a problem at home. Lord General Fairfax was known to be hesitant about going to war against co-religionists and former allies.

Cromwell arrived in England in late May and made his way to London from Bristol. He arrived there on 31 May. The issue of Fairfax's reluctance to fight the Scots occupied discussions for the next few weeks, but with news that the 'king of Scotland' was about to leave the United Provinces, the issue had become urgent. On 24 June as Charles Stuart landed in the Moray Firth, a committee of five, called by Cromwell and comprising himself, John Lambert, Bulstrode Whitelock, Thomas Harrison and cousin Oliver St John, met at Whitehall to try and persuade Fairfax to remain in command. Bulstrode Whitelock kept seemingly full notes. Cromwell led the discussion, asking, seconded by John Lambert, why the general was unsatisfied at the reasons for war. Fairfax argued that the two countries were united by the Solemn League and Covenant and that to invade Scotland without the Scots having provoked them, would be illegal. Cromwell countered:

> But (my Lord) if they have invaded us as your lordship knows they have done, since the national covenant, and contrary to it in that action of duke Hamilton, which was by order and authority from the parliament of that kingdom, and so the act of the whole nation by their representatives.

He went on to argue that they knew that the Scots were preparing armed forces and raising money to 'carry on their design'.[24] The other committee members joined in with Cromwell's argument but the lord general still pleaded that the intentions of the Scots were not clear: defence against invasion and even a pre-emptive strike to prevent one would be justified 'but what warrant have we to fall upon them unless we can be assured of their purpose to fall upon us'. In response to claims by Harrison that there was a great assurance of 'human probability' that the Scots intended to invade, Fairfax replied:

> Human probabilities are not sufficient grounds to make war upon a neighbour nation, especially our brethren of Scotland, to whom we are engaged in a solemn league and covenant.[25]

Fairfax was not moved by the three main arguments of Cromwell and the others that the covenant was broken in 1648: that even though the estates had repudiated the Engager invasion it could not repair the damage especially as it seemed that some Engagers were back in favour and that they had allied with the king's party. Nevertheless, Fairfax stated that this was a personal matter, for his conscience alone, and that he could not see the justice of a pre-emptive strike:

> every one must stand or fall by his own conscience: those who are satisfied of the justice of this war may cheerfully proceed in it; those who scruple it (as I confess I do) cannot undertake any service in it.[26]

The committee failed to move Fairfax and parliament failed to do so as well when the committee reported the lord general's decision to it. Fairfax resigned and two days later Cromwell was appointed in his place. This was an occasion when critics of Cromwell once again claimed that his promotion to the post of captain general and commander in chief was a part of his grand design. There was of course the same problem of trying to explain away Fairfax's role by continuing to claim that Cromwell 'kept him (as it was said) in praying and consulting ... Cromwell takes on him to be for a commonwealth (but all in order to the security of the good people) till he had removed the other impediments which were yet to be removed ...'[27] Even Whitelock, present at the discussions with the former lord general described Cromwell's promotion as a 'contrivance'. Lucy Hutchinson, certainly no supporter of Cromwell by the time she wrote her account of the period, was far more perceptive when discussing the way Cromwell succeeded Fairfax:

my Lord Fairfax, persuaded by his wife and her Presbyterian chaplains, threw up his commission at such a time, when it could not have been done more spitefully and ruinously to the whole Parliament interest. Colonel Hutchinson and other parliament men, hearing of his intentions the night before and knowing that he would thus level the way to Cromwell's ambitious designs, went to him and laboured to dissuade him ...

To speak the truth of Cromwell, whereas many said he undermined Fairfax, it was false; for in Colonel Hutchinson's presence, he most effectually importuned him to keep his commission lest it should discourage the army and the people at that juncture of time, but could by no means prevail, although he laboured for it almost all the night with most earnest endeavours. But this great man was then as immovable by his friends as pertinacious in obeying his wife; whereby he then died to all his former glory, and became the monument of his own name, which every day wore out. When his commission was given up, Cromwell was made general ...[28]

The speed in which this was undertaken was necessary, for Cromwell had not exaggerated when he had tried to convince Fairfax to remain in charge: the Scots were preparing for war. Cromwell's motives were probably complex: that he was needed at home would be beyond doubt, and despite the debacle at Clonmel he must have been aware that he could command an independent army, and of course he had been over the territory quite recently. Retaining Fairfax as commander was another matter. For the Commonwealth Fairfax represented continued aristocratic support for the actions of parliament since the beginning of the wars. Despite Fairfax's ambivalent role in the trial and execution of the king he had remained in post since the trial. Fairfax's links to Presbyterians too were important as his co-religionists were at the conservative wing of the republic and not all approved of the revolution: the general was therefore a link to this group. For Cromwell Fairfax, for whom he had nothing but respect, was an important part of his tolerant approach: the general had often been the lynch-pin of Cromwell's calls for parliament to recognise the efforts of all its soldiers in battle. For all concerned having a Presbyterian commander in the forthcoming war would make it difficult for Scotland to claim that there was a sectarian anti-Presbyterian motive behind the Republic's intentions.

Nevertheless it was Captain General Oliver Cromwell who travelled north rapidly. In mid-July he moved the army from Newcastle to Berwick on Tweed. Fairfax had not been the only officer who gave up his commission. Colonel John Bright resigned his commission, and he was only the most well-known, other men resigned even as the army crossed the borders: Cromwell replaced Bright with John Lambert. On 22 July the army crossed the border and headed along the coast road and as it did beacons spread the news across Scotland: the Republic's army was expected. The Scots had decided to draw the enemy into Scotland and deprived it of supplies. Scottish forces were based around Edinburgh and Leith in well prepared defences, but it was the countryside south of the capital that impressed itself upon the invaders. There were no men, no crops and no cattle. The Scots had united again in a national effort, harvesting or destroying crops and driving cattle north. This was problematic for Cromwell; the further he advanced into Scotland the further his supply lines became. It was necessary to get to Dunbar as quickly as possible so that he could reach a port large enough for supply ships. But even this port was small and the amount of supplies shipped there was small.

On 27 July Cromwell pressed on to the market town of Haddington and from there on to the capital's outworks at Gladsmuir, but even there the Scots withdrew. Mussleburgh was occupied. On 29 July Cromwell advanced on Edinburgh to confront David Leslie and the Scottish army. An attack on the defences was driven back and Leslie attacked the retreating army. Moreover, upon reaching Musselburgh the invaders found that the town had shut its gates against them. Cromwell had to fight his way back into the town, but that night he was attacked in the town by Scottish horse regiments determined to keep up the pressure.

Cromwell had not expected this type of campaign and he may have thought that there was more common ground between himself and the Scots: at least, unlike the Irish, they were Protestants. The military campaign had been supported from the start by a letter campaign. Before the invasion a declaration of good intentions had been sent into Scotland but during the early stages of the invasion, the General Assembly had rejected the overtures. Cromwell and several ministers responded to this rejection, questioning the judgement of the Kirk leaders and the Covenant, with which Cromwell had been long familiar, was the focus of the response. Cromwell asked 'I beseech you, in the bowels of Christ, think is it possible you may be mistaken'.[29] He suggested in response to similar accusations, that the Scots may have been drunk on spiritual matters rather than alcohol, but nevertheless misled. He advised the General Assembly to read Isaiah 28 verses five to fifteen which focussed on the errors of priests and prophets made through strong drink who when falling back on the word of the lord would be 'broken and snared'. Cromwell was suggesting that the faith of the Kirk in its covenant may be mistaken. Unsurprisingly the Kirk answered quickly and sent its response through David Leslie, rejecting Cromwell's accusations and declaring the reasons why it was prepared to fight the invaders: the General Assembly wanted this read out to the army officers, and Cromwell gathered as many of them together as he could at short notice to do so. He then replied to Leslie on 14 August. This time his letter centred upon the practical elements of the alliance with Charles Stuart. Cromwell was more subtle, he claimed to respect the covenant when it touched upon the worship of ordinary Scots, which he was accused of preventing. Instead Cromwell tried to work on the political angle questioning the General Assembly's declaration against malignants when it was now allied to the chief malignant himself.

The literary battle failed and so had the initial military campaign. Cromwell had attempted to get Leslie to advance from the defences linking Edinburgh and Leith, but the Scots refused to be drawn out for long. Early in August Cromwell had left Mussleburgh to return to Dunbar, but on 11 August he advanced again on Edinburgh camping south of the city on 13 August, it was from here that his soldiers travelled down to discuss the Scots' inactivity with representatives of Leslie's forces. It seems that there were loud accusations of cowardice levelled at the Scots, so much so that under flag of parley some Scots officers came over to explain that they would certainly fight if only the invaders could wheedle them out of the defensive works. The next fortnight was spent in Cromwell's fruitless attempts to probe a weak spot in the defences, moving to try and cut off western approaches to Edinburgh and out flank Leslie promised the chance of a battle on 27 August but Leslie's strategy left Cromwell on the opposite side of boggy ground. When over the space of three days Cromwell returned eastwards, Leslie followed slowly and by placing himself on the Carlton Hill defences even got slightly ahead of Cromwell and could have raced for Mussleburgh. He did not and Cromwell marched back to the town unmolested by Leslie but with an army beset by illness. With his army reduced in size from 16,000 to 12,000 by sickness and supplies running low, Cromwell retreated to Dunbar. The Scots misinterpreted this as the retreat of the defeated army and followed, initially harrying Cromwell's rearguard. Then Leslie decided to trap the invaders in Dunbar. As Cromwell marched into the town, Leslie marched south, establishing his main forces on Doon Hill south of the town and a smaller force at Cocksburnpath blocking the route to England. Given the bedraggled state of Cromwell's army when it arrived in Dunbar, and the continual transhipment of diseased soldiers from the town, it looked as if Leslie had cornered the invaders.

However, Cromwell's horse was filtered out of the town to the west to face Doon Hill. Whilst Leslie might have known the ground well, republican scouts quickly ascertained the nature of the ground between themselves and the Scots. It was realised for instance that the ravine upstream on the Brock Burn, which ran north of the Doon Hill was impassable, and the burn itself only fordable in its lower reaches. This meant that Cromwell would be able to pivot his forces at the eastern end of the hill and attack the Scots in their flank. This was not the action of a cornered and defeated army. It was the meticulous planning of an officer corps at its best. During the day of 2 September Leslie began to bring his forces downhill. Cromwell would not attack uphill and now Leslie was keen on fighting. The Scottish commander was firstly concerned because his army was declining in strength the longer it was in the field, the army had also been purged of 3,000 soldiers the Kirk thought morally dubious, and of these eighty were experienced officers, men disbarred because of association with Charles I, Charles Stuart or the Engagement. Secondly, Leslie thought the invaders might be intending to make a dash for home, which would have only postponed the war to another time, when Scotland would be less economically capable. The war had been expensive because of the cost of keeping an army in the field for so long and because of the scorched earth policy of July and August, and such a strategy, whilst successful, probably could not be mounted again.

On the night of 2–3 September under cover of darkness Cromwell withdrew the regiments facing the Scottish units across the burn and moved them to the rear of his army which now chiefly faced the Scots on the Cocksburnpath road. With the east end of the hill as a pivot, Cromwell had Monck's foot and Lambert's regiment of horse cross the burn and smash into the Scots forces on the main road. This hammer blow fell in the early hours of the darkening late summer morning, under the cover of September rain which had battered the motionless Scots all night. Nevertheless the attack slowed and when the Scots' foot moved forward to support their horse it faltered and Lambert and Monck were pushed back to the burn. This was probably what Cromwell anticipated, for he reinforced Monck and Lambert then led a reserve force across the burn east of the road, where there were no opposing forces. This brought him into contact with the flank of the Scots fighting Lambert and Monck, at ninety degrees to Leslie's army's front in effect a flank attack of enormous magnitude. Leslie's entire army was now enfiladed in a narrow field between the burn and the hill. There was little room for manoeuvre. The attack was relentless and as the front ranks of Leslie's army collapsed inwards they did so onto the regiments that were now ranged behind them. The Scottish horse were pressed from two sides and when they broke under the pressure they rode over some of the foot to their rear, these demoralised soldiers then faced an onslaught from Cromwell's horse and they too broke.

Cromwell kept up the pressure as the Scottish army imploded and then broke into fragments and fled. J.D. Grainger argues rightly that Cromwell remained incredibly calm despite what must have been an exhilarating experience. His control over the regiments was superb, honed in the past eight years to perfection. He calmed Francis Hacker's regiment down by making them sing the short Psalm 117, Grainger believed it to be just the right length, a melodious intake of breath before leading in renewed pursuit. It was the most destructive battle of the civil-war period, an astounding but bloody victory. Three to four thousand Scots were killed on the field and in the pursuit, 10,000 were captured and the remnants pursued almost to within sight of Edinburgh. Leslie's patient plan had not only been thrown away, the months of frustrating march and counter march overturned at one blow but Scotland's finest chance of having an army capable of matching the New Model had gone. And there was worse. In the wake of defeat Scotland's unity, its greatest strength in the face of Charles I and Oliver Cromwell came to an end within days of the disaster at the foot of Doon Hill.

Cromwell was undoubtedly impressed with what he saw that day:

> Thus you have the prospect of one of the most signal mercies God hath done for England and His people, this war. And now may it please

you to give me the leave of a few words. It is easy to say the Lord hath done this. It would do you good to see and hear our poor foot go up and down making their boast of God. But Sir it is in your hands, and by these eminent mercies of God puts it more in your hands to give Glory to Him; to improve your power, and his blessings to His praise. We that serve you beg of you not to own us, but God alone.

Such an astounding victory required an equally dramatic reaction:

we pray you own His people more and more; for they are the chariots and horsemen of Israel. Disown yourselves; but own your authority, and improve it to curb the proud and the insolent... relieve the oppressed, hear the groans of the prisoners in England... be pleased to reform the abuses of all professions: and if there be any one that makes many poor to make a few rich, that suits not a Commonwealth. [30]

This is a radical statement and probably influenced by the exaltation of his greatest victory; a victory which he saw as presenting the Commonwealth with an unprecedented opportunity 'to do these things and not be hindered'. Historians are also impressed by what happened at Dunbar. Frank Kitson is not alone when he believes that Dunbar proved Cromwell to be a tactician of the first order.

The Scottish cause imploded, with so many experienced men and officers lost the task of creating a new army was more difficult. One answer would be opening the ranks to former royalists and Engagers and also to Charles Stuart's followers, but this was opposed by the hardliners in the Kirk who abhorred such lassitude. There was no choice if Cromwell were to be opposed and Charles Stuart's role in Scottish politics grew steadily over the winter as the Scottish polity crumbled under the dichotomy. Cromwell had been known to compare his forces to those of Gideon, implying that there were an embattled minority gaining strength solely through their association with God. This was clearly a rhetorical technique designed to both underline the army's godly credentials and understate the size of the enemy. With the Scots hardliners this was more than an allusion they seemed to feel that the solution to this crisis imposed by the crushing defeat at Dunbar was to have a small godly army to take on the sectarian forces. The core of this belief was to be found in the south-west from where a Remonstrance emanated setting forth this very idea.

The Remonstrance protested about the intentions of the Resolution and the Marquis of Argyle's supporters in both Kirk and the estates who had opened the army up to engagers and royalists.

Cromwell occupied Edinburgh in the wake of the battle as the devastated Scottish army fled to Stirling in the company of the government and Kirk leadership. Cromwell's forces continued to shrink and decline in effectiveness: new regiments were sent from northern England after Dunbar, but garrisoning Edinburgh, repairing defence works at Leith and tackling the small garrisons in the occupied territory took valuable time and men. The initial aim had been to pursue the Scots and continue the destruction of the army begun at Dunbar, but the decline in strength halted the advance. By mid-September, Cromwell was in retreat from Stirling having declined to assault the town in the mistaken belief that there were far more soldiers there than there were. He had also heard that the western remonstrants had assembled an army in the western shires and whilst Edinburgh was an occupied city, the castle had stayed in Scottish hands.

In early October Cromwell marched west again from Linlithgow to Glasgow and occupied the city. This was, according to J. D. Grainger, an attempt to show that he could move around southern Scotland at will, and came in the wake of Charles Stuart's attempt to seize control of Scotland in a move reminiscent of his father's bungled coup d'état, 'The Incident' back in 1641. As with the father so with the son and 'The Start', as it became known, was an equally ignominious failure. Cromwell lost no opportunity to pursue his theme of the incongruity of the alliance of the godly Kirk and the reprobate Charles:

> ... it is evident your hearts had not that love to us as we can truly say we had towards you; and we are persuaded those difficulties in which you have involved yourselves, by espousing your King's interest, and taking into your bosom that person in whom (notwithstanding what hath or may be said to the contrary) that which is openly malignancy and all malignants do centre; against whose family the Lord hath so eminently witnessed for bloodguiltiness, not to be done away with such hypocritical and formal shows of repentance ... [31]

This, like Cromwell's other efforts to persuade the Scots that the English were the real brothers in Christ, fell again on deaf ears. The prospect of a covenanting king seemed to promise greater security than an alliance with a sectarian republic that Cromwell had promised in the later paragraph of the same letter of 9 October. The Western Association responded to Cromwell's assertions that if Scotland guaranteed the security of England and eschewed its alliance with 'England's' enemy then 'you may have a lasting and durable Peace'. Cromwell's response to the Remonstrants showed signs that he thought that there was a potential meeting of minds here than with the corrupted government at Stirling even though 'we are looked upon and accounted as enemies'. He believed or gave out that he believed that with 'ingenuity and clearness' there could be a meeting of minds in a 'Friendly and Christian Conference' of equal persons, a 'Friendly Debate' which would lead to a 'better and more clear understanding betwixt the godly party of both nations'.[32]

Cromwell was still acting as if he regarded the Scots as brothers, despite their failure to eschew Charles Stuart, but he seemed to be working on the principle that 'my enemy's enemy is my friend' and interpreting the Remonstrants as enemies of Charles. However, it was a difficult proposition because these hard-liners abhorred what they saw as the sectarianism of the republic. Cromwell was not their friend but a greater enemy, for Charles might yet be encompassed in the covenant and his adherents disposed of: there was no prospect of encompassing Cromwell. Moreover his proclamation of 5 November directed at the guerrilla warfare in the occupied territory conducted by those known by the twenty-first century occupying powers as insurgents, but by Cromwell as 'outlaws and robbers' would not have endeared Cromwell to the supposed brothers.[33] The Western Association did not reply. During November Cromwell launched a campaign to defeat the association's forces and on 1 December the association attacked Lambert's men at Hamilton. The Scots were defeated comprehensively and the Western Association as a military force collapsed. In Edinburgh too there was success, the castle surrendered on Christmas Eve.

Strangely the defeat of the Western Association and the surrender of the castle led to a recovery in Scottish forces. On 1 January 1651 the Scots crowned Charles Stuart and this coupled with the firm decision to create an inclusive army in the wake of the defeat of the western radicals, created a new impetus. By contrast it seemed as if now the invaders were in the doldrums, attempts to enter Fife came to nothing and in February Cromwell fell ill during another march westwards. He was to remain ill until May. During Cromwell's illness Monck did much of the work, but the work was small scale, the capture of minor outposts had propaganda value and brought in weapons and supplies, but they only marginally improved the invaders' situation. In April Cromwell, alerted to the possibility of royalist action in the west marched his army to Glasgow and occupied the city which was at the heart of the Remonstants' territory. They stayed for eleven days. Cromwell attended services in the High Kirk, to hear a range of anti-English sermons and invited the ministers to come to a personal meeting: when they refused, they were compelled to attend where Cromwell and Lambert tried to engage them in debate along the lines laid out the previous year in Cromwell's letter to the association. They got nowhere. Ironically the invaders played the role of peacemakers in Glasgow where the town's traditional government had been replaced by an emergency committee, leaving mutually antagonistic rivals for power. When the provost tried to wrest power back from the committee it was Cromwell's soldiers that stopped the scuffling outside the Tolbooth twice on 29 April. A day later Cromwell began the march back to Edinburgh, leaving Glasgow paralysed by confusion and apathy. This left the west coast largely unoccupied by the invaders, as much of the army was concentrated in Edinburgh and in the southeast. Cromwell's complete failure to secure the hearts and minds of the Scots Remonstrants was underlined when he met Archibald Johnston of Wariston, one of the framers of the National Covenant and a Remonstrant, to discuss the return of Scottish government papers to him as Lord Register of Scotland. On 5 May just after Oliver's return from troubled Glasgow the two met. Cromwell tried to convince Wariston that his invasion of Scotland mirrored the Scottish invasion of England back in 1640. Wariston underlined Cromwell's still poor grasp of history as well as the massive gap between them in his retort:

> ... becaus then Ingland had refused our offer of treatyes, imprisoned our Commissioners, decklared us rebels and traitors, raysed an army against us and was marching to our Border, and the Deputy of Irland coming in upon the West-land; then out of meir necessity beset by sea and land, wee was forced to goe for out defence, just as if wee had prevented them at our Borders when they wer now marching upon us ... [34]

Cromwell's health fluctuated during these months, in March he had felt better and he was clearly capable of making the journey back and forth to Glasgow in April and early May. He claimed in a letter to John Bradshaw on 24 March that he had feared for his life, but claimed that God 'seemeth to dispose otherwise'. In a letter to Elizabeth on 12 April he claimed that he felt physically stronger, but that he was not really fully recovered. Upon the return from the second march to Glasgow he again fell seriously ill with a fever and dysentery. Parliament sent two doctors in Lord Fairfax's coach to Edinburgh to tend the 'fit of sickness'.[35] Indeed they offered to let the general come home for 'a change of air'. Cromwell's illness affected the conduct of the campaign, he described himself as being useless to parliament during the bouts of sickness: 'a dry bone' was one phrase he had used and an 'unprofitable servant' was another. That it was a serious illness there is not doubt and certainly Cromwell was convinced that he had been near to death. In his letter to Bradshaw thanking him for sending Dr Wright and Dr Bates, he said that God had 'plucked him out of the grave', which was a paraphrase of either psalm 30 or 86. Cromwell was only fully recovered in July when he took to the field again, although he was feeling better in early June.

David Leslie had offered to resign in the wake of Dunbar, but there was no real alternative to him and his resignation had been refused. It was Leslie who masterminded the bluff which drove Cromwell from Stirling in October 1650 and despite Charles Stuart being given titular command along with the crown, Leslie remained effective commander and continued to defy Cromwell's attempts to wheedle him out of Stirling or draw him into battle. Failure to cross into Fife further frustrated the invaders' attempts to force Leslie out of Stirling. It was to Fife that the recovered Cromwell turned his attention in July 1651. His aim was to get the Scots to lessen their guard on the crossing points on the Firth which prevented a successful incursion into Fife. This he did by pressing forwards to Stirling, then marching to Glasgow, and back again. Thus J.D. Grainger argues, he became the centre of attention, forcing the Scots to draw their forces together at Stirling. This had the desired effect and a successful incursion into Fife was made at the Battle of Inverkeithing by Lambert on 20 July and Cromwell began to ship his forces across the Forth from Leith to join him. Yet it is questionable who was playing whom at this point. Cromwell had several aims: occupying Fife; it might draw Leslie into battle to regain control of the relatively untrammelled area of Scotland from where the Scottish army got its supplies, or he might simply prevent Leslie from getting the supplies he needed; he might even outflank Stirling. On the other hand, Leslie had marched straight into Fife as if to attack Lambert's outnumbered forces, knowing that Cromwell would then support Lambert: he of course did. Whereupon Leslie withdrew. Cromwell had deliberately left the route into the west open when he marched into Fife, and Leslie seized the opportunity. But Cromwell had left the west open long ago, knowing the king of the Scots wanted to march into England, before the recurrence of his illness in early May: it was a long game Cromwell was playing, and it had just turned his way. Cromwell was jubilant at every stage: upon the securing the Fife side of the Forth, he wrote: 'This is an unspeakable mercy'; when the Scots left their fortress at Stirling he claimed that the Scots were 'heart-smitten by God' whereas the republic's cause was the 'Providence of God'. Lambert was sent in pursuit, troops in northern England were to shadow the Scots and Cromwell would follow with the main army whilst Monck remained on campaign in Scotland.

Charles Stuart believed that there would be an upsurge of royalist support in England if he could only get to it. Prominent royalists such as the Earl of Derby encouraged this belief, but Cromwell was probably on far surer ground when he believed that England was far more capable of defeating an invader than back in 1648 when it was 'more unsteady than now'. The Scots crossed the border on 6 August but so closely were they pursued that when they arrived at Penrith two days later, Lambert was immediately behind them. Lambert then marched east, leaving Robert Lilburne to take over. Cromwell was taking the eastern route into England. He had reached the Tyne by 13 August when Lambert and Harrison, who had marched into eastern England first and had been at Newcastle before the Scots had even crossed the border, joined forces. They had both outpaced the Scots and joined forces near Bolton and began to destroy systematically the bridges ahead of the advancing invaders. However, when the Scots arrived on the scene Lambert and Harrison withdrew, apparently allowing an open route ahead. On 22 August the invaders arrived at Worcester.

For the royalists it had been a disappointing campaign. The recruits had been few and the desertions tended to offset even these low numbers. There was a more potent source of hope however, the Earl of Derby had gathered a small force in Lancashire and Edward Massey was also recruiting troops in the county, but the majority of these new recruits were defeated at the Battle of Wigan Lane on 25 August. Charles had intended to stay only briefly in Worcester to await recruits, but now the options were closing down; other cities were to refuse him access. Already there were republican forces based in a circle of towns around Worcester: Hereford, Gloucester, Ludlow and Bristol. Cromwell was approaching from the northeast and on 22 August parliament, which had been coordinating the holding actions in England, passed all military authority to Cromwell. Cromwell passed through Mansfield on the day the Scots reached Worcester, three days later he arrived at Warwick and joined Harrison and Lambert: together they marched on the trapped invaders. This was a consummate campaign. The invasion had been shadowed, slowed, harried and finally stopped and encircled. All available troops had been gathered down the eastern side of the county to shadow the enemy army as it proceeded down the west. As Cromwell approached Worcester, his army was double the size of the invading force. Cromwell knew it. His letter of 27 August to Lord Wharton is exultant:

> ... you have the opportunity to associate with His people in His work and to manifest your willingness and desire to serve the Lord against His and His people's enemies. Would you be blessed out of Zion and see the good of his people, and rejoice with His inheritance ...[36]

This is so reminiscent of his radical invocation after Dunbar: it was almost as if he had won. In many ways he had. The Scots had been lured out of their stronghold to where the resources of England could be turned on them. Cromwell moved his army to Worcester on 28 August and secured the southern approach to the city at Upton. Most of Cromwell's army was assembled to the east of the city, but a sizable force was to the south opposite Powick Bridge, scene of the first pitched fight of the first civil war nine years earlier. Two bridges of boats were assembled at Timberdene and close to where the river Theme and Severn joined. These imperilled the Scots based at Powick and on 3 September once the bridges were completed the Scots began to withdraw north from Powick to the western approach to the city. Charles Fleetwood's forces followed. Pressure on the city was increased, but the quick march across the meadows left Cromwell's forces increasingly divided. It was a division that Charles Stuart noticed and sought to exploit with a dramatic attack on the northernmost section of Cromwell's right. The royalists scattered the opposing forces and established themselves on Red Hill east of Worcester. Cromwell had seen this setback from the meadows where he was accompanying Fleetwood's advance. Leading his horse regiment back across the River Severn, Cromwell organised a counter-attack on Red Hill. This was successful and by sheer weight of numbers the royalists were pushed back into Worcester.

In the west Fleetwood completed his march up to the western bridge into Worcester. Over the river, Cromwell's counter-attack was carried into the city itself and the two armies reached the gates together but Cromwell's men forced their way in with Cromwell himself present at the storm of Sidbury Gate. Some royalists, including Charles Stuart and David Leslie's brigade of horse escaped through Foregate and headed north, but the majority of the invading army was caught in the city and taken prisoner. Cromwell was once again exultant: '... this hath been a very glorious mercy ... The Lord God Almighty frame our hearts to real thankfulness for this', he wrote to Lenthall on the day of the battle. [37] A day later he confirmed this; 'The dimensions of this mercy are above my thoughts. It is for aught I know, a crowning mercy'.[38] It was a crowning achievement for a military career for Cromwell had fought his last battle.

9

OH, WOULD I THE WINGS LIKE A DOVE
1651–1654

Cromwell made his expectations clear in the wake of both the battles of Dunbar and Worcester. After Dunbar he had told parliament what the commonwealth should become:

> own your authority and improve it to curb the proud and the insolent ... Relieve the oppressed, hear the groans of the prisoners ... Be please to reform the abuses of all professions: and if there be any one that makes many poor to make a few rich, that suits not a Commonwealth.[1]

He was to return to this theme after Worcester:

> I am bold humbly to beg, that all thoughts may tend to the promoting of His honour who hath wrought so great salvation, and that the fatness of these continued mercies may not occasion pride and wantonness, as formerly the like hath done to a chosen nation but that the fear of the Lord, even for His mercies, may keep an authority and a people so prospered, and blessed, and witnessed unto, humble and faithful, and that justice and righteousness mercy and truth may flow from you, as a thankful return to our gracious God...[2]

There was, Cromwell implied, a duty to develop the Commonwealth in the wake of these victories. He did acknowledge the war was not quite over yet, but he was confident that it would soon end because of Worcester. He had grounds for such confidence too. On 14 August Monck captured Stirling Castle and just as Cromwell closed in on Worcester, he captured the most important members of the Scottish executive, the Committee of Estates, at Alyth on 28 August. On 1 September Monck had stormed Dundee. In the wake of these victories, Montrose and Aberdeen had also fallen. By mid-November the war in Scotland was largely over. With the exception of several minor sieges military resistance was at an end. The republic had begun a month earlier to discuss absorbing Scotland into the republic. This 'anschluss' had not been a war aim; the point had been to prevent a royalist Scotland imposing its will on England and Wales rather than the other way around. The Scots' persistence with an aggressive alliance with Charles Stuart had changed this premise and Worcester facilitated a new direction, especially as the end of fighting in Ireland coincided with the collapse of Scotland. For the Cromwell family the Irish war brought tragedy: Bridget's husband, Oliver's close colleague Henry Ireton, had died. This was a great loss for Oliver: Ireton and he had fought together since 1643 and perhaps, despite Ireton's relative youth, it is not overstating the case to suggest that Cromwell had lost his most dependable political mentor. After Cromwell left Ireland, leaving Ireton in command, the royalist–confederation alliance fragmented further, with the Old Irish and the bishops refusing to accede to Ormond's demands to turn Limerick into his base.

The defeat and destruction of the Ulster Army at the battle of Scariffhollis in June 1650 prevented the alliance from any possibility of united action with Charles Stuart and the Scots, but in any case the appointment of the Bishop of Clogher as the army's commander had angered the Scots forces in eastern Ulster, the army of whom now abandoned the royalist cause and sided with the republic. By the end of summer 1650 the war was confined to western Connacht. In April 1651 Galway fell and by the summer of that year Ireton had invested Limerick and began to starve the city into surrender. In October, Ireton stormed the city and brought the siege to a bloody end. The long defiance had clearly angered him and he was vengeful towards the defenders, having seven executed in the wake of the siege: he had attempted to have Hugh O'Neill, Oliver's Irish nemesis killed too, but Ireton's fellow officers refused to accede to murdering the talented young commander. Ireton however, was ill by this point; having contracted a fever, he died on 26

November 1651 at the point at which his father-in-law could have done with his advice. On a personal level, Cromwell was saddened. Whitelock summed up both issues:

> [Ireton] was stout in the field, and wary and prudent in his councel, and exceedingly forward as to the business of a commonwealth; he married Cromwell's daughter, who had a great opinion of him; and no man could prevail so much nor order him so far as Ireton could.
>
> His death struck a great sadness into Cromwell; and indeed it was a great loss to him of so able and active, so faithful and so near a relation and officer under him.[3]

Although fighting in both peripheral nations continued into early 1652, the Republic could be seen as on the verge of complete victory at home when Cromwell wrote of the crowning mercy. The Channel Isles ceased their resistance in late 1651 and much further off, the West Indian Colonies submitted to the republic and the North American colonies would follow in 1652.

The victory at Worcester did impel discussions about the future of parliament and the political settlement of early 1649. There had been some discussion after Dunbar, but much of this was to focus on 'recruiter elections' similar to those at the end of the first civil war which would fill vacant spaces rather than call a new parliament. In mid-1651 the threat of Charles Stuart's invasion ended these discussions too. However after Worcester, the subject was reopened and Cromwell became involved. Whether or not Cromwell realised that at Worcester he had fought his last battle, he moved quickly into the world of politics. A bid to introduce a bill to set a terminal date for the present parliament and create a new one was debated for five weeks and passed by a bare majority in mid-November; Cromwell acting as a teller for the ayes. When the terminal date was set, however, there was broad agreement, but it was set for 3 November 1654: three years away and no less than fourteen years after it was first assembled. This would not please the radicals of the army, but neither would the discussions that followed.

On 10 December apparently at Cromwell's insistence a meeting was held at Speaker Lenthall's house to discuss 'a settlement of the nation'. The meeting included politicians Sir Thomas Widdrington, Oliver St John and Whitelock as well as the Speaker and officers Edward Whalley,

Thomas Harrison, John Desborough and Charles Fleetwood, as well as Oliver. Whitelock set the agenda: was there to be what he called 'an absolute republic' or would there be any 'mixture' of monarchy? Cromwell seemed open to the idea of a monarchy and the issue of 'in whom that power shall be placed'. Widdrington thought that a mixed monarchy was the best solution, and that it should be one of the sons of Charles I. St John agreed that the best way to govern England and Wales was a monarchy, for 'without something of a monarchical power, it will be very difficult to be settled as not to shake the foundations of our laws and the liberties of the people'. Lenthall concurred, but the officers were not convinced; Desborough asked why England was unique in being seemingly impossible to govern as a republic. Whitelock's response was extremely cautious and conservative arguing that the laws were so 'interwoven' with the 'power and practice' of a monarchy that making a new government without 'something' of a monarchy in it would lead to 'inconveniencies'. Whalley was sceptical. He asked who could be chosen but the dead king's eldest son? Charles and James, the second son of Charles I, were enemies who had fought against the republic. Widdrington suggested the third son Henry, but Whitelock suggested that there may yet be a treaty with Charles or James. Cromwell seemed to think this was very unlikely, but was prepared to go for a monarchical settlement.

Whitelock's notes of the meeting were brief, and he concluded that the officers were generally opposed to a monarchy, whilst the lawyers wanted a mixed monarchy. Cromwell, Whitelock suggested, had 'fished' for information about the participants' intentions. The diarist is not totally reliable: he had been a party to the 1644 conspiracy against Cromwell and he disliked the officers, claiming that it was ironic that the officers opposed a monarchy despite as he put it 'though each of them was a monarch in his own regiment or company'.[4] For conspiracy theorists past and present Whitelock provided a steer. Cromwell's aim would be interpreted as part of his own monarchical ambitions, using the meetings to see who supported the principle of a monarchy and to identify potential rivals. However, Austin Woolrych is probably correct when he interprets Cromwell's words as part of his generally conservative political approach: influenced here by his cousin St John's arguments, Cromwell was still looking for the stability that a mixed monarchy could bring by offsetting the power of each element of government through balancing them against each other. The question of course was who could be trusted, and for Cromwell the Stuarts were really suspect, despite the lawyers' preference for the family. Barry Coward also sees this as consistency within Cromwell dating it back to the *Heads of the Proposals* in 1647, and sees St John as central to Cromwell's role. Oliver St John was one of the few political allies Cromwell had retained from the early 1640s; in the mid-1640s Oliver St John had needed Cromwell more than ever. The 1648–1649 revolution had driven a wedge between Cromwell and the senior opponents of Charles I 1640 who had led the political revolution of the early 1640s. These men, lords Wharton and Saye and Sele included, had supported Cromwell throughout the war and been associated with him until the eve of the 1648–1649 revolution, but had eschewed the revolution itself. Barry Coward thinks that Cromwell's and St John's new allies in parliament, as well as being moderates, were political lightweights, and unable to work towards Cromwell's aim of promoting the interests of the army within parliament. On the other hand the army officers were unpopular and suspect. Moreover, Cromwell's work with parliament and his apparent conservatism was not popular with the radical members within the army.

Amongst certain sections of the army and civilian population the role of the army in the destruction of the British monarchy was nothing short of divine. Back in 1648 Mary Cary had elaborately worked out that the period of the first civil war equalled three and a half biblical days, referring to the period between the slaying of God's witnesses by 'the beast' and God's having resurrected them through breathing life back into them as described in *Revelation* Chapter 11. The implication of her exegesis was that the soldiers were Jehovah's witnesses bearing testimony to the millennium. Cary was not alone: even in the first civil war there had been some hopeful souls who identified such an unlikely figure as the Earl of Essex in the role of John the Baptist heralding the arrival of Christ. Then there were men like Thomas Harrison in the army who saw the defeat of the king in millennial terms heralding the second coming of Christ and the thousand-year reign of the saints. Harrison was part of a movement known as the Fifth Monarchists which believed that the fall of Charles I was the end of the fourth monarchy thereby combining Charles with the papal Roman 'monarchy' that had in turn succeeded the Babylonian, Egyptian and secular Roman 'monarchies'. The fifth monarchy would be that of Christ and the saints: Harrison and others had little trouble defining themselves as saints, but they were not always able to define who was a fellow traveller. For some people Cromwell was a case in point. Whilst he was seen as working in the army's interest then he seemed to be a saint; but there were times, back in 1647 for example, when Cromwell seemed to be running a different course. Now in 1651–1652 as Oliver attempted to turn the course of the anti-army feeling in parliament observers thought he had sold out to the enemies: the parliament which was becoming seen as an adjunct of the fourth monarchy rather than the forerunner of the fifth.

Cromwell personally left few contemporary clues to how he behaved between September 1651 and April 1653, the last eighteen months of the Rump Parliament. His views on the period were given in speeches he made in later years. Parliament, he argued later when he opened the Little Parliament on 4 July 1653, simply refused to exploit the victory given to them at Worcester:

> we came fully bent in our hearts and thoughts to desire and use all fair and lawful means we could, to have had the nation to reap the fruit of all that blood and treasure that had been expended in this cause; and we have many desires and thirstings in our spirits to find ways and means, wherin we might anyways be instrumental to help it forward. [5]

Occasionally MP soldiers reminded parliament that it should follow victory with reform, but parliament refused to deal with the issues the army wanted resolved: 'we had no at all that was satisfaction for us…'. Cromwell was concerned to point out that the army was patient. It waited until 'July or August last' said Cromwell who could not remember (it was August) before the army even petitioned parliament. Officers called a meeting of the Council of Officers on 2 August 1652 and drew up a list of demands, printed it and presented to Cromwell. As John Morrill has recently pointed out: it bore an uncompromising title 'Declaration of the armie to the lord general Cromwell for the dissolving of this present parliament'. Clearly as Austin Woolrych pointed out Cromwell approved of it, for he had chaired the meeting, but he did not sign it because he was an MP himself, and on subsequent days he had the language toned down. The more respectful version of the petition dealt with a series of social issues, the removal of ineffective ministers and their replacement by godly men supported by a new revenue system replacing tithes. Better treatment for the poor, old and infirm expanded the army's concern beyond its usual litany of requests for pensions for widows and orphans of soldiers (it still asked for the settlement of arrears of pay – an old army request). It wanted a cleansing of the corrupt and ineffective from the civil service and reform in the nation's fiscal machinery. Finally it wanted parliament to call new elections sooner than the November 1654 deadline set the previous autumn. This is the main area which Cromwell had had altered, and it was important that he did so. Whilst the petition did move along the track Cromwell had laid out after Dunbar and Worcester, it did not go all the way he intended, not mentioning reform of the law and practice of law as he had, Oliver wanted this to influence parliament. For a while it did.

A committee of influential soldier-MPs including Cromwell and civilian MPs under the chairmanship of John Carew was established to act on and report back on the army's points raised in the petition. The committee investigated action on the appointment of ministers, took over the responsibility for electoral reform and preparations for the new elections looked at provision for the poor. Nevertheless the same general torpor that had infected the Rump as a whole gripped Carew's committee and those temporarily reinvigorated by its enquiries: one by one the good intentions fell by the wayside, abandoned or sent into stasis on the floor of the house.

The frustration with parliament's broad-based failure to enact further reform divided the army from it, and drove Cromwell, who tried to nudge parliament along the path of reform, to side with the most disaffected. At this stage Cromwell was still working with both the remaining old parliamentary colleagues, like Henry Vane, and the more radical soldiers like Thomas Harrison, a man confidently expecting the arrival of Christ to rule with the saints for a thousand years. Yet he was losing his closeness to both. Vane was being alienated by Cromwell's apparent proximity to the army and its constant incursions onto parliamentary territory, whilst conversely, Cromwell's adherence to the 'parliamentary way' was driving a wedge between him and radicals like Harrison.

As has often been the case with Cromwell, people were trying to second guess his position and several accounts of Oliver's views about a monarchy or interpretations of what people thought he was saying about a monarchy survive. However, as with other such important periods, contemporary perception was quickly mixed with the clarity of vision conveyed by hindsight. Whitelock thought Cromwell was sounding him out about a seizure of power in the autumn of 1652 as the fog of inertia enveloped parliament's promising movements toward, if not reform itself, then discussions of reform. Cromwell and he met in St James's Park one November evening. Cromwell clearly wanted to discuss matters with Whitelock whom he flattered and with whom he tried to establish common ground; emphasising their service to the commonwealth. Cromwell moved to the specifics: 'there is very great cause for us to consider the dangerous condition we are all in'. He suggested that the commonwealth was now on the verge of bringing 'those mischiefs upon ourselves which our enemies could never do'. Whitelock and Cromwell quickly showed the gulf between them for the parliamentarian straight away took it, or seemed to imply that he understood that Cromwell was referring to the army, remarking that he was surprised that there were no mutinies, 'few thinking their services duly rewarded'. Cromwell on the other hand was thinking along a contrary route. He saw (or Whitelock portrayed him as seeing) parliament as the problem. The soldiers were not duly rewarded and parliament was filled with 'pride and ambition and self-seeking'. Worse was to come:

> Their delays of business and design to perpetuate themselves, and to continue the power in their own hands; their meddling in private matters between party and party, contrary to the institutions of parliaments; and their injustice and partiality in those matters, and the scandalous lives of the chief of them; these things, my lord, do give too much ground for people to open their mouths against them and dislike them.
>
> Nor can they be kept within the bounds of justice and law or reason, they themselves being the supreme power of the nation, liable to no account to any, nor to be controlled or regulated by any other power; there being non superior or coordinate with them.
>
> So that unless there be some authority and power so full and so high as to restrain and keep things in better order, and that may be a check to these exorbitances, it will be impossible in human reason to prevent our ruin.

Whitelock appeared a little taken aback: 'I am sure your excellency will not look upon them as generally depraved ... I hope well of the major part of them'. But Cromwell pressed on continuing to suggest that the potential for ruination of the commonwealth lay within parliament. Then suddenly he changed tack and asked, 'What if a man should take upon him to be king'. Some alternative authority could act as a brake on parliament's seeming arbitrary behaviour, establishing a check and balance as in the old system of a mixed monarchy. Oliver's question could be seen to presage the single person and a parliament idea enshrined in the Instrument of Government a year later. Yet the phraseology is odd, if Whitelock did, or ever intended to, remember it exactly. Cromwell did not ask in a neutral sense, a question such as 'What if we chose to have a king or monarch?', but asking what if someone should decide to be a king, perhaps to see what Whitelock's personal reaction to such a scenario would be. It is really impossible to know if Cromwell was seriously thinking of himself as a candidate for taking 'upon him to be king'. Whitelock's record of the conversation kept it personal, which might suggest that he thought Cromwell was thinking of himself: Whitelock seems to either be opposing Cromwell's thinking or to have changed his mind in order to come to this position before writing up a final record of the meeting. A year earlier Whitelock could be counted upon as cautiously monarchical, now he said 'I think that remedy would be worse than the disease'. He pointed out that Cromwell already had monarchical powers: he was commander of the army, a position in peace time held by the monarch; his candidates for civil office were usually chosen; legislation he did not like was usually unsuccessful; foreign embassies played court to him. Cromwell returned to an argument he had probably heard a year earlier at the last meeting where he and Whitelock had been discussing monarchy: that it was recognised in England that the state was more secure when the head was called a king, even if that king was not a direct descendant or a conqueror, than if the head of state had any other title. This was, Cromwell acknowledged, a lawyer's argument. Whitelock admitted it was a strong general argument, but in specifics it was weak. If Cromwell declared himself king then it would act as a destabilising factor: for it would alienate the supporters of the commonwealth who had opted for a free state and not a monarch. Moreover the monarchical faction would not necessarily support Cromwell, whilst there was an alternative monarch with a claim to the throne: 'and the question will be no more whether our government shall be by a monarch or by a free state, but whether Cromwell or Stuart'. It would be better to approach the king of the Scots and invite him to take the throne on severely restricted terms. This would have a double positive effect, getting the monarch on their terms and maintaining traditional legality. Cromwell, concluded Whitelock, had many secret enemies who could provoke rebellion if Cromwell were to become king. It is difficult to assess how accurate this record is. Whitelock clearly wrote some of it well after the event, for he added confirmation that Cromwell tended to treat him cautiously afterwards, sending him out of the way on important but distant tasks such as the embassy to Sweden: Cromwell's daughter Mary indicated as much to him.

Other observers certainly thought Oliver was a candidate for such a post: the German diplomat Herman Mylius thought of him as a potential doge whilst leading administrator John Dury saw him as in effect a king. But the conversation between Cromwell and Whitelock could have been completely hypothetical, using Cromwell as a convenient, appropriately placed, hypothetical candidate for a hypothetical job. That the basis of Cromwell's argument appeared so closely to resemble the role of a 'single person' of the Instrument of Government could have been instrumental in thinking yet to come, or the product of some degree of hindsight upon the part of the diarist is probable. Whatever the case, Cromwell was still some way from being a monarch in name or practice that November in St James's.

The political impasse that prompted Cromwell's constitutional musing continued to develop over the winter months as one by one the discussions on progress faltered. The frustrations of the army did not abate, but they were held in check by Cromwell, because for at least some of the time he was able to tell the soldiers that parliament was discussing the establishment of new elections for a new parliament. At the same time he pursued the aims he had attempted in 1647 to bridge the gap between the army and parliament through a series of 'conferences' whereby the two 'sides' communicated with each other. It is clear that he believed in a cause that subsumed the rivalries of these two elements within the state. He probably believed at least in late 1652 that both sides had the true interests of the nations at heart. There is much to commend J.S.A. Adamson's argument that Cromwell's view of the relationship between parliament and God's cause had changed after the end of the second civil war in 1648. Adamson suggests that parliament's sudden reopening of negotiations with the king changed Oliver's attitude to the 'legal proprieties of parliamentary authority' in an important way, and one that made his actions in April 1653 possible if not exactly comfortable for him. The authority of God and that of parliament that had appeared to be synonymous in 1642 were no longer so closely entwined, for how could it be if parliament felt able to negotiate with Charles I whom God had so clearly borne witness against? After Dunbar and Worcester, Cromwell suggested that God had granted power to parliament: but in trust not as an absolute. The implication was therefore that it could be removed. God had similarly placed trust in the army and the victories it obtained proved that this trust was still in place. If one or the other sacrificed that trust then the other could claim authority over it. As the winter continued Cromwell seemed to have worked on the basis that both bodies still shared in that trust.

By the spring the problems seemed to be about to be resolved. Parliament was discussing elections. But Whitelock seemed to detect a change. As the fighting in Scotland and Ireland came towards an end the army began to grow more confident, referring to its part in the defeat of the king's forces and the commonwealth's enemies. In Adamson's terms this would be an expression of the confidence that it had God's authority invested in it. The opposite side of the coin for Whitelock was that the army was now 'scarce owning the parliament'.[6] This was clearly more dangerous, for if the army saw itself as solely responsible for victory and the creation of the republic, then it could declare that parliament had lost the trust of God. The danger would really be if Cromwell could be brought to a similar belief. Whitelock approached Oliver on 7 April, but found him to be 'in distaste with the parliament and hastening their dissolution'.[7] Yet at this point Cromwell was probably thinking still that parliament would organise the means of its own dissolution and succession: back on 11 March he and Desborough had persuaded the army Council not to expel parliament by force, but on the other hand Cromwell had stopped attending either the Council of State or parliament within days of securing their agreement.

At the same time parliament was pursuing an intolerant approach to freedom of worship, something at the core of Cromwell's belief in God's intention and therefore his fiduciary relationship with parliament. On 1

April the Commission for Propagating the Gospel in Wales came to the end of its term and instead of being continued, parliament threw out the bill for its renewal. For Cromwell and more so for the Fifth Monarchists in the army the commission had been at the forefront of religious reform in the country; but parliament had harboured mistrust of its support for radical ministers, particularly Fifth Monarchists. Parliament did little to keep Cromwell happy. It had even proposed selling Hampton Court, which it had awarded Cromwell after his victories over the Scots. Suspending the sale was one of the few things parliament had done to try and keep Cromwell contented as April 1653 wore on. The discussions in parliament on the plan for its dissolution and the election of its successor had proceeded very slowly, with only a regular debate each Wednesday. At the end of March MPs had decided on the property qualification for electors and upon the geographical and demographic redistribution of constituencies, but on 6 April, the following Wednesday, they devoted the afternoon to other business. Austin Woolrych believes that this might be a final straw for Cromwell and the army and that it was now that he and they planned a more drastic solution. The debate did continue on 13 April, but somewhat ominously, Cromwell attended the sessions later that week. On the Monday and Tuesday of the following week Oliver convened meetings of the Council of Officers and a meeting of twenty MPs and an equal number of officers. The plan he discussed was an immediate appointment of an executive committee to govern in the absence of a parliament and charged with holding elections, followed by the immediate dissolution of the house. Whitelock and Sir Thomas Widdrington argued that such an action was dangerous and of dubious legality, whilst Oliver St John supported Cromwell as did most, if not all of the officers. The MPs present were pressured into agreeing and to presenting this to the house on 20 April. Moreover, they were expected to steer this proposal through the parliament that day and secure the implementation of it.

On the morning of 20 April Cromwell met with some officers and MPs, including Whitelock, to draw plans for the interim government which would have consisted of forty officers and MPs. Whitelock claimed that he continued to oppose the move; whilst other MPs began to approve of the plan because they believed that they would be included in the forty, Whitelock opposed it on exactly the same grounds, he effectively accused compliant MPs of venality, whilst painting himself as a concerned constitutionalist claiming that there would be no legal basis for the interim government and he did not want to be in such a parlous position. During the morning's discussions news came from Westminster that parliament was in session. The MPs with Cromwell left for the house but found it not to be discussing dissolution, but suddenly hastening through its own bill setting up a new parliament.

When Cromwell heard what was happening he gathered a squad of soldiers and marched down the road to parliament. He left the soldiers outside and took his seat in the chamber. There were about a hundred MPs there, double the usual number for the weekly sessions on the bill. It would seem that Cromwell's plan had prompted concerted opposition and the parliament was determined to complete its own bill that day. As the bill was about to be put to a vote Cromwell stood up and began to speak. He opened by praising parliament's past actions, but swiftly turned to an attack on its recent negligence. Then came the point: 'It is not fit that you should sit here any longer. You have sat here too long for any good you have been doing lately'. As a profound mark of disrespect he put his hat on and turned on three MPs in particular, Thomas Chaloner, Henry Marten and Sir Peter Wentworth, the latter of whom had tried to interrupt Cromwell's attack on the house. 'Some of them were Whoremasters', he looked at Marten, 'living in open contempt of God's Commandments', embracing Wentworth in his gaze, 'others of them were drunkards',[8] he looked at Challoner. It was also thought that Whitelock was encompassed in a glance made while Oliver spoke. In the course of the outburst he had got Harrison to call in soldiers, whose presence began to persuade reluctant and confused MPs that it was probably safest to leave. It must have prayed on the minds of older MPs including Cromwell that there were two instances in the recent past that bore similarity: the expulsion of the 1628–9 parliament when the speaker was sat upon and held in his chair, and 4 January 1642 when Charles I had burst into parliament to arrest the five members of the commons. There were distinct differences to the latter: Charles had not dared to bring the musketeers into the chamber, and then Speaker William Lenthall had held his seat in defiance of the breach of authority. This time Lenthall was prized out by the simple technique of being offered an elbow to lean on by Thomas Harrison. Cromwell picked up the mace and mused, 'What shall we do with this bauble?' before commanding a musketeer to take it away.[9]

For much of Cromwell's life if is difficult to assess his motivation because of the accidental absence of firm evidence. In this instance we are left bereft of the central motive to Cromwell's actions because he firstly stole the evidence and then later gave contradictory versions of his explanation of events. In the clerk's hand was the bill that was under discussion: Cromwell snatched the Act of Dissolution, which was ready to pass, out of his hand, he put it under his cloak, and having commanded the doors to be locked up, 'went away to Whitehall' and presumably destroyed it.[10] The possibility is that the spur to his actions on 20 April could have been a misunderstanding. Cromwell claimed that the bill under discussion was a new version of the recruiter ordinance of the 1640s designed to fill vacant seats in the current parliament. We cannot be certain, but the implication of Cromwell never producing the actual bill, which would have been an easier way to settle the argument, is that the bill was a genuine proposal for a new parliament and dissolution of the present one. Cromwell may well have over-reacted in the wake of weeks of growing frustration with the slowness of parliament to embrace the trust placed in it by God for the reformation of society. It would have been difficult for Oliver to accept that the house genuinely expected to finish the work on a bill that had taken months to progress so far in a single day, and that this had caused him to expect them instead to be discussing something simpler. Yet another image from Cromwell's past comes to mind: his outbursts in Huntingdon in 1630 when he attacked the beneficiaries of the new borough charter. We have no record of the scene when Cromwell made his allegations about the new councillors, but it probably was a forerunner of 20 April 1653.

There is no doubt that 20 April was a disturbing incident. Cromwell found it deeply depressing. As the last MPs left the chamber that day, he looked at Sir Henry Vane who had been at his house the previous day discussing the interim government. Vane had protested, 'This is not honest'. Cromwell responded, 'Oh Sir Henry Vane! Sir Henry Vane! The Lord deliver me from thee Sir Henry Vane!' Oliver may have felt that Vane had let him down that day, because he added he 'might have prevented this extraordinary course' or alternatively 'that you might have prevented this extraordinary course, but he was a Juggler and have not so much as common honesty'.[11] There were more than just earthly considerations. Cromwell felt instantly the need to justify what he had just done in the face of clear reproach from shocked MPs against whom he could probably not launch vitriolic personal attacks. 'It is you who have forced me to this. I have sought the Lord night and day, that he would rather slay me than put me upon the doing of this work'.[12]

It was not over when the great doors of St Stephen's Chapel closed. The Council of State still met later that day and the MPs and other members on it were angry. Cromwell arrived at the meeting and more or less told them they could meet quietly as 'private persons' but as there was no parliament, nothing that derived authority from it could still act. Bradshaw attacked Cromwell: ' Sir we have heard what you did at the House in the morning, and before many hours all England will hear it: but, Sir, if you are mistaken to think that the parliament is dissolved, for no power under heaven can dissolve them but themselves; therefore you take notice of that'.[13] Bradshaw was technically right: it was what the revolution of 1640–1641 had been about – no creature of that revolution should have been able to overturn that truth and Cromwell and the army were both creatures of that revolution, but Cromwell would be dead before that essential truth would out and the Long Parliament sit again. For the time being it was the revolution of 1648–1649 and its creator, the army, which was in the driving seat and its rules would be followed. The council of state was also expelled that day.

April 20 was a watershed: the culmination, some would argue, of Cromwell's overall plan. It was no such thing: there was no plan. There were ideas, held by members of the army which included expelling the Long Parliament, and ideas about what would succeed it which would surface as days passed, but on 20 April Cromwell himself had no plan to expel parliament: he usually let others take such dramatic actions whilst he stayed away, like at Holdenby House in June 1647 and parliament in December 1648. This time there was no son-in-law around whom ideas coagulated: the expulsion had been Cromwell's work; probably an explosion of anger inspired, perhaps by a mistaken impression, based on months of discontent and frustration, but not upon months of planning. Colin Davis suggests that 20 April saw Cromwell as a 'political actor' throwing caution to the wind, Christopher Hill saw it as the culmination of Cromwell's growing self-confidence, they and Barry Coward agree, in the end it was a spontaneous act. Cromwell was under contradictory pressures by this point. He seemingly remained convinced that he was a man of God: his letters in the 1650s invoke far more direct references to biblical precedents as if he were attempting to assure his readers that the he was not acting alone. People told him that he was acting in God's interest: minister William Erbery had told him that God had granted him great victories; relatives, John Desborough and Henry Ireton had implied the same thing, but both wisely had reminded him of the perils of the self-confidence this might inspire: Desborough of the slipperiness of high places, Ireton, using a reference to Hezekiah king of Israel who squandered his God-given victories, warned him of the sin of self-reliance. Cromwell seems most of the time to have heeded this advice, it is something which kept him working with parliament until 20 April. It would seem that that day's action was neither consummate nor confident.

Of course on 21 April there had to be a plan. Cromwell remarked of the expulsion 'there was not so much as the barking of a dog'.[14] Nevertheless it was a momentous act, which had to be followed by action no less important: a new government had to be created. There had been discussions of creating an interim government, both within the army and between officers and MPs, particularly on 18–19 April, but often these had generally assumed that the Long Parliament would have had some role in its own expulsion and thereby in setting up the successor. Now the slate was clean. Two days afterwards the army issued a statement claiming that it had been driven to expelling parliament. In the meantime a group of ten officers and former MPs closely associated with Cromwell began to meet and act as an executive. On 30 April it declared itself to be a Council of State: it is important to note that it did so through Cromwell alone, underlining the impression that Cromwell was central to the expulsion of the Long Parliament and post expulsion-government. It is of course a great fillip to the notion of Cromwell's conspiracy and fits with the most restrictive reading of Whitelock's discussion with Cromwell. However, for a man so seemingly obsessed with obtaining power, Cromwell was quickly giving it away. The Council of Officers played a more crucial role in creating the new 'constitution' than the new Council which acted only as an interim executive. The senior officers in some ways played the role of a constitutional assembly; however it was really a fore-runner to a constitutional assembly for it was to create an assembly that would create the new constitution. There was civilian involvement; Cromwell called in his cousin former Solicitor general Oliver St John to discuss a new constitution. For a would-be king such a method would be fraught with impediments and delays with no guarantee of eventual success.

The officers decided to create a compact assembly of representatives from across the British Isles – it would be the first assembly of the four united nations. The members would represent the counties, towns and regions of the isles, but they would be nominated by the officers, not elected. This gathering of the Godly would be controversial, but temporary, for if the assembly fulfilled the role planned for it an elected assembly would follow by the mid or late 1650s. The plan owed much to Thomas Harrison's theocratic approach: he had suggested an assembly of godly men chosen by the independent congregations across the country: a combination of Presbyterian structures and the biblical Sanhedrin. Harrison being a Fifth Monarchist thought that this group would rule until Christ returned to dwell on earth, in the not too distant future. But a more practical sense dictated the notion of a fixed term and an invocation to establish a successor body. Any ambitious dictator would ensure that he or she nominated the majority of members, but whilst Cromwell played a role in the process, he was no more that *primus inter pares* in this process and this is probably an indicator of the role he was playing during these few months. From around the British Isles, the occupying forces began sending in declarations supporting the expulsion and subsequent actions of the officers and Cromwell. That these expressions of support came from Edinburgh, Leith, Dalkeith, Ireland, Durham and other counties of the country masks the fact that they largely came from one constituency: the army. Also whilst the navy also sent its approbation, the effect was that support came from the armed forces not the country as a whole. In particular neither Scotland nor Ireland were really appreciative of the historical nature of what the officers were doing by establishing a one nation assembly. Ireland had been offered no choice in its political future as in the wake of the collapse of the Kilkenny government there was no body or collective political elite that the republic was prepared to do business with. In Scotland, whilst there was a political elite, the proposed union was not truly a 'take it or leave it' affair: it was a take it or have it imposed matter. In all the two conquered nations were represented by just eleven men: Englishmen from the occupying power chiefly.

The new assembly would have 140 members. The writs calling the assembly together were issued in June and the date for the assembly set for 4 July. When the assembly opened the temporary Council of State would cease to exist, for the assembly was to be both legislative and executive. Cromwell welcomed the members with a speech that was to be both a history lesson and an optimistic call for action. He used the speech to legitimise what he had done. The blame for the Long Parliament's expulsion lay with the parliament itself for it planned a series of recruiter elections to fill the vacancies, rather than a completely new representative. This plainly 'was not according to God'. Later in the speech, Cromwell elaborated. This perpetuation was not the only worry, although even a good parliament would have been abusing its trust by such an act. The concurrent problem was that there appeared to be no safeguards established in the proposed election plan to exclude royalist voters from electing a parliament of erstwhile enemies to the state. Cromwell could not or rather would not prove this. The bill on the clerks' table on April 20, which he had picked up, never saw the light of day, but not one of the former MPs in the new assembly contradicted the story.

After the history lesson, Cromwell reminded the delegates in front of him that they were here to do God's work. Thus it was he rather than the Council of Officers that had called them hence. The army officers whom he implied were 'saints' had been 'somewhat instrumental to your call'. The army he was suggesting was the manifestation of God's witnesses, a reference that recalled Mary Carey's prophesy back in 1648 when she had likened the army to Jehovah's witnesses. The new delegates were to join with the army. The assembly was, however, not to think of itself as somehow special. In the way that Ireton and Desborough had warned Oliver about becoming drunk on the sense of power Cromwell reminded the assembly that it was to govern justly and in the interests of all:

> ... have a care for the whole flock. Love all the sheep, love the lambs, love all and tender all, and cherish all, and countenance all in all things that are good. And if the poorest Christian, the most mistaken Christian, should desire to live peaceably and quietly under you, soberly and humbly desire to lead a life in godliness and honesty, let him be protected.

This seems to reflect Cromwell's tolerance; it did not even prescribe Protestantism, for a mistaken Christian could encompass a Roman

Catholic. Cromwell expressed unbounded confidence in the assembly who were owned by and owned Jesus Christ; he underlined the unique situation of their being together. The number 140 looks small when compared to a parliament, but Cromwell saw it as an executive and commented on its size: 'there never was a supreme body, consisting of so numerous a body as you are'. He acknowledged the diversity: 'indeed I am confident you are strangers, coming from all parts of the nation as you do'. He ended by informing the assembly that the council would sit to ensure caretaker management until the assembly asked it to disband.[15] Cromwell had great hopes for the assembly and he seemed in his speech to be rejoicing at its assembly, almost Barry Coward suggests being swept along by Harrison's millennial enthusiasm. It was to sit for up to sixteen months and three months before the end of its session it was to create the means of appointing a successor. The day following the assembly kept a fast and appointed a chair: Francis Rous and co-opted Cromwell, John Lambert, John Desborough and Thomas Harrison as members.

The new assembly took on the name parliament, which it had not been expected to do and created a new council of state, which included Cromwell, and it began to enact a series of reforms; marriage became a civil ceremony, debtors were to be provided with relief in prison, creditors were to be assisted, proposals were made for the reform of the law, and by December the funding of the churches of England was being discussed. Parliament had committees on education, law, poverty, trade, the army, Ireland and Scotland (the unions with these two nations were left incomplete at the end of the Long Parliament), prisons and treasuries. It was a busy parliament. However, it was not a complete success: it failed to bring the war with Holland to an end, it faced a rebellion in Scotland and its relationship with the army was problematic. It also attracted some derision: the best name for the assembly was the Little Parliament, although it referred to itself or allowed others to call it the parliament of the Commonwealth (sometimes of England!). However, others called it Barebone's parliament. This was a reference to Praise-God Barebone, or Barbon, a London merchant. Through him the name referred to the Fifth Monarchist group in parliament which included Thomas Harrison. These men formed part of a radical minority that pressed for the radical changes to the law and finance and pressed for particular severity towards royalists and Catholics. The title Barebone's was an attempt to tar the parliament with accusations of religious fundamentalism. In contrast the majority of members was less radical, but as Ronald Hutton says, only conservative when compared with the radicals. This majority comprised Cromwell's nominees and relatives, including Desborough. The disputes between these factions began to slow the output of legislation and the work of the assembly declined in effectiveness.

Oliver Cromwell sat rarely in either the parliament or the council of state, although he did attempt to become involved in diplomatic moves relating to the war with Holland – unlike Harrison and his colleagues, Oliver did not see it as part of a millennial struggle with the antichrist, not least because the Dutch were Protestants, and of course he was directing the affairs of the army. He was also Chancellor of Oxford University and active in its business. But he was, even before the summer was over, growing despondent with his hopeful saints. On 22 August he wrote to his son-in-law Charles Fleetwood, second husband to Ireton's widow and now commander in chief there. It purported to be an informal family letter apologising for the long gap between correspondence and including the sending of love to Bridget and the baby. Affairs in parliament, Cromwell felt were beset by the factionalism and felt that both directed their ire at him: he claimed to feel like Moses beset by arguing Hebrews and berated when he tried to act as mediator. He even included a reference to Psalm 55: 'Oh, would I the wings like a dove'.[16] He was a man truly fed up and disillusioned, with a parliament which was through its own factionalism failing to heal the rifts in post-war Britain and Ireland. This dove was very different to the dove of satin and gold he had envisaged in his speech to parliament on 4 July. Moreover, this parliament like those before it was not heeding Oliver's demand for tolerance: Presbyterians were being attacked physically with tacit approbation from factions in the assembly, despite Cromwell's calls for them to 'love the sheep, love the lambs'.[17] Cromwell was forced to intervene through his clerical associates. If he had hoped to be able to withdraw from the front rank of national politics, and remain a faithful servant of the state, he would soon be disabused of this too. The factions in the nominated assembly soon split apart irrevocably.

As the weeks passed attendance amongst the moderate majority began to fall away leaving the radicals with more chance of success of introducing new legislation. An early decision to retain the tithes as a basis for funding the ministries in England and Wales was by November being debated, and with moderate majorities falling, in danger of being revoked. Indeed this was a harbinger of a greater threat, the idea, held by some Fifth Monarchists, that the reforms to the law and treasury would end in the introduction of Mosaic Law – a code of laws derived from Moses's ten commandments and other biblical injunctions. Disaffection had, in some quarters, led to the discussions of the competence of the assembly to pass legislation when some had perceived its chief function to be that of a constitutional assembly rather than a legislative in its own right. It was during a debate on tithes and upon the establishment of a series of commissions into the state of the ministry and the tithes, that a section of the moderates sabotaged the assembly on 12 December. When the first part of the bill, that which dealt with the suitability of ministers fell, it looked likely that the support expressed for the principle of tithes in the later part of the bill might fail also, thus opening tithes to attack. Before this could happen a motion was proposed suddenly: 'the sitting of this parliament any longer would not be for the good of the commonwealth, and that it would be fit for them to resign their power to the Lord General'.[18] The motion was put to the vote and passed. With seeming ease a large number of representatives accompanying the speaker who carried the mace left the chamber and went to Cromwell with a prepared statement ceding their powers to him. Apparently the lord general was thunderstruck. Cromwell always maintained that he had no idea that this was about to happen.

Others had known that it would, for a replacement constitution was at hand. The Instrument of Government had dry ink. This new work was probably principally the creation of John Lambert, and despite what it portended for Oliver, was not therefore something that came from his own immediate circle of colleagues. Peter Gaunt and other historians and biographers are rightly more sceptical and accept that Cromwell had been occasionally consulted about the form of a new government in the second half of November, largely because of hints dropped by them and even Cromwell later. Within a week of the collapse of the Nominated Assembly a new constitution was approved by the army and Cromwell was offered the post of head of state, using an old monarchical caretaker title, last used during the minority reign of Edward VI: Lord Protector.

The Instrument of Government was ready within days and the ceremony installing Oliver Cromwell as Lord Protector was held in Westminster Hall on Friday 16 December 1653. This was in effect the first public acknowledgement that Cromwell's position in British and Irish society was as unique as the situation the four nations found themselves in during the 1650s. Oliver had been central to the relationship between parliament and the army since 1647. Initially he had not been quite unique, but as the revolution pressed on and the army became thoroughly alienated from the parliament, the conservative Cromwell, versed in the post-reformation monarchical state, became unique. As his military rivals fell by the wayside, on the battlefield or voluntarily, he became the centre of the soldiers' focus, even if not entirely trusted. There was no figure in parliament to rival him, indeed no one to provide the house with a leader in its own right. After Pym's death there had been important figures in parliament, colleagues and relations of Cromwell's such as Oliver St John, Saye and Sele, who would support Cromwell up to a point, and political opponents like Holles. There were strong characters in the republican parliaments and governments, men like Henry Marten or Sir Arthur Hesilrige, but if they led anyone then they were factional leaders only, not uniquely placed to lead the whole house. Of course neither was Cromwell, he could not command the house, and nor did he command a particularly strong faction that could steer the house. His strength lay in the army, even if his loyalty lay in the legitimacy of parliament (and his heart in a monarchy). In 1640 Cromwell was a gentleman cum administrator turned politician, but by 1653 he was a soldier politician. In the early forties Cromwell was a man used to working in the often petty worlds of urban and rural politics and Westminster's intricacies may have seemed familiar. He was also part of a parliament well led and part of a dominant political impetus. By contrast, by the end of the decade he was a changed man: it would seem that he had become accustomed to the clarity offered by military structures; the certainty of the relationship between command, order and action had been central to the victories he had gained on the field, the Gordian knot of politics, in a parliament that was not well led and contained no dominant impetus, was so entangled that command and action were not clearly linked if they were linked at all. In the end he acted as a soldier, drew his sword and cut through it. In turn this made him the man to whom soldiers and some politicians turned to by default. The problem that would be increasingly important from now on was that Cromwell had never learned to be a politician.

The Instrument of Government has been described as a monarchical system. It has been claimed that the title of king was included initially in the document only to be excised by Cromwell. It bears similarities to the Heads of the Proposals given to the king, but it bears unmistakable republican traits. The structure at the heart of government was certainly familiar. Government was to be in the hands of a single individual, a council and parliament, outwardly similar to a monarch, privy council and parliament. Yet this was a revolutionary structure, the single person was not of royal blood, there because of talent (although not political or civil administrative ones), the council of state was likewise assembled because of the members' talents, and parliament was unicameral. There would remain no automatic role for the aristocracy in the executive or legislature. The distribution of parliamentary seats would be reorganised along lines suggested amongst others by the Levellers, and for the first time in English history the county of Durham would have elected representatives: it would no longer be a fiefdom of the Bishop of Durham and represented only in the House of Lords. Moreover, like the Little Parliament the protectorate parliaments would be imperial, representing the whole British Isles. But the monarchical traits were there: Oliver was lord protector for life, and his investiture was the first state event since the trial of the king and the first state celebration since the coronation of Charles I in Scotland in 1633. Oliver was led into Westminster Hall behind the architect of the constitution, John Lambert who carried the sword of state. Ahead of him gathered around the old royal throne were the civil and military leaders who had survived or supported the radical changes of government for the last four years: generals and other officers, parliamentary officials and lawyers, members of the Council of State. Cromwell's subordination to the constitution was affirmed whilst as he stood, the Instrument of Government was read out. He was then invited to take the throne after which the assembled new elite swore loyalty. Tinges of royalty mixed with the revolutionary. Unusual men in almost recognisable traditions: no crown, a constitution in written form read out before the leader took office, reform that many of the king's opponents in 1640–1642 would have liked to have been able to put in place, but not many of these men were there, they had been left behind by the revolution. After the ceremony His Highness Lord Protector Oliver Cromwell returned to Whitehall Palace the seat of his government. He and his council would work alone for nine months: parliament would sit on 4 September 1654 the day after the Lord Protector's and the republican states' auspicious day.

From 16 December 1653 the state was a protectorate, with a forty-two-clause constitution. The first clause confirmed the single person and parliament idea; the council of state that was to rule with Oliver was established in clause two, with a quorum of thirteen and a top limit of twenty-one members. The commonwealth parliament's executive powers inherited in turn from the king, passed to the lord protector in the third clause. Parliament was to have a role in the 'disposition' of the armed forces when sitting, the council, by majority rule in its absence, and foreign policy too was to be undertaken by consent and advice: both aims of the wartime parliament. Parliament was to be triennial, and had to sit for a minimum of five months unless it consented to its own dissolution, again both facets inherited from the early 1640s. The representation of English and Welsh counties was standardised, whereas the representation of Scotland and Ireland was to be decided in the meantime by the lord protector and the council. The transfer of authority was stressed both within the constitution and in the proclamation that followed the ceremony; a few days later Oliver issued a proclamation confirming the retention of local administrators in office to affirm the continuance of order in the change of regime. By Christmas the new state was in place.

The new state had inherited two wars, one in the highlands of Scotland and the war with the United Provinces provoked by the Navigation Act of 1651. Oliver sought to end both. He had not been in favour of the war with the Dutch and was keen to bring an end to it. But the war in Scotland was the most immediate and threatening. By the time the protectorate came into being a coalition of highland clans with royalist backing was able to dominate certain areas of the highlands and raid the lowlands as far as the English border. Limited military resources were the benefit of the perceived 'peace dividend' in Scotland and this looks like a case of over confidence on the part of the commonwealth as it enabled the spread of the war. In 1654 this coalition of chiefs was consolidated into a single rebellion under the leadership of John Middleton. Oliver sent George Monck, the man who had delivered a conquered Scotland to the Commonwealth, back to the scene of his impressive victories in April that same year to build upon Robert Lilburne's sound strategy of isolating the rebellious clans, and to cap this with a vigorous campaign. Victory would follow, but it took thirteen months.

By contrast the war with the Dutch was soon over. In the same month as Monck was sent to Scotland the Treaty of London was signed. By its terms the Protectorate gained ownership of an island, Pula Run in the East Indies, compensation for merchant shipping attacked by the Dutch navy, and acceptance of the Navigation Act by the United Provinces. Moreover, the United Provinces would exclude the House of Orange from government to end working relations with their in-laws the House of Stuart. There was little that really hurt the provinces, it was in their interest to end the war and exclude the House of Orange that tended to try to dominate politics. The money was a significant loss, but the return to normal lucrative trading would have offset that. Pula Run was never ceded *de facto*. Nevertheless, the protectorate gained a reputation for success in the field of foreign diplomacy and a string of trade deals followed, with Sweden and Portugal in the summer and Denmark in the autumn.

April was a busy month, for Oliver. The new state gave him the palaces of the royal family: Whitehall, Westminster, St James's Palace, Somerset House, Greenwich House, Windsor Castle and the King's Manor, York. He had already been given Hampton Court. The Cromwells remained at the Cockpit by St James's until April when they moved to Whitehall. This became the official state residence, although later in the regime Oliver tended to use Hampton Court for business as well. Cromwell generally did a working week at Whitehall and retired to Hampton Court for the weekend as the regime wore on. The protectoral household resembled a royal court and the family a royal one. Elizabeth became her Highness the Lady Protectoress; together she and her husband moved to the refurbished Whitehall apartments on 14 April and became the head of the household at the palace, which had a steward to run the 'below stairs', the kitchens and the logistical arrangements and a chamberlain to administer 'above stairs', the domestic and state affairs in the protectoral apartments; which included diverse elements such as the wardrobe and the provision of music as well as the organisation of state banquets. Also living with Elizabeth and Oliver were the young daughters, Mary and Frances; and also Mrs Elizabeth Cromwell the fifty-five-year-old protector's eighty-eight-year-old mother. Wife Elizabeth was apparently never comfortable with being the wife of the head of state, although no-one who knew her ever levelled criticism. She and her husband found it faintly embarrassing if necessary to be surrounded by the trappings of a royal court. Often too cowed to attack the protector directly, some attacked Elizabeth instead, presenting her as a coarse countrywoman out of her depth in a royal household in a city. She was labelled Joan, thought to be a typical country wife's name. A cookery book was published by Randal Taylor under her name a decade later in a continuation of these slurs.[19] It is an odd collation, political invective levelled at Elizabeth and Oliver combined with recipes that have little direct connection with the protectoress except for hints that they were favourite dishes, such as Marrow Pudding (which she had for her Breakfast) or the insinuation that the dishes were somehow rustic. Even in this Taylor was inconsistent because some of the recipes were for sophisticated meals. The imputation that Elizabeth was a plain Joan is really quite a bizarre one and probably only served as a vehicle for labelling her husband the one time 'lord of the fens'. For unlike Oliver, Elizabeth's move to London in the 1640s was a return. She was a city-girl, daughter of a prosperous merchant. If either were more sophisticated than the other, then Elizabeth would be the candidate. But Oliver was a gentleman, versed in the qualities of gentility, a nephew of the owner of the courtly Hinchingbrooke House, courtier Sir Oliver. In any case, aping the high-born is hardly a difficult task compared to the roles Cromwell had experienced since 1640.

The new protector's real detractors came not from the scurrilous fourth estate or their royalist pipers. In England the royalist cause was largely moribund, although it would make one sustained attempt to revivify itself during the protectorate; no challenge on the scale of the highland rising could be mounted in England or Wales. The royalist secret service the Sealed Knot would be continually outwitted by the protectorate state. No, Cromwell's real enemies came from amongst the ranks of the army and those groups who believed that he had betrayed them. Cromwell at several points in the 1650s doubted that he was truly taking the path God had ordained and read into failures of the regime evidence of apostasy. Others were even more convinced. The Fifth Monarchists believed themselves betrayed. Until December 1653 there had been at least a residual belief that Cromwell was a part of the regime of saints that would witness (bring about) the second coming of Christ – in effect the fifth monarchy predicted in the Revelation story of the four horned goat. Each of the horns represented the major pre-Christian monarchies and the Roman Catholic church. The appearance of a small horn on the fourth of the goat's horns had been interpreted as

Charles I's regime: because it was an appendage of the Church of Rome. From the end of 1653 the small horn of the fourth horn was increasingly identified with Cromwell. In twenty-first century common parlance Cromwell was now recognised as 'part of the problem' not 'as part of the solution'. More secular versions of this belief in Cromwell's apostasy were held by sections of the army that demanded a radical outcome to the revolution. By becoming protector, Cromwell seemed to be dragging the revolution back to the monarchical state from which it had escaped. The protectorate was to have a difficult birth.

Peter Gaunt has argued that at the creation of the protectorate the personal Cromwell all but disappears. The private letters dry up and we are increasingly thrown back upon the official papers and speeches of a head of state, which betray little of the man whose rise to power is so remarkable. To historians and those others interested in Cromwell it is almost as if the biography is over: the fascination with Cromwell is how he achieved such a remarkable position; once there the story ends. Moreover, according to some historians, the protectorate is an anticlimax, for Cromwell fails to make a mark. Worse, his very presence dooms the republic to being consigned to the role of an experiment: an experiment that failed. There is truth in all of this: Cromwell was swept from the military environment in which he had been a striking success into one marked in the past at Huntingdon, in the first two sessions of the Long Parliament, 1647 and 1651–1653 where he had met with failure and frustration. From commanding an army that worked precisely because of obedience and order to managing politicians something akin to herding cats. Yet this is not the whole story. Getting into power is not what makes Cromwell so fascinating; his government could have been swept away or crumbled just as the republic was to do after his death: no, it was the success of the Lord Protector that gave Oliver's name to the whole period. No one striving for success or achieving a brief tenure in government can achieve that. It is the protectorate that gave us the Cromwellian era: for that reason the biography has to continue.

Of course other people made observations of Cromwell the man and head of state. Richard Baxter was determined to try and fathom the man, when he went to see Oliver early in the protectorate to give a sermon, but also to explore the protector's religious intentions. He was subjected to two speeches, both long and tedious. The first centred upon God's will and the creation of the protectorate. Baxter asked about the monarchy: 'we took our ancient monarchy to be a blessing and not an evil to the land, and humbly craved his patience that I might ask him how England had ever forfeited that blessing, and unto whom that forfeiture was made'. Cromwell argued that God had changed his mind over the nature of government, rather than England being forfeit. Baxter's observations are interesting for they describe Cromwell's manner of speaking 'speaking this slowly', 'slow tedious speech' occasionally 'awakened into some passion'. But there was another observation, that Cromwell seemed not to listen to others 'being more disposed to speak many hours than to hear one, and little heeding what another said when he had spoken himself'.[20] Is Baxter describing introspection and self-reliance, Cromwell's need to relay all he read and heard to God, or a slow reflective process? The answer lies in perspective. Cromwell was not an original thinker, he absorbed political and perhaps religious ideas from those around him, involving a reflective period; in his own terms he would be wrestling with God over the issue. Baxter was there to be milked for ideas. It is also possible that Cromwell's long slow speeches were part of the mental process of working out an idea. It is possible that his speeches to parliament were part of the same process of working through ideas, and this might explain the contradictions within reason, especially those that explained the end of the Commonwealth.

In the meantime the council was busy. It would be 4 September before parliament sat, but there had to be a great deal put in place. On 20 December Oliver and the council proclaimed that all law officers and administrators were to remain in place for the time being and all laws and ordinances in place on 10 December were to remain in effect until further notice meaning the country continued to function during the transition. An investigation of constables' accounts across the country conveys a picture of smooth transition between commonwealth parliament, Barbone's and the protectorate's executive government. At Upton in Nottinghamshire constables Gervaise Cullen (1653) and William Parlthorpe (1654) passed the weeks of the establishment of the protectorate in the usual round of duties: paying assessment levies, attending the Court Leet, making payments to soldiers going home from service in Scotland, and importantly being present at the plough day quarter sessions at Newark where Cullen handed over to Parlthorpe. These same accounts reflect the intensity of national events and their impact upon the village during the 1640s and early 1650s. The fact that nothing remarkable is noted as 1653 moved into 1654 and commonwealth transformed into protectorate is important. Cromwell came to power against the background of stability. The constitution was published on 2 January for this was to be a public visible act like the execution of the king. Moreover some of the local administrators and officers were actively ensuring not only that the protector was acclaimed publicly by local authorities, but used occasions like assizes to explain the new regime and give 'great satisfaction' to 'the people'. The council continued to define the new rules, in late January it defined the nature of treason; the next month the army's treasury was sorted and commissioners for the nation's assessments came into place. The council established rules for the custody of idiots and lunatics, established the values of assessments and explained some of its earlier ordinances as February continued. In March its committee for approving church ministers began to sit, it ensured that wills and probate matters were dealt with and prohibited cock-fights, yet another prohibited the growing of tobacco in England protecting the economy of far-flung colonies absorbed into the republic. Crucially the proposals for union with Scotland were presented to the Scots, and the war with the United Provinces was brought to an end.

Cromwell had probably opposed the Dutch war at its inception: he certainly wanted it to end quickly and he was disappointed that the Little Parliament had failed to end it. The war had begun in summer 1652 in the wake of failed attempts to form a close alliance with the United Provinces, and the failure of negotiations over the October 1651 Navigation Act. The war was popular with the republic's commercial sector that wanted to force the United Provinces into acceding to the tight restrictions imposed by the Navigation Act and hoped for a successful war against the carriers of European trade. War had mainly gone in the merchants' favour, over a thousand Dutch ships were captured in the two years it lasted and the general turned admiral, Robert Blake proved to be a match for the famous admiral Martin Tromp, defeating him in three major clashes in home waters in 1652 and 1653. Tromp's death in summer 1653 effectively ended the conflict between navies, even if the capture of trading vessels continued. The United Provinces were divided over Tromp's replacement and there was little enthusiasm for continuing the war to be found within the states.

With Cromwell in office, moves toward ending the war completely began in earnest. God was obviously continuing his favour toward his republic, and Cromwell pointed this out to the Dutch and so the treaty of Westminster was outwardly tough on the Dutch. Their ships would have to strike their colours in the presence of British ships in the channel and British home waters. No Dutch (or indeed any other nation's) ships would be allowed to trade with the Republic's territories without passing through London's port, nor would the Dutch be allowed to carry other nations' goods into British ports; the British were determined to muscle in on the carrying trade. There was also a secret element to the treaty and this involved intervention in United Provinces' politics. Cromwell insisted that the Dutch debar the Prince of Orange from government. The House of Orange was married into the Stuart royal family, facilitating the stadtholder's wife Mary offer of refuge for her brothers Charles and James. The outcome of Cromwell's insistence on withdrawing the Stuarts' welcome was not wholly unpopular in the provinces, but the interference in internal matters was generally resented.

In the end the commercial benefits of the treaty were not that great: Cromwell was accused of putting religion before trade: he saw the treaty as being a way of fostering a pan-European protestant federation somewhat in the mould of James VI and I. One author, Slingsby Bethel believed it was personal interest that drove Cromwell. Bethel argued that trade was in a good state when Cromwell came to power or 'began his usurpation'. The 'Hollanders' were 'upon their knees', but Cromwell 'misimproved the Victory God had given us over the *United Provinces*, making peace (without striking stroak) so soon as ever things came into his hands upon equal tearms with them'. One point Bethel considered to be particularly foolish was the neglect of reclaiming reparations for losses incurred by English merchants: a demand Oliver had dropped in the negotiations. Oliver's motivation, Bethel explained, was based in ignorance. Bethel would be implying that Cromwell's motivation was his belief in placing the godly motivation, the drive for unity of Protestant states before trade. Bethel believed the purpose of international diplomacy was the advancement of trade, not God.[21]

Whitelock noted the change of pace after the conclusion of peace: 'the lord protector and his council did not sit so frequently as formerly, and all things went according to their desire'.[22] Except in Scotland where the situation in the highland continued to get worse. However the matter was in the hands of the local forces, who from spring onwards were back under the command of George Monck, the man who had 'pacified'

Scotland in the wake of Cromwell's departure in pursuit of Charles Stuart in late July 1651. Cromwell was the target of a plot that spring by a group of royalists who had intended to kill him and other members of the government and in the confusion proclaim Charles Stuart king. The conspirators John Gerrard, Somerset Fox and Peter Vowell were tried by a high court and the plot to murder Cromwell en route to Hampton Court was uncovered. All three were sentenced to death on 6 July: two were executed on the 10 July. The main noticeable fall-out of the plot for most people was the six-month prohibition on horse race meetings, where would be plotters could gather. This came at around the same time as an attempt to enforce godly manners on people: commissioners of customs and other officers to prevent cursing and swearing amongst their staff. Duels and provocations to duels were also prohibited. The godly society was promised.

By the summer plans were being made for the calling of the first parliament of the protectorate, intended for early September to coincide with the anniversary of the 'crowning mercy'. On 28 June the number of Scottish and Irish seats in parliament was set at thirty each. The elections in England and Wales were held in mid-July, but the writs for the Scottish seats only arrived in Edinburgh on 24 July. During August the council investigated the outcome of the elections and the returns of MPs in order to vet the membership of the crucial parliament. Cromwell apparently took no part in these proceedings. The council kept only twelve of the election winners from taking their seats. This was a small amount but an unseen crisis within days of the parliament opening would be far more controversial and reduce the number of representatives.

10

A GOOD CONSTABLE TO KEEP THE PEACE

1654–1658

Cromwell opened his first parliament on 4 September 1654. Just as he had been on 4 July 1653 when he opened the Little Parliament, Cromwell was optimistic. By now he was perhaps more prepared to believe that he would 'see such a day as this', after all this parliament had been planned for about nine months: nevertheless, he greeted the MPs with 'You are met here on the greatest occasion that, I believe, England ever saw'. For to Cromwell the occasion was an opportunity. The MPs had upon their 'shoulders the interest of three great nations'. More than that they had 'the interest of all the Christian people in the world'. The job was highly personal to Cromwell because it was all about 'settlement and healing'. It was clearly to be a conservative settlement focussed on strong government, arguing that in the past years of war magistracy had been trampled under foot. Then in a fairly rambling piece of the speech Cromwell turned to discussing the Levellers. His view of them now seemed to have consolidated around an erroneous and very basic conservative view of the venality of political opponents: a politics of envy.

> I beseech you, for the orders of men and ranks of men, did not that Levelling principle tend to the reducing of all to an equality? Did it think to do so, do did it practice towards it for propriety and interest? What was the design, but to make the tenant as liberal a fortune as

the landlord? Which I think if obtained, would not have lasted long. The men of that principle, after they had served their own turns, would have cried up propriety and interest then fast enough.[1]

Indeed it was a similar claim to that which royalists had made of him: that the destruction of the existing system would serve only to advance the destructive group which would then re-establish the system with themselves in it. It is a cynical view, but it is consistent with a man who had been a part of an established governmental system, and who had chaired the Putney debates where his son-in-law had attempted to question the basic principles of the Agreement of the People. It is a view completely in keeping with the essential reformed-monarchy basis of the Instrument of Government and moreover it is a clear attempt by Cromwell to get the support of the parliament behind the constitution which they had had little part in bringing about by playing up the need for stability. But Cromwell was also embracing the more radical elements of parliament into the term Leveller – the Commonwealthmen who resented the dissolution of the Long Parliament and had always wanted a parliament to be sovereign: they and Levellers were labelled 'egalitarian'. Gaining a wide basis of support was essential, reminding MPs of anarchy in the hope of winning the parliament to the constitution was essential if Cromwell was to shift the agenda into creating the godly nation and his own project, a religiously tolerant state. This was the next part of the speech, a reminder that there had been a religious anarchy to match that of political anarchy: and here he turned on the Fifth Monarchists, although his main theme was the intolerance that excluded the godly from preaching. The Second Coming to Cromwell as expressed in this speech was an internal event 'that Jesus Christ will have time to set up his reign in our hearts': this was the means by which the corruptions, lusts and evils would be defeated.[2] The solution to this was to be in the hands of a parliament with God in its hearts. However, Cromwell was, as David Smith claims, pursuing a minority agenda; one which was to bring him into conflict with parliament.

The optimism was again misplaced, if indeed Cromwell was expecting his words to win over parliament: he had experience of launching an assembly in a spirit of optimism only to wish for the wings of a dove later. However, crisis came about quicker than Cromwell may have expected. The parliament quickly turned on two of Oliver's chief principles: the legitimacy of the Instrument and religious toleration. Sir Arthur Hesilrige, a convinced republican who resented the expulsion of the Long Parliament, and the old Council of State of which he had been a member, proposed the creation of a state church and the suppression of the sects, a direct challenge to Cromwell's desires and the Instrument's clauses. However, other of the principles of the Instrument were quickly under attack. The Instrument was a confirmation of some elements of the reform of the monarchical system desired by the king's English and Welsh opponents in 1640–1642 and reflected some elements of the Heads of the Proposals of 1647. However, there were some significant differences. One of the sparks for war in 1642, and a source of disagreement with the king in 1647, was the issue of the control of the armed forces. In the tradition of the 1640s, parliament wanted to control the armed forces, but the Instrument had clearly placed it in the hands of the lord protector and parliament naturally challenged this. MPs also questioned the role of the protector vis-à-vis him and the council, suggesting that parliament was superior to the executive as it embodied the will of the people: the direct expression of this was the suggestion that a new parliament should select a new council when it opened. All of this contravened the conditions imposed by the council on candidates at their election, which bound them to forebear interfering with the constitution.

On 12 September Cromwell summoned the MPs to the painted chamber at Whitehall. His speech this time was set against the background of potential mutiny in the army. Fifth Monarchist Major General Thomas Harrison, had harboured deep misgivings about the expulsion of parliament on 20 April, had tried to stop Cromwell once in the chamber that day before becoming swept up in his commander's actions. Now Harrison, further alienated by the abrupt end to the Little Parliament, encouraged the creation of a petition demanding that the protectorate, which he described as a 'present tyranny' be brought to an end as it was worse than the government of Charles I. Cromwell had finally been apostatized in the eyes of Harrison and his colleagues, Cromwell was not a saint bringing in the second coming: he was part of the fourth monarchy: the small horn on the fourth horn of the goat to use the parlance of the Fifth Monarchist's interpretation of *Daniel* 8, v8–9. Harrison was arrested and the truculent MPs lectured. It would appear from part of the speech that Cromwell saw the blame for the discussions on the nature of the constitution as laying with the men who had been a part of the Long Parliament.

There were 125 Long Parliament men in the house, although the majority were relatively new men, elected in the closing stages of the first civil war, rather than traditional family representatives, like Cromwell. Moreover at the core of this group was Sir Arthur Hesilrige an old-family opponent of monarchical rule: he and his father were prominent in opposition to Charles I, and now Sir Arthur was an opponent of the protectorate leading a cadre of what Cromwell had called 'commonwealthmen' who wanted the return of a sovereign parliament. It was this argument that Cromwell turned to in his speech, claiming that this supposed paradigm of commonwealth government was flawed. Despite his attempts to get parliament 'to period themselves' the Long Parliament ignored Cromwell after Worcester:

> I knew it better than any one man in the Parliament could know it, because of my manner of life, which was to run up and down the nation, and so might see and know the temper and spirits of all men, the best of men, – that the nation loathed their sitting; I knew it ... And that there was high cause for their dissolving is most evident, not only was there a just fear of parliament's perpetuating themselves, but because it was their design. And had their heels been not trod upon by importunities from abroad, even to threats, I believe that there would never have been thoughts of going out of that room to the world's end. I myself was sounded and by no mean persons tempted, and addresses made to me to that very end, that it might have been thus perpetuated, that vacant places might be supplied by new elections and so continue from generation to generation.

The old system was corrupt and in no ways represented the sovereignty of the people as Hesilrige and the others might pretend. It was to bring about an end to this that Cromwell and the army had expelled the Long Parliament and sought to bring together a civil government, first through the Little Parliament and then through the Instrument. At each point that Cromwell had been given supreme authority, he had sought to ensure civil government and the approval, not just of God but of representatives of the people in the three nations, civil and rural authorities and the army. He rounded upon the critics in the house by claiming they themselves had, as he expressed it, born witness to this truth by subscribing to the principles within the Instrument that had established their elections: 'for you to sit and not own the authority by which you sit, it is that I believe that astonish more men than myself and does dangerously disappoint and discompose the nation ...'.

Cromwell said he was prepared to discuss some elements of the constitution, those things which he regarded as not being fundamental. He referred to two in the speech, the position of a single person telling MPs he did not mean that he personally was indisputably part of the constitution, only the office was, and reminding them that any change to the nature of parliament had to acknowledge that perpetual parliaments were out of the question. Religion, at least freedom of worship, was however a fundamental. Cromwell decried the way that sects had called for freedom, but used their own positions, when free of an overweening church, to suppress others. The episcopacy, and Scottish and English Presbyterians had all done this in their turn. What Cromwell argued he did not want was a situation like that of the 1620s and 1630s when people 'were necessitated to go into a vast howling wilderness in New England'[3] and had fled to the wilderness of north America.[4] The other indisputable fundamental was the control of the militia. On the other hand some essential elements of governance, including finance were regarded as circumstantials.

The speech was not to stand alone. Cromwell had used troops to close the house that morning. MPs were not to be allowed back in unless they subscribed to an oath of fidelity to the protector and commonwealth, and to the Instrument of Government's fundamentals, briefly categorised as the single person and parliament. Only 190 of the 460 MPs signed in the next two days, a further fifty took a month to sign, others even longer and eighty never did and were banned from sitting. It was a subdued house that continued sitting after Cromwell's intervention, but it still did not fulfil Cromwell's desires. It is not surprising. Austin Woolrych thinks that Cromwell had in mind Elizabethan parliaments, those of his father's generation which he believed were good examples of the single person and parliament working together. The problem was that Elizabeth's parliaments were brought together through the shrewd and successful manipulation of members of her council who possessed enough personal, social and economic power which could be converted into the political manipulation of electors and elected. Woolrych is probably right. The new executive was not comprised of the same stature of men, and Cromwell was not a skilled politician at any practical level: this executive group were more akin to Charles I's privy councillors in England and Wales in 1640, and perhaps more like the dead king's Scottish councillors in the 1630s when it came to elections, unable to manipulate electorates into making the 'desired' choices.

As a result, parliament continued to disappoint Cromwell. Peter Gaunt thinks that Oliver perhaps ought to have directed parliament towards a clear set of targets; instead he tended to leave it alone believing perhaps that he had set it a clear course. Possibly he saw it as an army under a general's orders: with strategy outlined by him with subordinates directing various elements towards rendezvous and battlefields. Parliament continued to discuss religious conformity and the suppression of heresies despite Cromwell's desire for tolerance. The executive ordinances passed in March and August 1654 set up Triers and Ejectors to examine the suitability of ministers for incumbencies and to expel those who did not meet the requirements. Parliament discussed these ordinances and attempted to ameliorate their effect by insisting on a single interpretation of the true reformed Protestant Christian religion in effect creating a unified creed. It went on to lay out plans for indicting a number of heresies and blasphemies in a bill that once passed by parliament would go into effect twenty days after being presented to Oliver, 'although he shall not give his consent thereunto' thus both getting its way and subverting the 'single person'. Against this backdrop John Biddle's two books, *A Two-fold Catechism* and *The Apostolical and True Opinion, concerning the Holy Trinity, revived and asserted*, were examined by a parliamentary committee. Both books were adjudged heretical and burned, Biddle was imprisoned. Biddle clearly was outside Cromwell's own religious fundamentals, as he was a Unitarian. Trinitarian belief was at the core of the tenets Oliver regarded as essential or fundamental. Yet Cromwell tried to protect Biddle from parliament's wrath, he had him imprisoned on the Scilly Isles, a dependent territory not represented in parliament, and he ensured that he was provided with an allowance for necessaries. Cromwell was not alone in combating parliamentarian intolerance; the army petitioned for broad-based religious tolerance with the only exceptions being Roman Catholics. Cromwell waited for the statutory five months to elapse on 22 January – although he cheated a bit by using lunar months of 28 days rather than calendar months, thus knocking ten days off the sitting – and dissolved parliament. Gaunt used the phrase 'addled' to describe this parliament as it passed no bills despite its constant nibbling away at the constitution and its religious precepts: a nadir in Gaunt's eyes. Cromwell lectured the MPs in the painted chamber at Whitehall, greeting them as people he knew. He explained his hope at their first meeting, his frustration at the second. He continued the theme reminding them that he had left them alone, but that he had expected to be called in by them: 'I did not know whether you have been alive or dead'. This was unfair, no parliament had ever called in a monarch in such a way as Cromwell seemed to have been wanting them to call him in. He also blamed them somewhat for the recently discovered plans for a royalist rising, not so much because they had been a party to the plans but because they had unsettled the nation through their inaction. The people of Cornwall and Lincolnshire did not feel safe, he argued: a man could not go for a walk in the field nor travel, he cryptically declared, when his 'house is on fire'.[5]

Parliament was duly dismissed. Cromwell perceived them and their obsession with the constitution as a danger to the state, because he knew through the energetic activities of the master spy John Thurloe that royalists were planning to challenge him. Something of what Whitelock had warned Cromwell of back in 1652 had come true. There was a battle between him and the Stuarts for supremacy at the heart of the state and this had alienated parliamentarians and soldiers. Behind the opponents of the regime in parliament were a range of others: Levellers who thought that the people had been betrayed, soldiers thinking that the army had been let down, and the Fifth Monarchists who regarded Cromwell as apostate. Some of these groups were interlinked – Leveller John Wildman was talking to Colonels John Okey, Matthew Alured and Thomas Saunders who had circulated an anti-protectorate petition drafted by Wildman throughout the army. A second Fifth Monarchist petition, somewhat influenced by Wildman, Saunders, Alured and Okey, was being circulated in the navy. Cromwell's personal authority and timely payment of back pay curtailed much of this discontent in the armed forces and Okey and Saunders were cashiered. Wildman however was also meeting the parliamentarian malcontents, Leicestershire rebels, Sir Arthur Hesilrige and Thomas, Lord Grey of Groby and the former president of the Commonwealth Council of State John Bradshaw. There was also a Scottish angle to the rabble-rousing with batches of the colonels' petition carried northwards where a plan was hatched to arrest Monck and replace him with Robert Overton. Monck stopped this plot in its tracks and Overton served the next four years as an untried prisoner.

Royalists were also plotting the overthrow of the state and there was some communication between them and the internal enemies, however there were no substantial links, largely because the political intentions of the latter took the execution of the king as the springboard for further radicalism: the restoration of the monarchy was in no way part of their plans. The royalists were intending to stage simultaneous rising, in the north on the field of Marston Moor, with Hull, Newcastle and York as targets. This was to be the main rising, there were others planned for Lincolnshire and Cheshire and the southwest. Unfortunately for the royalists their plans coincided with the colonels' petition and the Levellers' plotting, so much so that Cromwell believed that they were linked together. In the latter weeks of the parliament, the State had sought to boost its own defences, recalling troops from Ireland and arresting Wildman in early February.

The royalists had established a management committee for subversive activities, the Sealed Knot, but one problem for the pretender Charles Stuart was that there were a series of factions within the movement, creating such fractiousness that leaks of information were common and thus information fell into the hands of Thurloe. Moreover as far as the Sealed Knot was concerned by the end of 1654 that there was no real chance of success for the rising planned for early 1655. Conflicting orders and advice crossed and re-crossed the channel from Charles Stuart in Cologne and other royalists in France, leaving the various protagonists somewhat confused. On March 8 the plan came to a lacklustre fruition and bore blown specimens. The great rally on Marston Moor brought only about 100 men. The rally intended to launch an attack on Newcastle brought together even fewer men and the other targets were relatively untroubled that night. The largest group of would-be cavaliers met at Rufford Abbey in Nottinghamshire, but the putative leaders had stayed away and the group dispersed just as all the others in the north had. Only one benighted rising got underway: that in the southwest led by determined royalist Colonel John Penruddock four days later in the early hours of Monday 12 March. Somewhat over 200 men marched on Salisbury where they arrested protectorate officials and symbolically burned their commissions. Their numbers doubled over night and they began to divide their numbers into troops to act as embryos for full regiments. Local officials, from sheriffs to town criers, proved loyal to the protectorate and refused to proclaim the king even when threatened. The thousands of expected recruits proved a pipedream and on the Wednesday it came to an end. Desborough had been hastily appointed major general of the west, but when he arrived local initiatives were already underway and in any case the rebels were reduced to aimlessly wandering the region. Penruddock's men were caught by a troop of horse under Captain Uncton Croke who attacked them in their night's quarters at the village of South Moulton. After three hours of street fighting the royalist resistance ended, the local leaders were captured whilst the incomers from the Stuart 'court' escaped to the continent. About fifteen people were executed for the western rising, but remarkably they were tried by local courts, rather than by special courts created for the purpose. The northern rebels were largely left to obscurity: a mark of confidence in the state, and newsbooks pointed out the unity of the people as a whole and even of disparate religious sects in the face of royalist aggression. However Cromwell had been frustrated by the rising and he was provoked into a change of gear; one that opened his government to accusations of being martial law and himself of being a military dictator.

Cromwell and his council's instigation of the major generals as local administrators was a response to both the rising and a shortfall of income necessary to pay the army wage bill as the regular army was reduced in size and replaced by county militias. One effect of the apparent loyalty to the regime was Cromwell and others' belief that the rebellion had been defeated by the Godly. Parliament had failed to work in the interests of these 'Godly' people, perhaps he assumed, extra parliamentary organisations could do so, and involve such loyal citizens more closely in the creation of a reformed state. About a year after the rising, Cromwell explained to the Lord Mayor, Aldermen and Common Council of London, that he believed that regional administrators and government officials were being lax, and the imposition of major generals was simply to act as a spur to such idle men into action and thereby inspire more rigorous government. He certainly believed that they had been effective in ensuring parity of local government across the regions. Moreover, he told his second parliament in September 1656 that the extra-parliamentary taxation which the major generals had been charged with collecting had been levied only on those who caused the sort of discontent that inspired the need for such taxation anyway: the royalists. Nevertheless, the major generals represented something of a failure for the policy of normalisation: it was divisive, when Cromwell strove for unity; it was outside the spirit of the constitution, and it went against the spirit of trust in local machinery evinced in the policy of leaving Penruddock and his men to the mercy of local courts.

Twelve regions were created in England and Wales in the summer of 1655, and in operation by the end of the year. Major generals had been put in charge of militia in associated counties slightly earlier, something similar to the system employed by parliament in the early stages of the first civil war, but in August they had been given the civil powers that Cromwell thought would be needed to ensure good government. They were asked to work with JPs, sheriffs and ministers to this end, but they were also expected to have their own committees – the commissioners for the securing of the peace of the commonwealth – to assist in the work. Moral regulation was clearly important; a sort of reform of manners was to be undertaken with clamp downs on vagrants, swearing and blasphemy. Royalists were subjected to additional regulation, as well as to taxation assessed at one tenth of their wealth: the decimation tax. The government knew that the system was problematic and the declaration announcing the system published in October laid the blame on royalists who, it was argued, had remained aloof from the settlement. Cromwell hinted at his state of mind in a letter to son-in-law Fleetwood in June. The letter was really an attempt to calm Fleetwood's apprehension that Henry Cromwell had been sent to Ireland to replace him: in reality he would, but Cromwell suggested in the letter that it was not what he had intended. Cromwell reflected on 'The wretched jealousies that are amongst us, and the spirit of calumny turn all into gall and wormwood. My heart is for the People of God...'.[6] It was a mark of his despair that he spent the first part of the letter on these sentiments, and then after a brief personal passage, returned to introspection. The last letter seems like a casual invitation to return to England with Bridget; but when Fleetwood took up the offer, his rumoured supplanting by Henry Cromwell came to pass.

The major generals worked with their commissioner assistants and local officials. They sat on the magistrates' benches within their associated counties, but the consensus is that they failed. Henry Cromwell thought that they perpetuated royalist hostility rather than quelled it. On the other hand the royalist cause did not reappear as a militant entity during their existence, nor whilst Oliver or Richard ruled. They were certainly unpopular. They carried the taint of overt militarism and Puritanism, both in the 1650s and afterwards. There seems, argues Christopher Durston, little question that they failed to create a society any more Godly than that in place before their inception or after their demise. Their existence has left the protectorate with giant, if misplaced stains on its character: all the taint of military rule is focussed on them and the general belief in the fun-hating Puritan regime is similarly focussed. For Austin Woolrych the major generals were triumphant in one sphere; the defeat of conspiracy: royalists were so tightly controlled that they were unable to act, and this in turn enabled the space needed to create a secret service so effective that the militia created in the wake of Penruddock's rising was not needed for the peace was won. The real fault Professor Woolrych maintained was that their job had been too large and ill defined.

Oliver embarked upon another experiment in 1655, that resulted in long-lasting consequences for Britain and its growing empire. The Western Expedition was an attempt to plant godly colonies in the West Indies to challenge Spain and her colonies. It was not the success that Cromwell expected, and it plunged him into desperate despair. The Western Expedition was criticised as an example of Cromwell putting religious issues before politics. Foreign affairs had been dominated at the beginning of the regime by ending the war with the Dutch, but there were other issues that had been ongoing. The decades of raids on the southwest coast of England by 'pirates' from the north African states, collectively referred to as the Barbary coast, were effectively ended by two naval campaign in the Mediterranean whereby Admiral Robert Blake forced the Dey of Algiers to release English captives and destroyed the fleet of the Dey of Tunis. Relations with the Swedish monarchy had been particularly promising, with Bulstrode Whitelock working as ambassador to Queen Christina. These dealings had secured rights to Baltic trade for English merchants, and the basis was mercantile rather than religious: Sweden was moving from the religious-centred foreign policy of its recent past and becoming more secular in its approach to foreign affairs, as the principal figures of its past aged and were replaced by younger men and a fairly cynical queen.

On the other hand Cromwell's policy towards the major powers of Europe was less secular. In 1654 an attack was launched on French colonists of Arcadia on Newfoundland and the long-established colony dispersed. This had been an opportunist use of an expeditionary force sent originally to attack New Amsterdam, that upon peace between the United Provinces and the Republic was redirected to Newfoundland. However, by 1654 France was prepared to overlook this in an effort to gain an alliance with the Republic. Opinion on such an alliance was divided. France harboured royalists, including the former queen Henrietta Maria, King Louis XIV's aunt. Moreover there was an active campaign of repression directed at the Protestant communities of Vaudois in the Savoy region. Cromwell had organised a financial collection to send aid to the embattled Protestants, contributing £2,000 himself. On the other hand the desire for a treaty in France was so strong that Cardinal Mazarin was forced to back down and leave the Vaudois Protestants to their faith.

The Council of State was split on the issue of alliances, some members favoured an alliance with Spain over France, but in general Cromwell favoured France. The issue of the Vaudois held up economic discussions until November 1655, by which time a major element of the developing relationship with France had gone wrong. In order to impress the French by challenging the Spanish Empire, Cromwell had sought to expand the Republic's position in the West Indies. A fleet left England in December 1654 and arrived at Hispaniola (now Haiti and the Dominican Republic) in the following April. The plan was to take possession of the island with a combined forces assault, but the commanders, William Penn and Robert Venables, leaders of the fleet and land forces respectively, had no experience of such a campaign and their attempt was defeated once they failed to capture the capital San Domingo. The Republic's forces enhanced by recruits from the Barbados colony, were driven from Hispaniola by 4 May. Penn and Venables did capture Jamaica on 17 May and established what would be a long term hold on the island, but it was by far an inferior prize. Cromwell took the failure hard, and sought reasons for God's seeming rebuff. Historians tend to look at the bad planning and logistical failures, Austin Woolrych was particularly cutting and apt when he suggested Cromwell ought to have looked to logistics rather than sin as a cause of the defeat. For a providentialist, of course, the defeat was clearly to be read as evidence of the loss of God's favour and Oliver shut himself in his rooms for some days when news reached him. In one of his letters to the governor of Jamaica Richard Fortescue, Cromwell practically narrated his own progress from despair over the failure to an optimism that seems a precursor to the development of the empire in the West Indies. Cromwell opened the letter with reference to defeat:

> ... our discouragements have been many: for which we desire to humble ourselves before the Lord who hath very sorely chastened us.[7]

Before praising Fortescue's character and work, Cromwell moved on to a prospective view. Fortescue had been sent supplies directly from the republic and from new England and Atlantic colonies, and with this he was expected first to fortify the island and them later go onto the offensive against Spanish colonies in Cuba. It had taken a long time for Oliver to get to this optimistic state of mind, the letter was written in November 1654, six months after the failed attack on Hispaniola and sometime after Fortescue had died.

The failed Western Expedition had an impact upon foreign policy as a whole, whilst it provoked Spain without any great return, it did not further the treaty with France which in any case was still bogged down in the Vaudois issue. The impressive effect of the Mediterranean victories had nevertheless been offset by the defeat. Nevertheless, by November 1655, just as Cromwell recovered his perspective in the west the trade deal with France was finalised. Coupled with the establishment of the major general regime, the republic, at the end of 1655, was moving into a new gear. There was one other major development that occurred late that year. Cromwell and the Council opened the republic up to Jewish people. At the end of the thirteenth century after being subjected to periodic pogroms Jews were expelled from England. By 1655 there were some Jewish merchants in the country, but no settled communities, and these merchants were officially identified as being denizens of what ever country they lived in, rather than as Jews. Cromwell's motives were probably manifold, and would be generally focussed on opening connections with major banking interests in the continent. There had been attempts to try and identify the tribes of Israel with American Indians, and much was made in millennial quarters about the biblical invocation that one of the precursors of the Second Coming would be the conversion of the Jews. An alliance of these two ideas was sometimes used to justify attempts to convert American Indians to Christianity.

For their part Jews were attracted by the prospect of the Republic's apparent tolerance, and the encouragement of Secretary of State Thurloe who had met leaders of the Amsterdam Jewish community in the early 1650s. Manesseh Ben Israel petitioned the Council on 13 November asking for the right to establish synagogues and 'reconcile differences according to Mosaic Law'.[8] Cromwell was very sympathetic to the idea of opening the borders and sought advice from the council, which debated the matter in December 1655, following a report on Ben Israel's petition. In the following year despite opposition from some religious leaders on theological grounds, seeing the Jews as blasphemous, and London merchants frightened of competition, tacit permission was granted for Jews to have a synagogue and burial ground in London. This was not the welcome that Thurloe and Cromwell had hoped for and the council of state was likely to actually have demurred if pressed to a vote. Some saw there being a 'generality' opposed to admission to the Jews: only a 'conivency' could secure their right to reside in the country.[9] Even so Jewish merchants were from that year recognised as such and not as Spanish or Portuguese traders.

In the country as a whole, 1656 was not going to be easy for Cromwell because the major generals were to prove very unpopular. The men in office were of very different capacities, some were very hard working, like Edward Whalley in the Midlands, who participated on local benches; others were less enthusiastic. Some of the appointees were already famous men like John Desborough, Cromwell's brother-in-law who was in charge of the west country, others were relatively unknown. However, there was, strangely for men that Oliver wanted to enact a 'godly' reform of the country, no seeming consensus amongst them of what Godliness was. Most importantly they were unpopular. The royalist community was angered by the decimation tax, and the general conservativeness of the gentry was provoked by the social standing of the major generals: they were not men from the social elite families that had traditionally governed society: some were related to such families, Whalley in the Midland was, and of course Desborough had married into the Cromwells, but then again the Cromwells were not by then at the apex of Huntingdonshire society and when Oliver had formed his first troop of horse he only accorded Desborough a quartermaster's place. This criticism of office holders was not new, gentry had always complained that members of 'inferior' social ranks had been given authority beyond their status; constables in particular had been abused, and mocked, for it. During and after the civil wars there had been criticism levied at the committees charged with county administration, often on grounds of social class. What was novel was the level of authority accorded the major generals. Cromwell appeared sensitive to this criticism. In London he spoke directly to the Lord Mayor and aldermen to try and assure them that the major general in charge of the city, the famous Philip Skippon, was there to assist: 'to the end that no misunderstanding may be had thereof; for that thereby the good government of the City is intended, and not at all to supersede them or at least to diminish any of there rights, privileges or liberties'.[10] Ronald Hutton has recently accused Cromwell of hypocrisy regarding the major generals, suggesting that Cromwell allowed the criticism levelled at them across the country to drive policy, and whilst verbally supportive he left them practically unsupported. It is probably more the case that the idea had never been fully worked out and the remit of the major generals remained ill-defined leaving Cromwell to become bored by the concept.

The fall of the major generals came with the second protectorate parliament of 1656. The need for parliament was the traditional one faced by Stuart monarchs: money. The decimation tax had proved insufficient even for its limited remit: the armed forces' arrears of pay grew and of course war with Spain continued to escalate. Foreign wars always proved expensive, and critics like Slingsby Bethel laid the blame firmly at Cromwell's feet:

> he pretended, and indeavoured to impose a belief upon the world, that he had nothing in his eye but the advancement of the Protestant Cause, and the honour of this Nation; but his pretences, were either fraudulent, or he was ignorant in Forreign affairs (as I am apt to think, that he was not guilty of too much knowledge in them) ...[11]

The costs of this war could not be met by taxation levied without the approval of parliament, and despite discussions in council about extra parliamentary levies, it was decided to hold elections. This would place a burden on the major generals who were expected to play a role in the selection of suitable candidates, somewhat of a legacy from the nomination of the Little Parliament, although not as successful. The emphasis, Hutton argues was on exclusion, rather than on ensuring inclusion of the regime's supporters and enthusiasts. The decision to call parliament had been taken in June, following the failure of attempts to steer a way through the financial maze facing the Republic. The major generals had been involved in the discussions and it had been pressure from them that persuaded Cromwell to call parliament believing, it has been argued, that they could influence the elections. They were, according to Christopher Durston, active in the election campaign of July and August, and all but one were elected. However these first impressions were misleading because the elections had not really gone their way. Opponents had called for the electorate to vote for 'no swordsmen, no decimators', thus betraying royalist origins for their opposition. Several of the major generals reported the strength of the opposition, when facing alliances of royalists, Presbyterians and enemies of the regime. This meant that after the polls Cromwell and the council had to sift the elected candidates. Unlike 1654, this time the council used the power of the Instrument to the full and over 100 MPs were debarred, stretching the powers of the council to the limit and embracing the excluded under the general terms of not being God-fearing or of good conversation: it was in the end republicans from whom the protectorate had to defend itself, not royalists, rebels or Catholics. The heavy handed approach persuaded another fifty to sixty MPs that parliament was unfree and they chose not to sit. Cromwell claimed that he had opposed the exclusions, but clearly did nothing to limit their effect.

Cromwell addressed the new parliament on 17 September, before it sat, and before the approved candidates were given a slip of paper confirming their election. The major generals must have felt vindicated. Not only had their dire warnings of opposition been heeded and many supposed enemies excluded, but Cromwell spent a good portion of the opening speech referring to them. They were the solution to the problem of royalists and papists who 'shake hands together' and the 'scum and dirt of this nation'. The major generals 'have behaved themselves in that work! I hope they are men as to their persons of known integrity and fidelity, and men that have freely adventured their blood and lives for that good cause'. Moreover his confidence seem confirmed as he said, 'If this were to be done again, I would do it!'.[12] The speech was not really about the major generals; Cromwell had tied the whole first part of the speech to one end, setting the case for the war against Spain. Spain was a traditional enemy with agents in England. The Catholics of England, Cromwell argued, were 'ever since I was born, Spaniolised ... They never regarded France, they never regarded any other Popish State. Where any such interest was, Spain was their patron'.[13] It was traditional English anti-Spanish tub-thumping, serving both as a deliberate attempt to gain popularity for the republic by proposing a jingoistic populist foreign policy, and an attempt to justify increased government expenditure. The speech also dealt with the reformation of manners in the republic, so much had been wrong that Cromwell declared that it had been a 'shame to be a Christian in these fifteen, sixteen, or seventeen years in this nation'. There was optimism about the young men in the universities looking to their hearts rather than to their books; whilst the MPs were to be 'as labourers in the work'. Cromwell assured them that they would be 'a blessing to the nation'.

Within weeks the MPs were to be much less of a blessing than Cromwell imagined. On 14 October a 38-year-old former soldier who had associated with the Ranters in London at the end of the 1640s, who had since become a Quaker, caused a national scandal. James Naylor accompanied by two women scattering rushes before him and many more accompanying him with song, rode on a small horse into Bristol in imitation of Jesus Christ's entry into Jerusalem. It was all to mark his release from Exeter prison where he had been incarcerated for attempting to visit Quaker founder George Fox who was imprisoned in Launceston. Not surprisingly Naylor was immediately imprisoned again; what was more surprising was that Oliver's second parliament decided to handle the case itself, after receiving a report from the Bristol MP. A committee deliberated the case for five weeks and then following its report to parliament a further nine days were spent in debate. The Blasphemy Act of 1650 prescribed six months in prison, but a hardline group wanted the death penalty. Cromwell's closest allies were divided too: several of the old soldiers wanted Naylor executed, whereas civilian members of the council including the chair of the council, Cromwell's old St Ives landlord Henry Lawrence wanted a more lenient sentence. In the end Naylor was savagely whipped and the plan was to brand him with a B for blasphemy and bore his tongue for having given voice to blasphemy. There was to be a similar bloodfest in Bristol too, but he was so savagely hurt as they whipped him at the cart's tail from Westminster to London that the further acts of butchery had to be delayed for nine days. The pause gave rise to an influx of petitions to Cromwell. The treatment of Naylor was a direct challenge to Oliver's sensibilities. Naylor's behaviour, like John Biddle's Unitarianism was to him abhorrent, but he did not want anyone punished for beliefs, certainly not to the extent imposed upon Naylor. On the very same day that Naylor was tortured Oliver had written to the corporation of Newcastle and the Presbyterian churches of the town confirming his belief in tolerance: the latter were told that the people of God 'should walk in the light of the Lord, each sort in their integrity seeking the best they can the promotion of an interest'.[14] Prompted by the petitions on Naylor's behalf, on 26 December he asked parliament through Speaker Thomas Widdrington, to explain the 'reasons whereupon they have proceeded'.[15] He was asking them to explain their source of authority: in reality they had no role in such a case, but parliament ignored him and Naylor was accordingly branded and his tongue bored in defiance of Cromwell. Naylor was then taken to Bristol and whipped there before being returned again to London and imprisoned. Cromwell and others, including those who had argued in parliament that parliament had no right to deal with Naylor's case, and that the case should have been left to local courts, thought that parliament needed reform, specifically a second house to prevent rash and unbridled action. In May Cromwell ensured that Naylor, in desperate ill health since his torture, got medical care from a Quaker nurse in Bridewell prison. Cromwell could do no more: unlike Biddle, Naylor could not be spirited away from parliament's sphere of influence. Naylor was allowed respite from prison for brief spells to restore his health, but he would only be freed when the Protectorate fell.

As Christmas 1656 passed attendance in the house declined and more and more members stayed away, despite attempts to impose fines on them. On 25 December John Desborough introduced a bill into the house to extend the decimation tax; which would of course entail the retention of the major generals. It was a point of contradiction that the decimation tax undermined Oliver's aim to heal old divisions, and several opponents of the tax pointed this out: arguing that it was against the principles of the Act of Oblivion. The speaker's illness over the next weeks prevented discussions of the bill, and it was only debated on 7 January, when it was attacked by Oliver's son-in-law, John Claypole, husband of daughter

Elizabeth. The bill was rejected by vote on 29 January. The bill had been killed off, as Austin Woolrych argued, by supporters of the state; but civilian ones in opposition to the military.

The puzzle is why Cromwell failed to support the bill and thus the major generals. He had been an effusive supporter of the major generals as recently as the opening of parliament. Ronald Hutton accuses him of nothing less than betrayal of the major generals: men most closely associated with Cromwell's godly plan. The betrayal he suggests was because Cromwell was aiming for better working relations with parliament, because within days Cromwell got the financial deal he needed to fund the war with Spain that he had wanted from parliament. It was part of a pattern, and on 23 January just before the major generals were killed off Cromwell spoke to parliament to thank it for the 'unexpected kindness' it had shown him. Cromwell had been preserved from yet another attempt on his life. Quartermaster Miles Sindercombe was a man with a grudge. In 1647 he had been one of the Leveller soldiers disappointed at Corkbush when Cromwell and Fairfax had barged their way through the rank and file of the regiments that had defied their orders to abandon the rendezvous which had been called to approve of the Agreement of the People. Ten years later he had been recruited by Edward Sexby a man disappointed too by the outcome of the Putney debates on the eve of Corkbush. Sexby was one of several radicals whose plans for the reborn England had been headed off at several climactic junctures, the spring of 1649, and December 1653 in particular. In January 1657 Sindercombe was the front man for Sexby's plot. The first plan to shoot Cromwell in his coach was abandoned in favour of burning down Whitehall Palace with Cromwell in it. The plan was betrayed; Sindercombe and Sexby were imprisoned. Parliament had congratulated Cromwell on his luck, and he in turn thanked them and praised them:

> And in this people, in the midst of this people, a people I know everyone will hear it, that are to God as the apple of his eye; and he says so of them, be they many or be they few. But they are many, a people of the blessing of God, a people under his safety and protection; a people calling upon the name of the Lord, which the heathen do not; a people knowing God, and a people, according to the ordinary expressions, fearing God. And you have of this no parallel, no, not in all of the

world. You have in the midst of you Glorious things, Glorious things. For you have the laws and the statutes and ordinances ...'[16]

At this point Oliver seems to have buried the major generals. God was working through parliament as a whole, not just them. In any case some of the very men whom Cromwell had trusted to bring about Godly reform had called for Naylor's death. They could not be trusted. He gave no support to the decimation bill and when it fell he made no move to rescue the major generals who fell with it. Could Cromwell have thought that their role in his plan had come to a natural end? Clearly the major generals had over-estimated their success in the community and clearly too they had failed to influence the elections. On the other hand, despite the Naylor incident, where the major generals had also let Cromwell down, parliament seemed to be far more cooperative (remembering that at least 140 MPs were missing): if it could be brought to godly reform at home as well as be committed to the war against Spain, then perhaps the major generals had become redundant.

The support parliament had given Cromwell was within weeks to be converted into a redrafting of the constitution along some of the lines Cromwell had been thinking. Almost simultaneous with the news of Sindercombe's plot there were moves within parliament to resurrect the 'ancient constitution', in other words make Oliver a king. This in turn became transformed into the creation of a reformed constitution, with the head of state being a hereditary post. Several prominent protectorate politicians were the authors of the new constitution, in particular Roger Boyle, Lord Broghill, one of the architects of the defeat of the confederation–royalist alliance in Ireland during Cromwell's campaign. He was in this parliament as MP for both Cork and Edinburgh. On 23 February 1657 Sir Christopher Packe, former Lord Mayor of London who had benefited from the civil wars by gaining position of Leicestershire estates from the royalist Skipworth family, proposed the new constitution in the house, opposition led by Lambert, Desborough and Fleetwood, was immediate, but the critics were defeated on a vote.

The Humble Petition and Advice of the parliament of England, Scotland and Ireland to his Highness was discussed in detail for the next few weeks in a committee chaired by Bulstrode Whitelock. Whitelock believed that the chief point of the petition was to get Cromwell to accept the title of king. It was the classic lawyers' argument from the inception of the republic, that stability and normality required a monarch. It ignored completely the recent publication of political philosopher James Harrington's *The Commonwealth of Oceana*. Within Harrington's argument was the assertion that the political structure of a nation should match the social structure. England with a relatively widespread distribution of property was ripe for a republican government. In the minds of those who pressed the royal title on Cromwell was also the attendant belief that a hereditary succession guaranteed stability. In the minds of many, recent history had associated a change of leader with regime change. Had Sindercombe been successful then the state would have been endangered by the death of Cromwell. A monarch would be succeeded immediately and the state thus secured. Cromwell was less convinced and had suggested the creation of the committee in the first place. On 27 February, Cromwell met with the army leaders who generally disapproved of the offer of the crown. Oliver was quite aggressive in the face of their opposition, but there is no doubt that he was influenced by their hostility, so that as the parliamentary committee was ready to present its argument to him, he addressed parliament, asking them to let him consult with himself and God on the issue. It was a great and important matter, and

> if these considerations fall upon a person or persons that God takes no pleasure in, that perhaps may be at the end of this work, that to please any of those humours or considerations that are of this world shall run on such a rock as this is without due consideration, without integrity, without sincerity, without approving the heart to God, and seeking an answer from him and for putting things as for life and death to him, that such and answer may be received as may be a blessing ...[17]

In other words, Cromwell was asking for time to consider the offer. Cromwell felt obliged to answer the army's concern about the offer the crown made within the Humble Petition and Advice, discoursing on how he saw himself as head of state. It was not the first time he had done so. In his second speech to the first Protectorate parliament on 12 September 1654 he had come around to speaking about his own position after the MPs had begun debating the constitution against his express instructions.

> I called not myself to this place. I say again, I called not myself to this
> place; of that God is my witness. And I have many witnesses, who I do
> believe could readily lay down their lives to bear witness to the truth of
> that, that is to say that I called not myself to this place.[18]

He would do so several times in the intervening years. To the army
he remarked: 'That for his part he loved not the title, a feather in a hat,
as little as they did', reminding them that it was a group of soldiers that
in drawing up the Instrument of Government had first offered him such
a title.[19]

Cromwell had often justified his position in providentialist terms,
reasserting his lack of personal ambition combined with a weary
readiness for a role that God had called upon him to undertake: but
the title of his office was not usually addressed. That Cromwell was
essentially a conservative in constitutional matters is little doubted.
He usually, when pushed, harked back to a monarchical system. His
supposed discussions with Whitelock in November 1652 were aimed
at cutting another Gordian Knot – the political impasse over continued
reform and new elections and the sword he promised was the installation
of a monarch. According to some accounts, including his own at the
meeting with the officers in February, it was Cromwell who removed the
title king from the Instrument of Government, but even so the system
was essentially a reformed monarchy limited by constraints demanded
since 1637 within Britain, with the notable exception of control of the
armed forces. The compromise over the title lord protector, a distinctly
interregnum-style name if ever there was one, was naturally an invitation
to reopen discussions. On 13 April 1657 Cromwell mused:

> I am ready not to serve as a king but as a constable. For truly I have
> as before God thought it often, that I could not tell what my business
> was, nor what I was in the place I stood, save by comparing it with
> a good constable to keep the peace of the parish. And truly this has
> been my content and satisfaction in the troubles I have undergone,
> that yet you have peace.[20]

The question in this case is what did Cromwell mean? Was he thinking
of a national level constable, a role not unlike a lord protector, babysitting
a nation on behalf of a monarch who was out of either the country or

his or her mind, or was it really the parish constable? The national level officer was not without recent precedent. The Earl of Essex had been given the office back in 1642 by parliament on the verge of war with Charles I and incorporated into the Nineteen Propositions alongside the Lord High Steward and lord chancellor. On the other hand the office of parish constable does suggest several appropriate comparisons. The constabulary was not without its critics. The combination of authority with social class or aspirant social climbers led to the office being held up to ridicule. It was not only Shakespeare's Dogberry that impressed himself upon the historians as well as contemporary observers' minds, John Earle had created a character study in 1628 that underlined the self importance of the 'jobs-worth' constable: 'No man stands more upon't that he is the king's officer'.[21] These officers were perceived as social upstarts or 'wannabes' in some communities, because the local gentry which was supposed to fill the office were either absent or studiously avoided taking up the post. It was a position at the lower end of national government, to be avoided at all costs in some places, yet it also could present the holder with authority over his (or occasionally her) neighbours, for it was at the upper end of parish government. This very dichotomy made it a risky position for the holder as conflict between the national and the local could be encompassed in this one office. In fact dichotomy might have been on Cromwell's mind in 1657.

There were of course several reasons for Cromwell's musing on the constable's position. There was a massive range of unpaid duties for which a constable could be responsible: law enforcement, peacekeeping and public safety, militia duties, highway and sewer management, agricultural administration and fiscal duties amongst them. The actual post varied from place to place, as did the title of the holder, the frequency and type of selection process and the number of officers per parish. In parts of Wales, brought into Anglified management during the sixteenth century there had been attempts to standardise the system, with two constables per parish, regularly rotated around the village hierarchy; but in England the system had grown piecemeal and there was no standard system in place.

Cromwell's experience of the constable's office was quite limited. In his Huntingdon life, Cromwell had been a borough JP, with authority over the town constables who would make presentments to the borough court. The reissue of the Huntingdon charter in

1630 reduced the role of the JPs. He could not and did not take up the post of JP, which in any case was not one which would have carried much prestige; John Morrill compared its authority to that of a village constable, but this may be understating the case. There would have been mundane ward-based duties, but an urban JP did have magisterial power too and would with his colleagues hold the borough courts, the urban equivalent of the county quarter sessions. When the Cromwell family moved to St Ives Oliver quickly appeared in the vestrybook, implying that Cromwell would have at some time held one of the parish offices, such as churchwarden or constable himself. However, because Cromwell's time in St Ives was brief (and may have incorporated a downward social trajectory) he was not appointed to any office. Nevertheless at two points in his pre-war career, Oliver Cromwell observed the work of the urban and rural constable at close quarters.

As Cromwell would understand the constable was the point of contact for the national and the local, what Keith Wrightson would refer to as 'two concepts of order'. Even in relatively stable times the demands of the law and fiscal authorities might meet with local opposition and constables bear the brunt of the dispute; facing arrest by one side and social oblivion from the other in case of default on his part. In the 1630s constables were the target of opponents of ship money for collection: distraint of goods in case of tax default was the responsibility of the constable. Ironically it was one of the protectorate's harshest critics, Sir Arthur Hesilrige, using his position as a deputy lieutenant who had arrested a constable working for the high sheriff of Leicestershire, collecting distraint for non payment with the consequent effect of deterring other constables from collecting the taxes. Of course it was not just the branches of local government that were in conflict, it could be larger sections of the constable's community which objected to national policy, placing the constable in an uncomfortable position. It could be this which impinged on Oliver's mind. The issue of the title of the single person placed him in the middle of two contending groups – the MPs who made the offer and the army officers, many of whom were absolutely opposed to using the title. This was not the first time that Cromwell had been in such a position. In 1647 he had been one of the soldier's champions in the argument with parliament over back-pay and conscription for the planned Irish campaign, etc., and therefore associated with the developing political radicalism in the New Model Army. At the same time he was still MP for Cambridge and an active member of the House of Commons, with which the army was in dispute. Cromwell strove to represent the army in parliament, but was part of a minority: Cromwell's attempt to bridge the growing chasm failed and the political impasse had to be broken by a limited purge of parliament and the occupation of London and Westminster by the New Model. Cromwell tried to maintain links between the army and parliament again in 1651–1653, pressing again for a radicalised political programme and a new constitution, whilst holding back demands from within the army for a forced dissolution of the house. In each case Cromwell had had a foot in both camps, and would have been seen as a servant of both, expected to do the bidding of each of the contenders. In 1657 Cromwell was in a similar position, expected to take the offer of the crown by parliament as a means of overcoming his opposition to their tampering with 'fundamentals' of the constitution, but expected by the army to reject the title of king which God had witnessed against. This was the background to the fairly ill tempered exchange on 7 March 1657 when he reminded the soldiers of 'the time ... they boggled not at the word for the Instrument by which the government now stands was presented ... with the title in it as some there could witness ...'.[22]

Of course there is one more dichotomy to be considered. Despite the rhetoric of unworthiness, Cromwell constantly reminded his audiences that he was there because God had willed it: 'if my calling be from God ...' (12 September 1653);[23] 'the burdens that have lain heavy on me, they have been laid on me by the hand of god' (13 April 1657);[24] 'and I did labour as well as I could to discharge my trust, and God blessed me as it pleased him' (13 April 1657).[25] Cromwell was thus an appointment of God's. However, Cromwell also acknowledged that there was a further approbation needed, that of the people: 'and my testimony from the people'. He was therefore again, like a constable, the meeting point of two sources of power. That the argument of whether or not power ascended from below or descended from above was not thoroughly worked out in the incomplete revolution of 1648–1649. There was seeming tacit agreement that it came from God, but through the godly people of the nation; but Cromwell's reference to his being there because of God's will (or hand) left the issue confused, but nevertheless dichotomous like that of the constable, the upper end of one source of power and the lower end of another.

This period is one of the most famous pauses in British and Irish history, and Cromwell appears to be incredibly indecisive. There are several schools of thought on Cromwell's attitude. One is that the meeting with the army had been the start of a concerted campaign by the officers to force or persuade Oliver to reject the crown. Prominent officers, including his brother-in-law Desborough and Lambert, probably thought that their meeting with him on 6 May when they told him they would resign if he accepted the crown had influenced him. Another contingent believed Cromwell was on the verge of accepting the crown until about the time of this meeting, even that Cromwell was warming to the idea by early May having previously sought to reject it. Of course Cromwell was an old conservative MP from a family with close post-reformation ties to monarchy, so such an argument is not without foundation: it had taken a long time for Cromwell to turn against monarchy *per se* as opposed to monarchy in the person of Charles I. Cromwell the oil-tanker would take an age to turn around again. Oliver had of course been involved in semi-public and private discussions on the practicality of recreating monarchy in Britain and Ireland in the 1650s. However, it is likely that Cromwell had no intention of accepting the crown: he was happy with the Protectorate regime and saw himself as its constable. The speech on 13 April seems unequivocal. Oliver did not want the crown. Austin Woolrych agrees with this, explaining that the long period of inaction was so that other aspects of the *Humble Petition and Advice* could be negotiated. Cromwell secured an increase in the fixed budget and he gained the right to nominate the first members of the new senate-style other house. His ongoing expressions of interest during negotiations and his praise for other sections of the document had led many to believe that Cromwell was beginning to favour the title. Friendly chats with Broghill and Whitelock did nothing to dispel this belief. On May 8 Cromwell formally rejected the title God had borne witness against. Heads of state like chief administrators in villagers had many names, but they essentially did the same job: Cromwell was to remain a constable.

This oil-tanker would not perform a *volte-face*. Coward thinks Cromwell erred on the side of staying with God's favour and God had so roundly condemned kingship in 1648. J.C. Davis thinks that Cromwell was sensitive to the wishes of godly colleagues and old soldiers (not 'the army') who urged him in spring 1657 to reject the title adding that there was no indication that he had ever wanted it. Peter Gaunt argues for a combination of the two. Hutton argues for Cromwell the pragmatist, there would have been a cataclysmic show down had Cromwell accepted the crown on 7 May. The confrontation with the three army commanders on 6 May when they threatened resignation was conducted against the background of a petition drafted by John Owen, a close colleague of Cromwell, and it was being circulated in the army by Thomas Pride, the colonel who with Lord Grey had purged parliament in order to bring about the king's trial. After the meeting Cromwell delayed giving his answer to parliament by postponing his scheduled meeting for a day. Hutton argues that Oliver had decided to accept the crown by 5 May and intended to tell parliament so. The meeting with the officers on 6 May therefore becomes very important as it alone deflected him. Such an argument has Cromwell in thrall to the army. He had accused it of forcing his hand at times when he met the 100 officers at the end of February, but then he was angry and overstating how he had acted with their interest at heart in 1648 and 1653 probably because he was intent on developing civil government and minimising the army's overt role in government, rather than being specifically angry about it opposing his acceptance of the crown. Over the next months Cromwell removed the lynch-pin of the army in government and opponents of kingship, John Lambert, from his command.[26] That Oliver could do so to a man who had threatened to resign if Cromwell had taken the crown suggests that there was no need to simply do what the officers wanted. Cromwell rejected the crown because it was a tainted title for God 'hath not only dealt so with the persons and the family, but he hath blasted the title': it had taken a long personally difficult battle for Cromwell to reach this position.[27] He would not abandon it now: 'I cannot undertake this government with the title of king'.[28] It is a mark of Cromwell's political consistency, rather than an indecisive reaction to conflicting pressures that ensured that Oliver remained a protector to the people not a king over them, the greatest pause in history was simply not a pause at all: it was a period of negotiation aimed at getting what Oliver wanted from the *Humble Petition and Advice* without having to adopt the royal title.

Enthusiasm for the *Humble Petition and Advice* waned once Oliver rejected kingship. Broghill and others wanted the *Humble Petition* accepted in full or not at all, but it was returned to parliament and debated on 15, 19 and 22 May. The title of protector was confirmed and it passed the house by 50–53 votes; a new parliament would be created and a government more civil in aspect would be in place. The final draft of the eighteen-clause *Humble Petition and Advice* was presented to Oliver on 25 May 1657.

Cromwell was reinvested in office on 26 June, again at Westminster, but this time in a more clearly civil ceremony, derived from monarchical precedent: few soldiers were present. The sword of state carried by Lambert at the first investiture was now carried by the Earl of Warwick accompanied by the Lord Mayor of London. The title and badges of office may have been presented by the Speaker of the House of Commons Sir Thomas Widdrington, as if to emphasise parliament's role in the massive changes wrought during the past eighteen years, but he used words similar to those cited by archbishops of Canterbury at royal coronations. The recipient too was dressed more like a king than he had been at the previous investiture, and he now sat on the coronation chair with its encased Stone of Scone. The symbols of regal authority surrounded this parish constable alongside the officers of state and ambassadors of the United Provinces and France. Nearby too was Oliver's eldest son Richard.

In some ways historians have tended to view this second installation as something of a climax to Cromwell's government, suggesting that the remaining period of Oliver's life was marked in government by drift, and in his personal life by tragedy. The momentum in both personal and political life had drained away. In some senses this is perhaps due to Cromwell's declining health in 1658, this had political consequences, partly because until them Oliver had been at the heart of government. The protectorate was not as some historians have claimed a personal rule, but Oliver was personally involved in government to such an extent that his absences delayed government. Peter Gaunt rightly challenges the view of drift. Cromwell was becoming experienced in international politics and the republic was making itself felt on the stage of the Western Hemisphere. This had consequences for the enemies of the state. The royalist cause had been dealt severe blows in England and Scotland. At the core of the exiled court there were deep divisions. France was closing its doors to them and Spain, in whose armed forces the brothers Charles and James Stuart enlisted was firmly identified as the republic's principal as well as the country's traditional enemy. Associating with

Spain lessened the Stuarts' credibility as a ruling family in waiting, and supporters at home were in any case exhausted by years of war and rebellion; restrictions upon them in public life and by fines imposed in the wake of Penruddock's rebellion. Perhaps worse still for the Stuarts, was the fact that the regime was becoming established. At the level where it mattered the regime functioned. For years local government had been overburdened with war and its consequences. There is no doubt that the need for a standing army was a continuous problem requiring as it did higher taxes. But in general the tax burden was declining.

Despite the differences in handwriting in the account books of the constables of Upton in Nottinghamshire, a glance shows how the constables' job had become harder in the 1640s. In 1641 the constable's records filled about four and a half pages in the account book. In 1642 this had increased to five pages, by 1644, fourteen and a half. By 1656 however the duties took up just one single page. The expenditure had also declined dramatically from a peak of £146-08-00 to £81-02-01 in 1649, only to rise to £112-01-05 in the year of the 'crowning mercy' before a general decline into the protectorate. The average annual total during Cromwell's rule was under £38, a sum more in keeping with pre-war years.[29] In Upton and elsewhere the protectorate began to reintroduce normality in taxation, even if the sums reflected more the early 1640s than the 1630s. In other communities, similar falls in charges and duties are noticeable. At South Kyne in Lincolnshire pre-war duties took up one or two pages, war-time ones an average of seven, with levy details taking even more. During the protectorate the levies still used up three to four pages, but the duty details had declined to about the same number: the assessments were running at a third of their war-time levels.[30] In Scotton, also in Lincolnshire, the rates collected by constables fell by over half in the mid-1650s compared with wartime levies.[31] Falls in expenditure did not always occur so early. At Thorpe in Nottinghamshire a fall in expenditure did take place but not until the protectorate was established was this really dramatic. Levies had remained high in the late 1640s and even increased in 1650 and 1651. The levy fell by £15 in 1653 from an average of around £70. There were further falls, but by 1656 and 1657 the amounts were almost back to pre-war totals.[32]

Of course there is also a legacy of disinformation to counter when looking at the acceptance of the regime. Godly reform which Cromwell believed would bring the nation into God's favour and create a nation

which was 'prospered and blessed' with a duty to 'relieve the oppressed …
reform the abuses of all professions …' and where no one would make
'many poor to make a few rich' a nation which would 'shine forth to
other Nations' has been reduced in the collective memory to a place
where maypoles were cut down, plays banned, horse races prohibited
and pubs closed. In short Protectorate Britain and Ireland or 'Cromwell's
England' was a dismal place.[33] The truth is far different, many restrictions
were temporary, plays were written and performed, music was composed
and played. Pubs opened and closed as they had always done.

One of the enduring myths of the protectorate remains the supposed
obsession with order. H.L. Mencken's aside in 1949 that Puritans live in
fear that somewhere, someone is having fun, remains a persistent line.
An examination of Coventry constables' presentments to JPs would seem
to confirm this. On 11 January 1657, of sixty individuals presented at
the General Sessions no less than eleven (18 per cent) were presented
for selling ale without a license. At the October sessions the same year
the constables presented sixty-one people, and thirty-three of them were
there for unlicensed selling of beer or ale. Whilst the presentments for
illegal distribution of alcohol continued under the restoration regime,
they were a short measure by comparison with 1657 and therefore seem
to underline the impression of a Godly clean up. Yet this is not the case,
back in 1629 of sixty individuals presented to the court, twenty-one
were cases of illegal brewing and selling of ale. In both 1629 and 1657
closing down alehouses was an economic not a moral issue. Alongside
the illegal purveyors in the courts of 1629 and 1657 were licensed
brewers and alehouse keepers hauled before the courts for selling ale at
the wrong price; regulation not oppression. The same trend can be seen
elsewhere, in Essex and Middlesex there is not suggestion that there was
a Godly clean up. In Scarborough, the picture is more complex, as the
numbers of alehouses reviewed annually declined by 42 per cent during
the protectorate, but few illegal brewers were presented to the courts,
although a batch of six were in July 1658.[34]

Against the traditions of the mythology of puritans, Cromwell loved
music and had employed musicians in his court. They were to play at
the lavish weddings of his daughters during 1657. On 11 November
forty-eight stringed instruments and fifty wind instruments played at the
Whitehall Palace wedding of Francis Cromwell to Robert Rich, grandson
of the Earl of Warwick. It was an occasion when Oliver's playfulness

reached the fore, he spilt drink over several dresses, stole his daughter's head dress and sat on it. He daubed chairs with food, just as people were about to sit down. Roy Sherwood playfully suggests that Oliver's court had thus adopted the habit of royal courts in that the 'monarch's' annoying behaviour had not only to be tolerated but applauded. A week later at the weekend home, Hampton Court, Mary Cromwell married Lord Fauconberg this time accompanied by Andrew Marvell's *Two Songs at the Marriage of Lord Fauconberg and Mary Cromwell*. The first song was a staged duet in which Oliver may have played a mute part as Jove. The two weddings provided an official kick start to the revival of court music and masques, following the war. The festivities undermined the royalist cause still further, underlining the acceptance of the traditional ruling classes of the new regime.

Parliament had not met since Cromwell's second installation as lord protector. It was summoned and assembled with a second chamber on 20 January 1658. This second house had sixty-three names selected by Oliver, but many of his old colleagues would not sit. Saye and Sele, his political ally, Manchester, his old commander, even Warwick father of Oliver's son-in-law refused to give their approval to the state; but cousin Oliver St John the renowned long-term opponent of the king did. Some forty-two other nominees did appear amongst them officers, like Henry Cromwell and George Monck, representatives of the 'army party'; Fleetwood the son-in-law, Desborough the brother-in-law, and Hewson, the victor of St Fagins in 1648. There were a collection of the regime's officials, Cromwell's ex-landlord Henry Lawrence, Bulstrode Whitelock and Lord Broghill included and some enemies: Sir Arthur Hesilrige who did not sit in the upper chamber but steadfastly remained in the lower house, and Scottish sceptic Archibald Johnston of Wariston. Again Richard Cromwell was present, slowly moving into public view. The lower house was different too, for the new constitution allowed only parliament to vet membership and so MPs elected to the house in autumn 1656 but excluded in September, returned to take their seats. Naturally they were likely to be opponents of the protectorate.

Cromwell's speech to the second session of the parliament is often regarded as downbeat, even Gaunt sees in it 'decline and emptiness', yet Cromwell seems optimistic: 'We hope we may say that we have arrived at what we aimed at'. He was even more positive about the previous year's constitutional changes:

You see that the Petition and Advice that brought us hither hath not through a little difficulty, restored us both in point of civil liberty as we are men, and liberty for all those that are of the Protestant profession amongst us; who enjoy a freedom to worship God according to their conscience.

God still favoured the nation: 'he hath given us peace', he had brought them 'unto a blessed and happy estate and condition, comprehensive of all the interests of every member, of every individual of these nations, as you very well see'.[35] There was a downside to the speech, twice Cromwell told the MPs that he was ill, explaining that this was the cause of his brevity, and he had to hand over to Nathaniel Fiennes to present policy.

Cromwell's optimism was knocked quickly. The return of the commonwealthmen opponents of the regime had brought experienced parliamentarians in to the Commons, they understood parliamentary functions and dominated debates over the next few days and attacked the form and structure of the other chamber. They had had no hand in setting it up as they had been excluded from the first session of parliament and moreover Cromwell had secured the right to nominate the members of the second house having originally had to have his decisions vetted by parliament. Commonwealthmen attacked this element of the new constitution led by Hesilrige who had refused to go into the new chamber. The new house they argued was a check on the sovereignty of the people rather than on the head of state. Cromwell spoke to the house again to try and get it to change tack on 25 January. His short speech was a determined attempt to turn parliament from its introspection by outlining the importance of foreign affairs, and the threats to the regime from external enemies and the still present cavaliers. Cromwell may have been exaggerating the internal threat, but nevertheless parliament was neglecting the state of the armed forces: the army was six months in arrears in England and Scotland and even more in Ireland where the iniquity of free quarter had been introduced. Parliament had more important tasks than debating the constitution that it had itself put in place. Cromwell was adamant that this was necessary for the preservation of the civil and spiritual rights of the people. Parliament ignored him.

A petition outside parliament was written and circulated amongst soldiers and Londoners arguing that the protectorate perpetrated the sins of the monarchy it aped. Like the Leveller petition of the late 1640s it was addressed to the Commons in terms that suggested that it was still the sole sovereign body ignoring the new chamber completely: the petition was fine-tuned to appeal to the army somewhat disingenuously on grounds of its lack of pay, but also playing on the fears engendered by the Humble Petition and Advice. The petition was ready to be presented to parliament on 4 February; but Oliver was apprised of its content and sought to head it off by going to parliament himself. This time he was not so much frustrated as angry. He had referred to the bad weather in his last speech to parliament: this time it stopped him going to Westminster by river as there was ice blocking the way. Grabbing a carriage Oliver arrived at parliament and summoned the judges from Westminster Hall and the commons from their chamber all to meet him at the new chamber. He was met by Fleetwood who tried to dissuade him, but Cromwell insulted his son-in-law calling him a milk-sop. The commons decided to meet Cromwell despite Hesilrige trying to stop them going. Cromwell was angry at the ingratitude and a failure of parliament was there for all to see: they had created the new constitution, begged him to take the position despite his having 'thought the burden too heavy for any creature' only to waste time now in going over all ground. The thankless task that had once found him wishing for the wings of a dove, now led him to exclaim:

> I can say it in the presence of God, in comparison of which we are here are like poor creeping ants upon the earth, that I would have been glad to have been living under a woodside to have kept a flock of sheep, rather than to have undertaken such a place as this was. But undertaking of it upon such terms as I did, known unto you all that did advise and petition, that I undertook it for the safety of the nation, I did look that you, that did offer it unto me, should have make it good.

He ended his speech by setting out it was clearly a conflict between him and the rogue elements of parliament: 'And I do declare to you here, that I do dissolve this parliament. Let God judge between you and me'.[36]

Potentially dissolving parliament so acrimoniously opened the state up to dysfunction. Enemies thought this is precisely what had happened, but Cromwell still had a working government and he secured army loyalty at a meeting two days later where he explained his actions before the session that turned into a drinking bout amongst friends. Fleetwood organised loyal addresses from the English regiments and votes of supports were sent in from Scotland, organised by George Monck. Officers of dubious loyalty were discharged and replaced; ironically six of them from Cromwell's own regiment. The commonwealthmen, whom Cromwell had taken to associating with Levellers with only a little justification had been defeated. Their only real strength lay in parliament and with no parliament they had no power and nowhere to present their petition. Their policy of wrecking had ended for the duration of Oliver's rule. They had failed to enhance their position in parliament through taking up posts in the new house and had wasted their energies on questioning it, thus blocking further business in the house and ending what had been a parliament full of promise. If the last of Oliver's parliaments had failed it was because of the very men he had wanted to keep out of it in the first place back in September 1656. The constitution was robust enough to withstand the shock of the dissolution and the council of state settled into government alongside Oliver.

Cromwell's illness began to affect him in the wake of his political victory over the commonwealthmen. His attendance at council meetings declined rapidly from January onwards attending just nineteen of seventy-two sessions of council between then and early September. Spiritually he was drained, deaths within the family weakened his morale. On 16 February both Oliver's niece Lavinia Whetstone and Robert Rich his son-in-law of only three months died. Robert's grandfather the Earl of Warwick died within months. These familial deaths and that of an old war comrade wounded the already ill Cromwell, and as his attendance declined in the council, government began to atrophy. The state's finances needed radical overhaul and parliament was really needed for such work. Discussions on holding new elections failed to develop into plans as the protector grew ill. Nevertheless, there were some spectacular successes to celebrate. In June the Republic's army defeated Spanish forces on the dunes of Dunkirk and took possession of the town: it was the first possession on the European mainland since Calais was lost over a century earlier, and it was a dramatic appearance on a greater stage for the New Model Army. Cromwell's protectorate was beginning to make an impression on the European stage to match its diplomatic successes.

However, amid rumours of renewed interest in the crown, Cromwell's personal world was shattered. Oliver's affection for all his children is evident in his letters, yet if any was closest to his heart then it was Elizabeth, known as Bettie, wife of John Claypole. Cancer claimed her on 6 August 1658 after a long and painful battle with the disease that drained her and both her parents of their energy. Oliver was so distraught that he could not attend the funeral, gout was cited as the excuse. For the rest of the month Cromwell's health declined. George Fox met him on 17 August on a day of relative good health riding in Hampton Court Park. Fox wanted to discuss the plight of fellow Quakers and obtained an invitation to Hampton Court for the next day. However, Fox noted, 'I saw and felt a waft of death go forth against him; and when I came to him he looked a dead man'. Cromwell was soon confined to his house and then his bed. On 3 September the propitious anniversaries of Dunbar, Worcester and the opening date of the first protectorate parliament, Oliver Cromwell Lord Protector of the Commonwealth, commander of the armed forces in four nations died amidst a great storm that rattled the casements of Thomas Wolsey's great palace. Seemingly Richard was confirmed as his father's successor before Oliver died.

CONCLUSION

MY DESIGN IS TO MAKE WHAT HASTE I CAN TO BE GONE

Oliver's death should not have had the shattering consequences that it did: it would have been better if he had been a constable for then the constablewick would have chosen the successor, not the incumbent. The state had proved robust when Oliver dissolved the second protectorate parliament in February 1658. The succession had been confirmed, a civilian Richard Cromwell became the second lord protector seemingly confirming the partial demilitarisation of the state. The ubiquitous John Lambert, the heir presumptive until the *Humble Petition and Advice* simultaneously deposed him and his brainchild the *Instrument of Government*, had been sidestepped and deprived of office and influence. Richard was not in the pocket of any section of civilian or military: the problem for his government was that no one was in his pocket either. He worked hard to overcome this. Richard met with the army leaders and raised army pay. This worked and the army pledged loyalty. The country seemed to have applauded Richard's succession and there was goodwill to be derived from that. In January 1659 a parliament met, elected on pre *Instrument of Government* principles, the new chamber was enlarged to include peers. After these adjustments the parliamentary constitution began to work and when the year-old petition that had prompted Oliver into dissolving parliament was presented in the Commons, it had no impact.

The protectorate was however doomed when in April the cumulative effect of the bombardment by commonwealthmen literature inferring that the protectorate was in reality an impending monarchical threat had led to discontent in the army, which combined with the massive arrears of pay still due to the soldiers. Richard succeeded in quelling immediate anger until the Commons began to question William Boteler about his actions whilst one of the infamous major generals, and then refused to accept the financial report that indicated a shortfall in revenue of almost one third of a million pounds and army arrears approaching a million pounds. Richard tried to head off the inevitable army reaction by sending the army council out of the city of London. Simultaneously parliament discussed taking control of the militia. The army reacted angrily and demanded the dissolution of parliament. Richard called upon the loyalty of the colonels. Few answered and in many cases they were overridden by their regiments who moved off to rendezvous. Parliament was dissolved by Richard's order and the army created a new council of state which ended the protectorate and put Richard out to grass, appointing John Lambert to command the army. The Long Parliament was recalled and sixty-five survivors turned up for duty.

The death throes of the republic were protracted over a further year. The Rump Parliament was at first seemingly prepared to take radical action: it opened discussions on law and religion, but very quickly, it became clear that this Rump, although small and potentially thereby capable of swift decisions was little different to how it had been in the great lull of 1651–1653, for it did very little to radicalise politics or society. Much in the way of decision making tended to mirror the early protectorate in form and parliament failed to tackle the dire financial situation the country was in. On the other hand, with a few exceptions the newly reorganised militia was put in the hands of radicals, including Quakers. Parliament was also in contrast with the reinvigorated press which proposed radical solutions to the issues parliament was so laggardly in solving. However, the implications of including Quakers on militia committees raised expectations of further radicalism in the provinces, prompting conservative Presbyterians to join a royalist group planning a rising. The rebellion occurred in August but was quickly defeated by the army, effectively ending any chance of a home-grown royalist revival. With Lambert in command of the army the radicals in it felt able to draft a petition pressing parliament for action: it was almost a replay of

1652–1653 with the army demanding expediency from a slow moving parliament. Parliament responded in a way reminiscent of 1647 by proposing to punish the authors of the petition, rather than deal with it. Naturally the army reacted badly to this treatment and a second petition was drafted condemning parliament's action. This time parliament really overreacted and dismissed these new petitioners from their offices and summoned loyal regiments to its defence, only to find as Richard Cromwell had that the army had greater loyalties. Lambert was in full control of his men and on 13 October closed parliament. This time there was no widespread support for the action as it was grounded upon army interests alone. The attempt to govern through the Council of Officers failed, because it could not forge a plan for a new parliament. Nemesis came in the form of George Monck whose army in Scotland condemned the expulsion of the Rump and threatened to bring it to England. There was a real risk of civil war as both the armies in England/Wales and Ireland remained loyal to the Council of Officers. Although Lambert marched to Newcastle negotiations prevented fighting but allowed the situation in London to deteriorate dramatically. In mid December the Army Council imploded and soldiers and civilians invited the Rump Parliament to return. This restored parliament offered Monck the post of commander in chief and he led his army into England in support of parliament.

By the beginning of 1660 whilst parliament was in the hands of some of the more radical MPs like Hesilrige, local government was in the hands of conservatives not aligned to the aims of the revolution, after many of the radical elements embraced in English and Welsh local administration after the fall of the protectorate were expelled and in Scotland and Ireland conservative groups took control of government. There was growing clamour for a free parliament. In February Monck hitherto loyal to the parliament, refused its orders to use the army against demonstrators calling for a new parliament and instead initiated the return of MPs purged in 1648. This had the effect of creating a conservative body which moved swiftly towards dissolving itself and setting up a Convention Parliament. In turn the Convention Parliament invited Charles Stuart to accept the throne. On 28 May 1660 the man who would-be king returned to England, instigating the Restoration of the monarchy and the reshaping of post-revolutionary Britain in a way that combined elements drawn from the pre-war years and the past two decades.

In some ways then, Cromwell's death precipitated the fall of the British Republic and the incomplete nature of a settlement or the lack of direction some have identified as existing in its last nine months could well be said to have brought about decline and fall. In such a case what is the contribution of Oliver Cromwell to this part of British and Irish history? At the outset we are beset by a problem. Ironically the man who has given the period its most enduring and public name never really encapsulated the dynamics of the period. Cromwell, as this book argued at the outset, was the product of three things: his gentry cocoon, the revolution and his own innate talents. All three were necessary: the latter could never have appeared without the revolution, and Cromwell would never have been in a place to exhibit those talents without having being placed there by members of his family and their political allies. In 1639–1640 Cromwell was brought into a political dynamic that was already in place: he was allied to it by his (probably new-found) religious perspective and became involved in its politics during the Long Parliament's sessions and its committee work.

Cromwell's political perspective was largely honed during the revolutionary period, but the evidence is that Cromwell remained wedded to the post-reformation political system with a parliament and monarchy closely united in government. For this reason it took a great deal of effort to shift Cromwell from firstly trying to negotiate with the king to considering bringing the king to trial and finally to eradicating the monarchy altogether. Convincing Cromwell was not an earthly task. He had earthly advisors, firstly his family members Oliver St John and John Hampden, and their associates, later it would be Henry Ireton. After Ireton's death it would be John Lambert but only briefly: after the inception of the protectorate, Cromwell broadened his perceptions, trusting his own judgement on grand strategy and leaving the detail to John Thurloe, and other trusted protectorate men. Cromwell's attempt to embody the republic was an attempt to assimilate the various strands of society in an inclusive settlement that overrode any of the vested interests that had brought about the revolution and victories in its train. Oliver would have interpreted this as God's will demonstrated to him in a series of providences. This had brought him full circle into an effective reconstruction of the monarchy.

One of the most striking elements of Cromwell's life is his apparent innate military ability. With no discernible background in anything more militaristic than riding a horse whilst hunting, Cromwell became one of the primary generals of his age within the British Isles. Some historians have speculated about Oliver's abilities in comparison with the period's great European leaders and even in comparison with other commanders in different ages. All have pointed out that as Cromwell operated within the British Isles only no true comparisons can be drawn. In many ways such speculation is irrelevant, Cromwell's importance is broader than his military reputation. However, in purely military terms Cromwell only had to be better or luckier than those he faced. He was rarely outmatched in battle. There were only a handful of commanders in the foremost rank: Waller, Leven, Leslie, Fairfax, Rupert and O'Neill. Cromwell was on the same side as two of these throughout; Leven was in decline when he was Cromwell's enemy, O'Neill died before confrontation between the two occurred, and Oliver defeated both Leslie and Rupert. Victory proved sufficient to elevate him to the role of head of state. Cromwell proved to be a fast learner, unlike some who progressed from troop captain to general command in a short time he did so through talent not birth, and that talent displayed itself in less than a year. Within months of taking up arms Cromwell demonstrated himself a competent regimental commander and quickly demonstrated leadership in the field in Lincolnshire during the summer of 1643, whilst simultaneously demonstrating the ability to arrange logistics, organise defence and selectively lobby for pay for his men. In 1644 Cromwell's talent at major battlefield level became clear at Marston Moor and this was confirmed a year later at Naseby and Langport. In between the disaster at Newbury was not his fault although unusually Cromwell was defeated on the field by Sir Humphrey Bennet whilst in command of his natural metier: the horse. Whilst this and Cromwell's apparent disobedience in the wake of the battle did provide his political enemies with a lever to try and dislodge him Oliver's reputation did not suffer.

The second civil war saw Cromwell move one stage further, into independent command of significant forces detailed to undertake what became the major campaign of the war. His success against the Scots at Preston ensured that the later campaigns in Ireland, Scotland and England were confirmations of rather than demonstrations of his ability. Dunbar confirmed his ability on the field of battle and Worcester consummate mastery of a campaign, which raises questions about Peter Gaunt's negative assumptions about Cromwell's mastery of a campaign. Victory was only one strand to Cromwell's military prowess: Cromwell's consummate grasp of leadership and logistics, coupled with his ability to make rapid and accurate decisions made him unique and explain his rise to power. Frank Kitson thinks that these qualities make Cromwell the father of the British army. He also cared for his soldiers' well-being. This is first indicted by his fantastic ability to recruit soldiers. From the outset Cromwell's troop and then regiment was always oversized. In a war when most units, especially before the creation of the New Model Army, were undersized, often ridiculously and expensively so, this was an extraordinary achievement. His respect for his men is shown in his comment that they be treated as men, his care for them in the constant reminders to his allies in parliament that they be paid, and his love for them in his boast that he had a 'lovely company'. That this regimental care carried forward into care for the army as a whole is probably demonstrated by Oliver's decision to side with the soldiers in 1647 on the grounds of their dire needs. That this was repaid is demonstrated by the way the army quickly came to order on Corkbush field in 1647 and remained loyal in May 1649. This relationship was crucial for the army trusted Cromwell for the most part and that allowed him the time to try and reach political compromise with parliament at times when army patience had almost expired in 1647 and 1652–3. Reliance on the army led to one of the problematic acts of the republic; the one which allowed later critics to label Cromwell a dictator and portray the regime as a military state; the major generals. Whatever their true role there is no doubt that Oliver felt that they had let him down, and through their failure understood that the army as well as parliament was a flawed vehicle for change. It was a double-edged sword for this relationship meant that the army felt that Cromwell should act on its wishes – Cromwell complained of such in 1657. It also seems to have made him feel that he could embody their wishes without having to consult them; the perils of this were clearly seen when his own regiment became estranged from him towards the end of his life.

In his early political career, Cromwell's chief concern was religion: he seems to have been convinced by 1640 that the church of England in its present form was endangering Protestantism, not just in terms of its present officials, but also its post-reformation structure: he wanted it sweeping away. However, this was a minority view: most opponents of the king's political and religious policy would have been content to have removed only the particular officials responsible for Charles's policies and to increase parliament's involvement in church management. Cromwell's more radical perspective was to be the model for his religious belief for the next eighteen years, he remained in a minority: his pleas for toleration were generally overridden in the 1640s by those who wanted to establish an alternative monolithic church in Presbyterian form. In the 1650s there was no dramatic progress, but a steady path was trodden. That this was fragile was shown by the fragmentation of the religious consensus in 1659 in the face of greater toleration and the acceptance into public life of known Quakers. Cromwell would have needed a great deal more time to bring about a tolerant broad church.

Cromwell's view of godliness was essentially internal. Whilst God exhibited his plan in various external manners, Cromwell was after all a providentialist, it was up to Cromwell and anyone else to wrestle with God in order to find out what it meant. In some cases this was easy: string of victories for a multifarious army was a clear indication that God favoured it. Other things, such as the failed Western Design were harder to interpret. We are not entirely sure about the way Cromwell interpreted the loss of his children, Robert, Oliver and Bettie or their partners Henry Ireton and Robert Rich, for unlike contemporaries Archibald Johnston of Wariston or Robert Baillie he left no detailed account of the way in which he interpreted them. We know they were hard blows, and Bettie's death did contribute to his own lack of will power at the end of his life.

A problem for Cromwell was his close relationship with God. Cromwell was convinced of the providential nature of God's relationship with the world. Only through studying the present, in conjunction with bible study, and interpreting God's work, could God's plan be understood. That this provided Cromwell with the confidence to act is undoubted. Through this working relationship Cromwell devised his political and religious perspective from the 1630s onwards. Confidence that God favoured the cause of his parliamentary allies in the early 1640s, and then the army from the mid-1640s onwards directed Cromwell's reaction to victory and the revolutionary demands of 1648–1649. That God awarded victory to the republic confirmed in Cromwell's mind that his actions and those of the army had been sanctioned, even if Cromwell could never break completely from his essential belief in monarchical structures. This imparted to Cromwell the responsibility of guarding the outcome of the revolution. Here the problems began. Cromwell associated victory ever more closely with himself and the army consequent upon God's handing victory to it in the face of parliament's hostility. At the same time death and the revolutionary actions of 1648–1649 removed from Cromwell his new and old familial allies, divorcing him from the intimate and broad range of moral, intellectual and political advice, that along with consultation with God had provided Cromwell with his direction. John Morrill quite correctly portrays the route of Cromwell's later career as paved with his cast-aside allies, Lilburne and the Levellers, the regicide revolutionaries and fellow travellers, the religious visionaries of the Second Coming, Lambert and the new constitutionalists: add to these the men his God deprived him of and this left Cromwell much more dependent upon his association with God, and the problem with such a close relationship with God is that it is essentially individualistic. What God wanted of Cromwell was essentially what Cromwell wanted of himself, and others. For an atheist there is no relationship to be had with any God and thus all of the conversation is one sided: Cromwell was talking to himself, feeding back to his own mind what he had witnessed and how he had interpreted it. But Cromwell's mistaken belief in God must not be belittled, for that is how he understood the world, for him there was a genuine conversation a constant struggle to work out God's plan, and it would be churlish to argue otherwise. Those who walk with God, however, have difficulty walking with mankind. Cromwell's perception was not an isolated one, but he was unable to carry a majority with him. And this was most unfair for Oliver spent probably as much time trying to understand what others wanted. Baxter may have found him boring, but he mistook what was going on: Oliver sought his understanding, not his attention. Whitelock saw it more clearly, even if he presented in a cautious light, perhaps because walking with Oliver might do him harm later in his life. Whitelock's Oliver was a questioner, posing hypothetical questions with direct relevance to his own thoughts and current events. Cromwell's walk in the park with Whitelock was not the same as Whitelock's grilling by Essex and Loudon, Cromwell sought genuine knowledge and understanding, not a legal certainty. In such a way did Oliver seek to find the route ahead. It was part of his magnanimity that Cromwell allowed others into his thought process as much as it was of his need to find answers and conviction. This was clearly linked to Oliver's need to find reconciliation. If we see his understanding of the state as being a mirror of his family then it becomes so. The Cromwells had been divided by war, whilst Oliver's nuclear family remained a coherent body the wider family had ranged on both sides. When Oliver sought to encompass old enemies in the settlement, this would include his family. With Oliver as head of state then the decline in the family fortunes could be halted. But Oliver like the war and revolution continued to drive in wedges, he left his cousin Oliver St John behind, the rule of the major generals would inflict pain on his royalist cousins, and just as in his political life his new family forged in war fell by the wayside.

It is difficult to agree with John Morrill's assertion that it is ironic that the destroyer of divine right of kings ending up as the exponent of the divine right of republicanism. Cromwell believed he had no divine right to the seat of government, just as neither the army nor parliament had sole right to be the arbiter of the state. Cromwell was there only as part of a fiduciary arrangement. If he failed in his duty to God then he would, like the king, the Rump, and the Little Parliament, before him be swept away; it is the extreme edge of what Peter Gaunt sees as Cromwell's strength: flexibility and his openness to be swayed in debate. Where John Morrill is undoubtedly right is in his suggestion that Cromwell is consistent. The central sinew of this biography has to create a consistent Cromwell from the very divergent perspectives possible. At least Cromwell was consistent in his behaviour for the final third of his life, and it was this third that matched onto revolution and public life: that both began once Cromwell eschewed his role as chief of sinners. From then on he was what James VI of Scotland had clearly wished to be: 'un homme de Dieu'. His loyalty was to God and God's plan, not to those whom he worked with and left behind: his duty was to discover exactly what this meant. But godly service was public service: just as he never swayed from the notion that God was a beneficent being, Oliver never lost view of the idea that mankind had the capacity to be godly or good. The purpose of Oliver as governor was to create a world in which British and Irish men and women could achieve godliness. The godly world Oliver dreamt of and strove for never arrived: elements appeared: changes in the practice of law, the banning of some bloodthirsty sports; and some disappeared too: new parliamentary boundaries, modernisation of parliament's second chamber, religious pluralism; things that were associated with radical religion but cannot truly be described as the offspring of a Puritan revolution. John Morrill is also right to claim that Cromwell did not see a social revolution as necessary. When repelled by the unicameral parliament and by the army's failed political interventions, Oliver returned to the security of the social cocoon that had advanced him as a young man: the 'traditional' governors of society: a conservative belief in the pre-war social hierarchy, in a way that was so ungrateful to the broadened social and political responsibilities of the war-generation that had advanced Cromwell beyond the social possibilities of his pre-war cocoon. Colin Davis sees this in a positive light as creating or affirming a civilian basis to government on the basis of the stand taken by the Solemn League and Covenant, including parliamentary government and protection for civil and religious liberties; and there is a good deal of truth in this, but the protectorate was marred by the inclusion at local level of people with no deep commitment for such broad and tolerant principles. Moreover it was probably this that doomed the revolution, for whilst this establishment group might tolerate Cromwell, they in the end baulked at his successors and welcomed a real monarch. But we cannot blame Cromwell for this, for had he lived longer his policy of healing, of not depending upon one group, but on the ideas of many filtered through conversations with God, might just have worked. Cromwell need not have died when he did, although his father died relatively young, Oliver's uncle did not. Old Sir Oliver who had walked at the shoulder of James VI and I lived to carry his nephew's pall on his own shoulder. Oliver's mother whose genes he carried lived into her eighties and Richard Cromwell the second and last commoner head of state (even if tainted unlike his father by being the outcome of hereditary succession) lived until he was eighty-six. Longevity could have been on Oliver's side.

Cromwell is often judged as having in the end failed. His tolerant church, even his limited approaches towards extending parliamentary franchise, and government came to an abrupt end in 1660, but by then he was dead, the failures were those of others; Oliver had not yet finished his search for a solution and left behind him lesser men, and men who did not share his vision. Cromwell cannot be judged against impossible standards. He came to his various posts with what is now termed 'baggage', the social, political, economic and cultural traits of the upper gentry in post-reformation England. His personal religious rebirth and his experience of revolution bashed about and restructured his understanding but it never could obliterate it: it is what provoked his anger towards Catholics in 1649, as much as his reluctance to reform the socio-political structures in a way that men with fewer ties to this old post-reformation regime demanded of him and others after the First Civil War. What Cromwell should be remembered for is his capacity to overcome this, to overcome prejudices and his openness to ideas. When he could not break out of this we cannot blame him. He is remarkable enough for what he did achieve, to ask more of him is churlish: no-one else came close to his achievements for they were either the defeated moribund royalists or the radical revolutionaries comparatively out on a limb without the support of a powerbase. They might have manufactured such a base for Cromwell's powerbase was forged by the same war that created the other victors of 1648–1649, his gentry-family cocoon had only provided for him so far in his career, much of Cromwell's advancement after 1642 had been his own work, through his own talents and that too must be remembered.

When Cromwell died his body was embalmed badly and buried hastily in the Henry VII chapel at Westminster Abbey. This was only the private element for there was a public lying in state of his effigy throughout October and an official and elaborate funeral, copied in almost every detail from that of James VI and I, thirty-three years earlier. Ironically the closed Imperial crown Cromwell never wore in life was placed on the effigy's head. Only in death could the arch-conservatives get their way with him. The body with its valedictory plaque rested only a couple of years. On 30 January 1661 Oliver's corpse was dug up, dragged to Tyburn, hanged and beheaded along with Bradshaw and Ireton. This was a monumental and dual act of cowardice, perpetrated by those who could not outface the protector in life and permitted by a restored king whom the protector had defeated in the field. The post-republic carrion reburied the body beneath the gallows and impaled the head on a pike and took it to Westminster. There are many tales of the rescue of the body: especially by his daughter Mary Falconberg whose husband rose to greatness during the Restoration, and of a secret burial on the field of Naseby but it is likely that the body remains beneath Marble Arch. The head blew down in a gale before the century was over, preserved in private hands before in 1960 ending up in Cromwell's old college, Sidney Sussex at Cambridge University. That there is no real tomb or funereal monument to Oliver

Cromwell, Lord Protector of the Republic is to the eternal shame of the nation. The only one of us Britons to reach the position of head of state, without dubious claims to divine right, should at least receive the rites accorded to the assembled good, bad and indifferent holders of the kingly office he so rightly rejected.

Notes

1 BY BIRTH A GENTLEMAN ...

1 Huntingdon Record Office (HRO), 3870/1 Huntingdon St John Composite Register, 1582–1682, n.p.
2 HRO, HB26/14 Survey of Huntingdon (10 May) 1572, p. 8.
3 Hugh Trevor-Roper '"The gentry" 1540–1640', *Economic History Review*, Supplement I, 1953.
4 HRO, 3870/1.
5 HRO, 4480 Sale of Property by Oliver Cromwell.
6 Lawrence Stone, *The Crisis of the Aristocracy 1558–1641*, Oxford University Press, Oxford, 1965.
7 Abbott, Wilbur Cortez, ed. *Writings and Speeches of Oliver Cromwell* (Four Volumes, Cambridge, MA: Harvard College, 1937–1947), vol. I, p. 27.
8 F. Heal and C. Holmes, *The Gentry in England and Wales 1500–1700*, Macmillan, London, 1994.

2 A CHIEF OF SINNERS

1 Abbott, I, p. 31.
2 S. Carrington, *The history of the Life and Death of His Most Serene highness Oliver, Late lord Protector*, London 1659.
3 James Heath, *Flagellum*, London, 1663.
4 A.L. Erickson, *Women and Property in Early Modern England*, Routledge, London, 1995.
5 Ibid., pp. 29–30.
6 Ibid., p. 36.
7 Ibid., pp. 50–1.
8 HRO, 4880.
9 Abbott, I, p. 46.
10 Richard Cust, *The Forced Loan and English Politics 1626–1628*, Oxford University Press, Oxford, 1987.
11 Ibid., p. 52.
12 British Library, Sloane Ms 2069, *Mayerne Ephemerid Morborum*, ff133, 149.
13 Ibid., f96v.

14 Abbott, I, pp. 61–2.
15 HRO, H Charter 17.
16 Abbott, I, p. 68.
17 HRO, 1983//1, 436 Certificate of Thomas Beard.
18 Abbott, I, pp. 68–9.
19 HRO HMR Vol/1/15 St Ives Manor Court book 1632–1661.
20 Abbott, I, p. 77.
21 HRO, 3734/8/1, St Ives Vestrybook, 1626–1765, n.p.
22 Abbott, I, pp. 80–1.
23 Ibid., pp. 96–7.

3 ... A GENTLEMAN ... VERY ORDINARILY APPARELLED

1 Abbott, I, p. 89–90, 95.
2 Ibid., p. 109.
3 Cope, E.S. and Coates, W.H. (eds) *Proceedings of the Short Parliament of 1640* (London, Camden Fourth Series, 1977), pp. 46–9.
4 Clarendon, Earl of, *History of the Rebellion and Civil Wars in England* (Oxford, Oxford University Press, 1992 reprint of 1888), vol. I, p. 183.
5 Abbott, I, p. 114.
6 Ibid., p. 121.
7 Ibid., p. 125.
8 Gardiner, S.R. (ed.) *The Constitutional Documents of the Puritan Revolution, 1625–1660* (Oxford, Oxford University Press, 1978), pp. 167–79.
9 Abbott, I, pp. 127–8.
10 Ibid., p. 133.

4 MY ESTATE IS LITTLE ...

1 Clarendon, History of the Great Rebellion (Oxford, Oxford University Press, 1992 edition), vol. 1, pp. 419–20.
2 Abbott, I, p. 163.
3 The list of the Army Raised under the command of his Excellency Robert Earl of Essex (John Partridge, London, 1642).
4 Abbott, I, p. 208.
5 The list of the Army Raised under the command of his Excellency Robert Earl of Essex (John Partridge, London, 1642.)

6 HRO, 455 Militia Certificate.
7 Abbott, I, p. 256.
8 Ibid., pp. 213, 215.
9 Ibid., p. 264.
10 Ibid., pp. 256–9.
11 Ibid., pp. 228–68.
12 Ibid., pp. 230–2.
13 Ibid., pp. 234–5.
14 Ibid., p. 241.
15 Ibid., pp. 256–9.

5 THE GREAT AGENT IN THIS VICTORY

1 Abbott, I, p. 240.
2 Ibid., pp. 277–8.
3 HRO, 3343/M80 Assessment of Oliver Cromwell's Character, anon. 1644.
4 *Newes from the Siege before York* (London, 14 June 1644).
5 Abbott, I, pp. 287–8.
6 Abbott, I , pp. 287–8.
7 British Library, Harleian Ms166 f87.
8 *A More Exact Relation of the Late Battle near York* (London, 1644).
9 *A Relation of the good successe of the Parliaments forces under the Command of Generall Lesley, the Earle of Manchester and the Lord Fairfax* (Cambridge, 1644).
10 *The Glorious and Miraculous Battel at York* (Edinburgh, 1644).
11 Abbott, I, p. 297.
12 Whitelock, Bulstrode, *Memorials of the English Affairs* (Oxford, Oxford University Press, 1853), vol. I, p. 343.
13 HRO, 3343/M80, ff9, 11.
14 Whitelock, II, p. 344.
15 Ibid., pp. 346–8.
16 Abbott, I, p. 310.
17 Ibid., pp. 314–15.
18 Ibid., pp. 339–41, 344, 345.
19 Ibid., pp. 342–4.
20 Ibid., p. 352.
21 Sprigge, Joshua, *Anglia Rediviva* (London, 1647), p. 34.
22 *Three letters from the Right honourable Sir Thomas Fairfax, Lieutenant General Cromwell ...* (London, 16 June 1645), p. 3.

23 Tibbutt, H.G., *Colonel John Okey* (Bedford, Bedfordshire Historical Society, 1955), vol. XXXV, p. 11.
24 *Three letters from the Right honourable Sir Thomas Fairfax, Lieutenant General Cromwell* ..., p. 3.

6 HE DID NOT OPENLY PROFESS WHAT OPINION HE WAS OF HIMSELF

1 Abbott, I, pp. 364–6.
2 Morrill, J.S. (ed.) *The Revolt of the Provinces* (London, Longman, 1980), pp. 199–200.
3 Abbott, I, pp. 368–9.
4 Ibid., pp. 372–3.
5 Ibid., pp. 371–2.
6 *Bristol and the Civil War* Historical Association (London, 1981).
7 Ibid., pp. 474–8.
8 Baxter, Richard, *The Autobiography of Richard Baxter* (London, Dent, 1985), pp. 49, 53.
9 Ibid., pp. 56–7.
10 Abbott, I, p. 468.
11 Ibid., p. 410–11.
12 British Library, Sloane Ms 1519, f147. Abbott, I, p. 430.
13 Abbott, I, pp. 428–9.
14 Ibid., p. 441.
15 Ibid., pp. 445–6.
16 Ibid., pp. 459–61.
17 Ibid., p. 510.
18 Woodhouse, A.H. (ed.) *Puritanism and Liberty Being the Army Debates* (London, Dent, 1938), p. 22.
19 Ibid., p. 56.
20 Ibid., p. 58.
21 Ibid., p. 59.
22 Ibid., p. 73.
23 Ibid., pp. 69–70.
24 Baxter, p. 62.

7 I NEVER IN ALL MY LIFE SAW MORE DEEP SENSE

1 Ashburnham, J., *A Narrative by John Ashburnham*, (London, Payne and Foss, Baldwin and Cradock, 1830), vol. II, pp. 104–19.
2 Whitelock B., *Memorials of the English Affairs* (Oxford, Oxford University Press, 1853), vol. II, pp. 233–4.
3 Abbott, I, p. 575.
4 Ibid., pp. 598–9.
5 Ibid., pp. 613, 616.
6 Ibid., pp. 620–1.
7 Ibid., p. 632.
8 Ibid., p. 634–8.
9 Ibid., p. 654.
10 Ibid., p. 661.
11 Ibid., p. 638.
12 Ibid., p. 678.
13 *The True Copy of a Petition promoted in the Army and already presented to His Excellency the Lord General by the officers and soldiers of the Regiment under the command of Commissary General Ireton* (London, 1648), pp. 5–6.
14 Abbott, I, p. 690.
15 Ibid., p. 707.
16 *The Humble Proposals and Desires of His Excellency the Lord Fairfax and of the General Council of the Officers ...* (London, John Rushworth, 1648).
17 Abbott, I, p. 690.
18 Ibid., p. 719.
19 Whitelock, II, p. 480.
20 Roots, Ivan, *The Speeches of Oliver Cromwell* (London, Dent, 1989), p. 7.
21 Essex County Record Office, D/DQs 18, p85f.

8 EVERYONE MUST STAND OR FALL BY HIS OWN CONSCIENCE

1 Essex County Record Office, D/DQs 18, p88f.
2 Jones, Henry, *A Remonstrance of Divers Remarkable Passages Concerning the Church and Remonstrance of Ireland* (London, Godfrey Emmerson, 1642).
3 Abbott, II, pp. 256–9.

4 Ibid., p. 163.
5 Ibid., II, pp. 103–4.
6 Ibid., II, pp. 124–5.
7 Ibid., II, pp. 125–8.
8 Abbott, I, pp. 386–7.
9 Abbott, II, p. 127.
10 Abbott, II, p. 142.
11 Abbott, II, pp. 125–8.
12 Abbott, I, pp. 230–2, 634–8.
13 Abbott, II, p. 145.
14 Ibid., p. 146.
15 Ibid., p. 173.
16 Ibid., p. 177.
17 Abbott, II, pp. 196–205, *A Declaration of the Lord Lieutenant of Ireland, For the Undeceiving of Deluded and Seduced People.*
18 Ibid., p. 203.
19 Abbott, I, p. 287.
20 Abbott, II, p. 218.
21 Ibid., p. 224.
22 Ibid., pp. 231–5.
23 Ibid., pp. 248–9.
24 Whitelock, III, p. 208.
25 Ibid., p. 209.
26 Ibid., p. 210.
27 Baxter, p. 64.
28 Hutchinson, p. 313.
29 Abbott, II, p. 303.
30 Ibid., p. 325.
31 Ibid., pp. 349–50.
32 Ibid., p. 356.
33 Ibid., pp. 359–60.
34 Wariston of Johnston, A., *The Diaries of Sir Archibald Johnston of Wariston* (Edinburgh, Scottish History Society, 1991), vol. II, p. 47.
35 Abbott, II, p. 400.
36 Ibid., p. 453.
37 Ibid., p. 461.
38 Ibid., p. 463.

9 OH, WOULD I THE WINGS LIKE A DOVE

1 Abbott, II, p. 325.
2 Ibid., p. 463.
3 Whitelock, III, p. 371.
4 Ibid., pp. 372–4.
5 Roots, I. (ed.) *Speeches of Oliver Cromwell* (London, Dent, 1989), p. 12.
6 Whitelock, III, p. 477.
7 Whitelock, IV, p. 2.
8 Abbott, II, pp. 641–4.
9 Ibid., pp. 642, 643 (it could also have been 'these baubles').
10 Ibid., p. 644.
11 Ibid., p. 646.
12 Ibid., p. 642.
13 Ibid., p. 646.
14 Roots, p. 43.
15 Ibid., pp. 8–28.
16 Abbott, III, p8. 9.
17 Ibid., p. 62.
18 Whitelock, IV, p. 54.
19 HRO, HUTCM: 90; Taylor, Randal, *The Court and Kitchen of Elizabeth Commonly called Joan Cromwell The wife of the late Usurper, Truly Described and Represented And now Made Public for general Satisfaction* (London, Tho Milburn, 1664).
20 Baxter, Richard, *The Autobiography of Richard Baxter* (London, Dent, 1985), p. 140.
21 Bethel, Slingsby, *The World's Mistake in Oliver Cromwell*, (London, 1668), pp. 3, 9, 11.
22 Whitelock, IV, p. 105.

10 A GOOD CONSTABLE TO KEEP THE PEACE

1 Abbott, III, pp. 435–6.
2 Roots, pp. 30–1, 32–3.
3 Ibid., p. 43.
4 Abbott, III, p. 459.
5 Roots, p. 76.
6 Abbott, III, p. 756.
7 Ibid., p. 857.
8 Everett-Green, M.A. (ed.) *Calendar of State Papers Domestic, 1655–6* (London, Longmans, 1882), p. 15.

9   Ibid., p. 82.
10 Roots, p. 79.
11 Bethel, pp. 3–4.
12 Roots, p. 92.
13 Ibid., p. 85.
14 Abbott, IV, pp. 261–2.
15 Ibid., p. 366.
16 Roots, p. 108.
17 Abbott, IV, p. 470.
18 Roots, p. 42.
19 Ibid., p. 111.
20 Ibid., p. 133; Abbott, IV, p. 470.
21 Earle, John, *Microcosmography* (London, 1628) in Morley, H., *Character Studies of the Seveneenth Century* (London, 1891), p. 180.
22 Roots, p. 111.
23 Ibid., p. 42.
24 Ibid., p. 134.
25 Ibid., p. 135
26 HRO, HUTCM 68.
27 Roots, p. 137.
28 Abbott, IV, p. 514.
29 Nottinghamshire Archive Office (NAO), PR1710, pp. 3–7, 9–13, 20–35, 85–95, 130.
30 Lincolnshire Archive Office (LAO), South Kyne, Par 12 passim.
31 LAO, ASW 2/59/15, passim.
32 NAO, PR5767, passim.
33 Abbott, II, p. 325.
34 Ashcroft, M.Y. (ed), *Scarborough Records, 1641–1660* (North Yorkshire County Council, 1991), pp. 217, 231, 238, 245, 246, 247.
35 Roots, pp. 169–70.
36 Ibid., pp. 189, 193.

Further reading

The importance of Cromwell's contribution to British and Irish History means that there are a wide range of books about him to suit every line of enquiry: his politics; his personal life; his religion; his campaigns in Ireland and of course his military campaigns and ability. There is a mixed collection of primary sources for his life, many of which are referred to in the notes to the chapters in this book, but it is worth referring to them again. Huntingdonshire County Record Office in Huntingdon is very near Oliver's old school and in conjunction with it in its role as the Cromwell Museum and other institutions in the county, provides an internet site containing a calendar of documents relating to Cromwell's life and details of how and where to gain access to them: http://www.cambridgeshire.gov.uk/leisure/archives/projects/cromwellcollection.htm.

The central source for Cromwell remains his letters and records of his speeches, and these have been published a number of times. The largest collection is Abbott, Wilbur Cortez (ed.) *Writings and Speeches of Oliver Cromwell*, Four Volumes (Harvard College, 1937–1947) reissued (Oxford University Press, 1989); a major collection, but not without its errors of transcription. A smaller, but nevertheless reasonable extensive collection readily available in second-hand bookshops is Carlyle, Thomas (ed.) *Cromwell's Letters* (Oxford, Ward Locke and Co, no date). This is one of several versions printed in the eighteenth and early nineteenth century. Again there are problems with the text and the editor's interpretation on occasion; but these are small problems when compared with Carlyle's annoying interventions and railings against his imaginary dullard of an historian Dryasdust. Ivan Roots has put together a collection of Oliver's speeches; Roots, Ivan (ed.) *Speeches of Oliver Cromwell* (London, Dent, 1989), which offers a modern and instructive record of Oliver's public utterances.

There are a number of great and useful biographies of Oliver, dealing with him from a range of perspectives. Fraser, Antonia, *Cromwell Our*

Chief of Men (London, Methuen, 1973, reprinted 1985) is useful for a very personal approach and remains a source of fascinating information, the main pitfall being that the book becomes less useful the further from the central subject the author ventures. In recent times three authors have produced very useful explorations of Cromwell: Coward, Barry, *Oliver Cromwell* (Harlow, Longman, 2000); Davis, J.C., *Oliver Cromwell* (London, Arnold, 2001) and Peter Gaunt's *Oliver Cromwell* (Oxford, Blackwell, 1995) all offer different and valuable interpretations of Oliver's life. Peter Gaunt's book is a straightforward biography analysing Cromwell as his life progresses, whilst both Davis and Coward have adopted an analytical approach throughout, with Davis choosing a thematic approach rather than a chronological one. Older biographies can also still present interesting insights, Maurice Ashley's *Oliver Cromwell and the Puritan Revolution* (London, English Universities Press), remains an incisive brief history and Charles Firth's *Oliver Cromwell and the Rule of the Puritans in England*, first published in 1900 (Oxford, Oxford University Press, 1953); still has something to offer, whilst John Buchan's *Oliver Cromwell* (London, The Reprint Society, 1941), is an entertaining read. Christopher Hill's *God's Englishman, Oliver Cromwell and the English Revolution* (Harmondsworth, Penguin, 1970) is perhaps dated somewhat, but the approach is still contentious and vibrant.

There are few attempts to examine Cromwell's early life in isolation, and one is thrown back on the complete biographies, usually. John Morrill's essay 'The making of Oliver Cromwell' in Professor Morrill's edited volume, *Oliver Cromwell and the English Revolution* (Harlow, Longman, 1990), is an outstanding exception, cutting through myth and succeeding in creating a realistic image of the unnoticed Cromwell. Another essay that serves a similar myth-busting purpose is Brian Quintrell's 'Oliver Cromwell and the Distraint of Knighthood' in the *Bulletin of the Institute of Historical Research* (57, 1984).

Books that deal with particular aspects of Cromwell's life include Frank Kitson's *Old Ironsides* (London, Weidenfeld and Nicholson, 2004), a perceptive attempt to explore the nature of Cromwell's military genius and to ask questions such as how good a general was he and where did he learn his military craft from? Robert S. Paul in *The Lord Protector: Religion and Politics in the Life of Oliver Cromwell* (Grand Rapids, MI, William B. Eerdmans, 1955), looks at the other major theses of Oliver's life. Roy Sherwood's two works *The Court of Oliver Cromwell* (Stroud,

Willingham Press, 1989), and *Oliver Cromwell: King in All But Name* (Cambridge, Sutton, 1997) focus on the stateliness of Oliver's regime.

In terms of Cromwell's military career John D Grainger's *Cromwell Against the Scots* (East Linton, Tuckwell Press, 1997), looks specifically at Cromwell's last campaign, but it is Ireland that draws much more attention as an examination of a campaign as a singular entity. The best of these works is James Scott Wheeler, *Cromwell in Ireland* (New York, Gill and Macmillan, 1999): this is an expert analysis of the campaign that has not yet been bettered. Thomas O'Reilly's two main contributions *Cromwell at Drogheda* (Dublin, Broin Print, 1993) and his book *Cromwell, An Honourable Enemy* (Dublin, Brandon Books, 1999) have attempted to raise Cromwell's reputation in Ireland by questioning long held assumptions, but not as deftly as either Wheeler or Jason McElligott in *Cromwell Our Chief of Enemies* (Dundalk, Dundaglen Press, 1994).

Blair Worden must be regarded as one of the foremost historians as far as delving into Cromwell's religious motivation goes. His essays, 'Toleration and the Cromwellian Protectorate' *Persecution and Toleration: Studies in Church History*, XXI (Oxford University Press, 1984); 'Providence and Politics in Cromwellian England' *Past and Present* (109, 1985); and 'Oliver Cromwell and the Sins of Achen' in Beales, Derek and Best, Geoffrey, *History, Society and the Churches* (Cambridge University Press, 1985), rank amongst the best studies of Cromwell. The section on Cromwell's reputation consisting in five chapters of *Roundhead Reputations: The English Civil Wars and the Passions of Posterity* (Harmondsworth, Penguin, 2001), is an exemplary study of historiography and Cromwell. Similarly John Morrill's work on Cromwell, including his already cited edited volume: *Oliver Cromwell and the English Revolution* (Harlow, Longman, 1990), has made a major contribution to demythologising Oliver, with essays by J.S.A. Adamson, David Stevenson, Anthony Fletcher, Derek Hirst, Johann Sommerville and J.C. Davis. Morrill's attempts to clear the myths surrounding Cromwell continue in an all-too-brief essay, 'Was Oliver Cromwell a War Criminal?' in the inaugural issue of *BBC History*, of May 2000, and his more substantial treatment of Oliver in the *Oxford Dictionary of National Biography* (Oxford, Oxford University Press, 2004).

Cromwell's most famous battles have been covered by several historians. Oliver's reputation was boosted by his work at Marston Moor, and this battle has been explored by several historians: Peter Young's

Marston Moor 1644: The Campaign and the Battle (Kineton, Roundway Press, 1970) was the first modern account of the battle and still has a great deal to offer the reader, but really it is the work of Peter Newman which surpasses all studies of the battle. His *The Battle of Marston Moor* (Chichester, Anthony Bird, 1981) was a starting pistol for work on battlefield archaeology and his last work a joint effort with archaeologist P.R. Roberts, *Marston Moor: The Battle of the Five Armies* (Pickering, Blackthorne Press, 2003) showed that historians rarely regard their own work as definitive: this is a great reassessment made possible by the combined approaches of the two authors. Peter Young's *Naseby 1645: The Campaign and the Battle* (London, Century, 1985) whilst containing useful information about the structure of the armies has been superseded by the work of Glenn Foard, whose *Naseby: The Decisive Campaign* (Whitestable, Pryor, 1995) is an excellent exploration of the field of Naseby and Cromwell's exploitation of it. S. Bull and M. Seed's *Bloody Preston: The Battle of Preston 1648* (Lancaster, Carnegie Publishing, 1998) is a useful study of Cromwell's first major independent victory. It is clear that the bias of individual battles fought by Oliver remains English in geographical focus and those wishing to examine the Irish and Scottish battles will have to work through Wheeler and Grainger.

A fertile area of controversy regarding Cromwell's career as head of state remains the period of the rule of the major generals. Ivan Roots's 'Swordsmen and Decimators, Cromwell's Major Generals' in Parry, R.H., *The English Civil War and After* (London, Macmillan, 1971) is worth reading as is Austin Woolrych's article 'The Cromwellian Protectorate: A Military Dictatorship?' *History* (75, 1990), which rejects the assertion that the major generals represented a militaristic state. The most recent works are those of Christopher Durston whose essays: 'The Fall of Cromwell's Major-Generals', *English Historical review* (113, 1988) and '"Settling the Hearts and Quieting the Minds of all Good People": The Major-Generals and the Puritan Minorities of Interregnum England', *History* (85, 2000) were in effect leading up to his major and incisive work *Cromwell's Major Generals* (Manchester, Manchester University Press, 2001). Other aspects of the government of the period have been examined by Peter Gaunt in articles such as '"The Single Person's Confidants and Dependants"? Oliver Cromwell and His Protectoral Councillors', *The Historical Journal* (32, 3, 1989); 'Cromwell's Purge? Exclusions and the First Protectorate Parliament' *Parliamentary History* (6, 1987); and 'Law-Making in the

First Protectorate Parliament' in C. Jones, M. Newitt and S. Roberts, *Politics and People in Revolutionary England* (Oxford, Oxford University Press, 1986) are all important contributions, as is Ivan Root's older essay 'Lawmaking in the Second Protectorate Parliament' in H. Hearder and H.R. Loyn's *British Government and Administration* (Cardiff, University of Wales Press, 1974).

Several of the essays cited above have been conveniently gathered together by David Smith in *Cromwell and the Interregnum* (Oxford, Blackwell, 2001), but another contentious essay by Ronald Hutton is contained in a very useful collection of essays written by Professor Hutton *Debates in Stuart History* (London, Macmillan, 2004). Chapter four is an examination of Cromwell which leaves him in a fairly unflattering light after making some very pertinent points: I am very grateful to Professor Hutton for allowing me to read a copy of the chapter before the publication of the book.

No man is an island as one of Cromwell's near contemporaries wrote and so anyone wishing to make a thorough study of the man must come to terms with the period in which Oliver lived. There are numerous important works on the civil war period and naming them all is impossible. As one theme of this biography has been positing the fenlander Cromwell in the wider world of Britain and Ireland the new wave of four nation history are recommended here, John Morrill's already cited *Oliver Cromwell and the English Revolution*, contains a useful essay by David Stevenson on the subject of Cromwell and Scotland and Ireland, and Ronald Hutton's *The British Republic* (London, Macmillan, 1990) takes a pan-national approach to the period. J.P. Kenyon and Jane Ohlmeyer's edited book, *The British and Irish Civil Wars: A Military History of Scotland, Ireland, and England, 1638–1660* (Oxford, Oxford University Press, 1998), presents the civil wars in the same wide scope. Conrad Russell's monumental *The Fall of the British Monarchy* (Oxford, Oxford University Press, 1991) sets the scope for the opening of the crisis which coincided with Cromwell's emergence from the shadow of obscurity. There is no finer single volume coverage of the period as a whole than Austin Woolrych's final great work; *Britain in Revolution* (Oxford, Oxford University Press, 2002). General coverage of aspects of the period are also to be found in M. Bennett's *The Civil Wars Experienced: Britain and Ireland 1637–1661* (London, Routledge, 2000) and *The Civil Wars of Britain and Ireland, 1638–1653* (Oxford, Blackwell, 1997).

But as with the biographical angle some of the older treatments remain important today such as C.V. Wedgwood's *The King's War*, originally published 1958 (Harmondsworth, Penguin, 1983), and *The Trial of Charles I*, originally published 1964 (Harmondsworth, Penguin, 1983). Samuel Rawson Gardiner's four volume *History of the Great Civil War*, originally published in 1893 (Adlestrop, Windrush Press, 1987) is useful as are his Cromwell's *Place in History*, 1897 (Oxford, Books for Libraries, 1969), and the *History of the Commonwealth and Protectorate 1649–1656*, four volumes, originally published in 1903 (Adlestrop, Windrush Press, 1988), completed after his death by Charles Firth.

INDEX

THE EARLY STUART KINGS, 1603-1642

GRAHAM E. SEEL

In 1603 King James I ascended the throne to become the first King of a united England and Scotland. There followed a period of increasing religious and political discord, culminating in the English Civil War. The Early Stuart Kings, 1603-1642 explores these complex events and the roles of the key personalities of the time - James I and VI, Charles I, Buckingham, Stratford and Laud.

ISBN10: 0-415-22400-4 (pbk)
ISBN13: 978-0-415-22400-0 (pbk)

THE ROUTLEDGE COMPANION TO THE STUART ERA, 1603-1714

JOHN WROUGHTON

The Routledge Companion to the Stuart Age, 1603-1714 is an invaluable, user-friendly and compact compendium packed with facts and figures on the seventeenth century - one of the most tumultuous and complex periods in British history. From the reign of James I to Queen Anne, this guide includes detailed information on political, religious and cultural developments, as well as military activity, foreign affairs and colonial expansion. Chronologies, biographies, key documents, maps and genealogies, and an extensive bibliography navigate the reader through this fascinating and formative epoch.

With complete lists of offices of state, an extensive glossary of key constitutional, political and religious terminology and up-to-date thematic annotated bibliographies to aid further research, this reference guide is essential for all those interested in the Stuart Age.

ISBN10: 0-415-37890-7 (hbk)
ISBN10: 0-415-37893-1 (pbk)
ISBN13: 978-0-415-37890-1 (hbk)
ISBN13: 978-0-415-37893-2 (pbk)

MARY QUEEN OF SCOTS

RETHA M. WARNICKE

In this new biography of one of the most intriguing figures of early modern European history, Retha Warnicke, widely regarded as a leading historian on Tudor queenship, offers a fresh interpretation of the life of Mary, Queen of Scots.

Setting Mary's life within the context of the cultural and intellectual climate of the time and bringing to life the realities of being a female monarch in the sixteenth century, Warnicke also examines Mary's three marriages, her constant ill health and her role in numerous plots and conspiracies. Placing Mary within the context of early modern gender relations, Warnicke reveals the challenges that faced her and the forces that worked to destroy her.

This highly readable and fascinating study will pour fresh light on the much-debated life of a central figure of the sixteenth century, providing a new interpretation of Mary Stuart's impact on politics, gender and nationhood in the Tudor era.

ISBN10: 0-415-29182-8 (hbk)
ISBN10: 0-415-29183-6 (pbk)
ISBN13: 978-0-415-29182-8 (hbk)
ISBN13: 0-415-29183-5 (pbk)

THE ROYALIST WAR EFFORT, 1642–1646

RONALD HUTTON

'Hutton's subject is the area which gave Charles I his most valuable support to that task he brings a thrilling intelligence, a powerful imagination and a bracing, epigrammatic prose.'

London Review of Books

In this reissue of the second edition of *The Royalist War Effort, 1642–1646* Ronald Hutton places his vivid account of the Royalist War effort in modern historical context, bringing the reader up to date with recent developments in the study of the English Civil War.

He analyzes the influences which affected his own interpretation of events, ensuring that The Royalist War Effort, 1642-1646 remains the most informative and compelling account of the Royalist experience in the English Civil War.

ISBN10: 0-415-30540-3 (pbk)
ISBN13: 978-0-415-30540-2 (pbk)

ENGLISH SOCIETY,
1580-1680

KEITH WRIGHTSON

Bringing together the results of recent historiography and much original research by the author, this second edition of a successful book paints a fascinating picture of society and rural change for students of sixteenth and seventeenth-century history.

Using contemporary diaries and texts Keith Wrightson brings his material to life as he examines the enduring characteristics of society and the course of social change. The book emphasizes a wide variation in experience between different social groups and local communities, and builds up an overall interpretation of continuity and change.

Covering every aspect of society and change in this period, students and general readers are treated to a fascinating read and an invaluable tool in the study of seventeenth-century history.

ISBN10: 0-415-29068-6 (pbk)
ISBN13: 978-0-415-29068-5 (pbk)

THE CENTURY OF REVOLUTION: 1603-1714

CHRISTOPHER HILL

'This is a book we have all been waiting for – a history of the political and religious conflicts of the seventeenth century that is rooted in reality; and it will be a long, long time before this brilliantly lucid and forcefully argued book is bettered.' – *Spectator*

'Lucid and economical ... his immense range of reading sits lightly upon him, revealed only in the frequent, telling quotation on every aspect of seventeenth century life ... ingenious and provocative.' – *Times Literary Supplement*

There is an immense range of books about the English Civil War, but one historian stands head and shoulders above all others for the quality of his work on the subject. In 1961 Christopher Hill first published what has come to be acknowledged as the best concise history of the period, The Century of Revolution. Stimulating, vivid and provocative, his graphic depiction of the turbulent era examines ordinary English men and women as well as kings and queens. Hill argued that the Civil War was driven by the conflict between the old feudal élites and the growing merchant classes. Society and the State are dissected alongside other aspects such as Protestantism and the rise of capitalism and the questioning of hitherto unassailable authorities such as the church and the law. Full of wit and insight, his treatment of what is regarded as one of England's most formative periods is one that is truly satisfying.

ISBN10: 0-415-26738-2 (hbk)
ISBN10: 0-415-26739-0 (pbk)
ISBN13: 978-0-415-26738-0 (hbk)
ISBN13: 978-0-415-26739-7 (pbk)